Anti-Inflammatory Chicken Cookbook

350 Chicken Recipes, Sides, and Sauces to Heal Your Immune System and Fight Inflammation, Heart Disease, Arthritis, Psoriasis, Diabetes, and More!

Stephanie Bennett

MINI TABLE OF CONTENTS

Introduction 1
The Complete Anti-Inflammatory Food List 10
Poultry Recipes 18
Sides 128
Sauces And Dressings 160
Seafood 174
About The Author 309

TABLE OF CONTENTS

Introduction 1
   Causes Of Chronic Inflammation 1
   Chronic Inflammatory Diseases 2
      Autoinflammatory Disease 2
      Autoimmune Disease 3
      Cardiovascular Disease 4
      Type 2 Diabetes And Obesity 4
   Managing Chronic Inflammation 4
   Anti-Inflammatory Eating Habits 5
   Anti-Inflammatory Ingredients 6
   Ingredients To Watch Out For 8
The Complete Anti-Inflammatory Food List 10
      Beverages 10
      Condiments 10
      Dairy And Dairy Alternatives 10
      Fats And Oils 11
      Fruits 11
      Grains And Starches 12
      Meats, Poultry, Fish, And Proteins 12
      Nuts, Seeds, And Legumes 13
      Sweeteners 13
      Vegetables 13
      Herbs, And Spices 14
   Pantry Essentials 14
   Tips And Tricks 16
   About The Recipes 17
Poultry Recipes 18

Adobo Lime Chicken Mix	18
Almond Chicken Cutlets	18
Apricot Chicken Wings	19
Asian Saucy Chicken	20
Avocado-Orange Grilled Chicken	21
Bacon-Wrapped Chicken with Cheddar Cheese	21
Baked Chicken Meatballs - Habanero & Green Chili	22
Balsamic-Glazed Turkey Wings	23
Basic "Rotisserie" Chicken	24
Basil Chicken Saute	24
BBQ Chicken Zucchini Boats	25
Blue Cheese Buffalo Chicken Balls	26
Boozy Glazed Chicken	27
Breaded Chicken Fillets	28
Buffalo Balls	29
Buffalo Chicken Lettuce Wraps	29
Buffalo Pizza Chicken	30
Cajun Chicken & Prawn	31
Capocollo and Garlic Chicken	32
Celery Fries and Chicken	33
Champion Chicken Pockets	34
Cheesy Bacon-Wrapped Chicken with Asparagus Spears	34
Cheesy Chicken Sun-Dried Tomato Packets	35
Cheesy Mexican-Style Chicken	36
Cheesy Pinwheels with Chicken	37
Cheesy Ranch Chicken	38
Chicken & Cheese Filled Avocados	39
Chicken and Snap Peas Stir Fry	39
Chicken Burrito	40
Chicken Cacciatore with Spaghetti Squash	41
Chicken Cheese Steak	42
Chicken Divan	43
Chicken Frittata with Asiago Cheese and Herbs	44
Chicken in Pita Bread	44
Chicken Korma	45
Chicken Parmigiana	46
Chicken Piccata	48
Chicken Pie with Bacon	49
Chicken Quiche	50
Chicken Scarpariello with Spicy Sausage	51
Chicken with Fennel	52
Chicken-Bell Pepper Sauté	53
Chili & Lemon Marinated Chicken Wings	54
Chili Chicken Kebab with Garlic Dressing	55
Chimichurri Turkey & Green Beans	55
Chinese-Orange Spiced Duck Breasts	56
Cilantro-Lime Chicken Drumsticks	57
Cipollini & Bell Pepper Chicken Souvlaki	58
Coconut-Curry-Cashew Chicken	58
Creamy Chicken & Greens	59
Curry Chicken Lettuce Wraps	60
Delicious Roasted Duck	61

Delightful Teriyaki Chicken Under Pressure	62
Double Cheese Italian Chicken	63
Duck Breast and Blackberries Mix	64
Duck Breast Salad	65
Duck Breast with Apricot Sauce	66
Duck Legs and Wine Sauce	67
Duck Stew Olla Tapada	68
Easy Chicken Tacos	68
Exquisite Pear and Onion Goose	69
Feta & Bacon Chicken	70
Flying Jacob Casserole	70
Greek Chicken Stifado	71
Grilled Chicken with Black Bean Mango Salsa	72
Healthy Turkey Gumbo	73
Hidden Valley Chicken Drummies	74
Home-Style Chicken Kebab	75
Honey Chicken Tagine	76
Honey-Mustard Lemon Marinated Chicken	77
Hot Chicken Meatballs	77
Keto Chicken Enchaladas	78
Lebanese Chicken Kebabs and Hummus	79
Lemon & Garlic Chicken Thighs	80
Lemon and Herb Crusted Chicken Fillets	81
Lemon-Garlic Chicken and Green Beans with Caramelized Onions	82
Mango & Lime BBQ Turkey	83
Middle Eastern Shish Kebab	84
Moroccan Turkey Tagine	84
Nacho Chicken Casserole	85
Nutty Pesto Chicken Supreme	86
Orange Chicken Legs	87
Pancetta & Cheese Stuffed Chicken	88
Pancetta and Chicken Risotto	89
Pan-Fried Chorizo Sausage	90
Paprika Chicken & Pancetta in a Skillet	91
Peanut-Crusted Chicken	91
Pesto & Mozzarella Chicken Casserole	92
Pulled Buffalo Chicken Salad with Blue Cheese	93
Red Pepper and Mozarella-Stuffed Chicken Caprese	94
Roasted Chicken	94
Roasted Whole Chicken	95
Rotisserie Chicken & Cabbage Shreds	96
Salsa Verde Chicken	97
Simple Turkey Goulash	97
Skillet Chicken with Brussels Sprouts Mix	98
Slow Cooker Chicken Cacciatore	99
Slow Cooker Chicken Fajitas	100
Slow Cooker Jerk Chicken	101
Spicy Almond Chicken Strips with Garlic Lime Tartar Sauce	102
Spicy Chipotle Chicken	103
Spicy Pulled Chicken Wraps	104
Spinach Chicken Cheesy Bake	104
Stuffed Chicken with Sauerkraut and Cheese	105

Super Sesame Chicken Noodles	106
Tangy Barbecue Chicken	107
Tangy Chicken with Scallions	107
Tarragon Chicken with Roasted Balsamic Turnips	108
Teriyaki Chicken	109
Three-Cheese Chicken Cordon Bleu	110
Tomato & Cheese Chicken Chili	111
Traditional Hungarian Gulyás	112
Turkey & Sweet Potato Chili	112
Turkey and Potatoes with Buffalo Sauce	113
Turkey Bacon Melt Sandwich	114
Turkey Breast with Fennel and Celery	115
Turkey Chili	115
Turkey Club Wraps	117
Turkey Crust Meatza	117
Turkey Ham and Mozzarella Pate	118
Turkey Meatballs with Spaghetti Squash	119
Turkey Sloppy Joes	120
Turmeric Chicken Wings with Ginger Sauce	121
Turnip Greens & Artichoke Chicken	122
Tuscan Chicken Saute	122
Vodka Duck Fillets	123
White Bean and Chicken Chili Blanca	124
White Bean, Chicken & Apple Cider Chili	125
Winter Chicken with Vegetables	126

Sides   128

Beet Hummus	128
Broccoli and Black Beans Stir Fry	128
Caramelized Pears and Onions	129
Cauliflower Broccoli Mash	130
Cilantro And Avocado Platter	131
Citrus Couscous with Herb	131
Cool Garbanzo and Spinach Beans	132
Couscous Salad	133
Creamy Polenta	134
Crispy Corn	134
Cucumber Yogurt Salad with Mint	135
Curry Wheatberry Rice	136
Farro Salad with Arugula	136
Feta Cheese Salad	137
Fresh Strawberry Salsa	138
Goat Cheese Salad	138
Green Beans	139
Green, Red and Yellow Rice	140
Hot Pink Coconut Slaw	141
Lentil Salad	142
Mascarpone Couscous	142
Moroccan Style Couscous	143
Mushroom Millet	144
Onion and Orange Healthy Salad	144
Parmesan Roasted Broccoli	145

Quinoa Salad 146
Red Cabbage with Cheese 147
Rice with Pistachios 148
Roasted Carrots 149
Roasted Curried Cauliflower 149
Roasted Parsnips 150
Roasted Portobellos With Rosemary 151
Shoepeg Corn Salad 152
Spiced Sweet Potato Bread 152
Spicy Barley 153
Spicy Roasted Brussels Sprouts 154
Spicy Wasabi Mayonnaise 155
Stir-Fried Almond And Spinach 155
Stir-Fried Farros 156
Tender Farro 157
Thyme with Honey-Roasted Carrots 157
Tomato Bulgur 158
Wheatberry Salad 159

Sauces And Dressings _____ 160
Apple and Tomato Dipping Sauce 160
Balsamic Vinaigrette 161
Bean Potato Spread 161
Cashew Ginger Dip 162
Creamy Avocado Dressing 163
Creamy Homemade Greek Dressing 163
Creamy Raspberry Vinaigrette 164
Creamy Siamese Dressing 165
Cucumber and Dill Sauce 166
Dairy-Free Creamy Turmeric Dressing 166
Herby Raita 167
Homemade Ginger Dressing 167
Homemade Lemon Vinaigrette 168
Homemade Ranch 169
Honey Bean Dip 170
Soy with Honey and Ginger Glaze 170
Strawberry Poppy Seed Dressing 171
Tahini Dip 172
Tomato and Mushroom Sauce 172

Seafood _____ 174
Ahi Tuna Poke 174
Amberjack Fillets with Cheese Sauce 174
Avocado & Salmon Omelet Wrap 175
Bacon and Jalapeno Wrapped Shrimp 176
Baked Tilapia with Cherry Tomatoes 177
Baked Tomato Hake 178
Balsamic Scallops 179
Basil Halibut Red Pepper Packets 179
Bavette with Seafood 180
Blackened Fish Tacos with Slaw: 181
Cheese Tilapia 182
Cheesy Tuna Pasta 183

Chili Hake Fillets	183
Chili Shrimp and Pineapple	184
Chili Snapper	185
Chunky Fish	186
Citrus & Herb Sardines	187
Citrus Salmon on a Bed of Greens	188
Clams with Garlic-Tomato Sauce	189
Clams with Olives Mix	189
Coconut Mahi-Mahi Nuggets	190
Coconut Rice with shrimps in Coconut curry	191
Cod Curry	192
Cod with Ginger and Black Beans	193
Codfish Sticks	194
Crab Rissoles	194
Crab Salad Cakes	195
Crab Stuffed Salmon	196
Crispy Fish Stick	197
Cucumber Ginger Shrimp	199
Curried Fish	199
Curry Tilapia and Beans	200
Daring Shark Steaks	201
Delicious Oysters And Pico De Gallo	201
Dill Haddock	202
Easy Crunchy Fish Tray Bake	203
Fish & Chickpea Stew	204
Fish Cakes	204
Fish Casserole with Cream Cheese Sauce	205
Fish Fingers	206
Fish Meatballs	208
Fish Sandwich	209
Fried ball of cod	209
Fried Codfish with Almonds	210
Garlic & Lemon Shrimp Pasta	211
Garlic Butter Shrimps	212
Garlic Crab Legs	213
Ginger & Chili Sea Bass Fillets	213
Ginger Salmon and Black Beans	214
Gingered Tilapia	215
Glazed Halibut Steak	216
Grilled Calamari	217
Grilled fish tacos	218
Grilled Salmon with Caponata	219
Grilled Squid with Guacamole	220
Grilled Swordfish	221
Haddock with Swiss Chard	221
Halibut Curry	222
Halibut Stir Fry	223
Healthy Fish Nacho Bowl	224
Herbed Coconut Milk Steamed Mussels	225
Herbed Rockfish	225
Honey Crusted Salmon with Pecans	227
Hot Tuna Steak	227

Irish Style Clams	228
Italian Halibut Chowder	229
Keto Salmon Tandoori with cucumber sauce	230
Keto Zoodles with White Clam Sauce	231
Lemon Butter Tilapia	232
Lemon-Caper Trout with Caramelized Shallots	233
Lemony Mackerel	234
Lemony Mussels	235
Lemony Trout	235
Lime Cod Mix	236
Mackerel Bombs	237
Manhattan-Style Salmon Chowder	238
Marinated Fish Steaks	238
Mexican Salad with Mahi-Mahi	239
Mozzarella Fish	240
Mussel Chowder	241
Nut-Crust Tilapia with Kale	242
Octopus Salad	243
Orange and Maple-Glazed Salmon	244
Oven-Baked Sole Fillets	244
Pan-Seared Scallops with Lemon-Ginger Vinaigrette	245
Parmesan Crusted Tilapia	246
Poached Halibut and Mushrooms	246
Popcorn Shrimp	247
Potato Dumpling with Shrimp	248
Prosciutto-Wrapped Cod	249
Proscuitto-Wrapped Haddock	249
Pumpkin Shrimp	250
Quick Chermoula Fish Parcels	251
Quick Fish Bowl	252
Quick Shrimp Moqueca	253
Roasted Salmon and Asparagus	254
Rockfish Curry	255
Rosemary-Lemon Cod	256
Salmon and Cauliflower	257
Salmon and Coconut Mix	257
Salmon and Roasted Peppers	258
Salmon and Shrimp Mix	259
Salmon Balls	259
Salmon Cakes	260
Salmon Ceviche	261
Salmon Croquettes	262
Salmon Patties	263
Salmon Rolls	263
Salmon Skewers in Cured Ham	264
Salmon Sushi	265
Salmon with Mustard Cream	266
Sardine Casserole	266
Sardine Fritters	267
Seafood Noodles	268
Seafood Paella	269
Seared Ahi Tuna	270

Sesame Ginger Salmon	271
Sesame-Tuna Skewers	272
Sherry and Butter Prawns	273
Shrimp and Beets	273
Shrimp and Black Beans Enchalada	274
Shrimp and Corn	275
Shrimp Pie	275
Shrimp Risotto	277
Shrimp Rissoles	277
Shrimp Scampi	278
Shrimp with Cinnamon Sauce	279
Shrimp with Spicy Spinach	280
Simple Founder in Brown Butter Lemon Sauce	281
Simple Squid Stew	282
Sole with Vegetables	283
Souvlaki Spiced Salmon Bowls	284
Special Oysters	285
Spicy herb catfish	286
Spicy Kingfish	287
Spicy Salmon Tempura Roll	288
Squid Rings with Potato and Spinach	289
Steamed Garlic-Dill Halibut	290
Steamed Mussels with Thyme	291
Stuffed Trout	292
Sweet Crab Cakes	293
Swordfish with Pineapple and Cilantro	294
Tender Creamy Scallops	295
Thai Chowder	296
Thai Salmon Fishcakes	297
Tiger Prawn Paella	297
Tilapia and Red Sauce	298
Tilapia Fillets	299
Tilapia with Parmesan Bark	300
Tilapia with Spicy Dijon Sauce	301
Trout with Chard	301
Tuna Cakes	302
Tuna Handrolls	303
Tuna Steaks with Shirataki Noodles	304
Tuna-Stuffed Tomatoes	305
Vietnamese Roll and Tarê	306
Wasabi Salmon Burgers	307
Whitefish Curry	307

About The Author   **309**

INTRODUCTION

Inflammation is your immune system's response to injury or unwanted microbes in your body. It is a natural process and vital part of your body's healing process. When inflammation becomes systemic and chronic, however, it becomes a problem, and measures need to be taken. This type of inflammation serves no purpose, and can cause a lot of harm to the body.

As a nutritionist, I have clients suffering from a wide spectrum of health issues, and inflammation is easily one of the most common issues. Some of these clients are in constant pain, often excruciating. Migraines are a regular occurrence, and they don't sleep too well either. Their energy reserves always seem depleted and even sleep doesn't help, even if they manage to get a few good hours in.

I always suggest these clients to get a blood test for C-reactive protein if they haven't got one already, and if you feel you suffer from any symptoms of inflammation, I suggest you go to a nearby lab and get this blood test done right away. Chances are that your C-reactive protein levels are higher than normal, and the best way to manage this is diet. Shouldn't be hard though, considering how delicious anti-inflammatory foods are! Even if you do not suffer from chronic and systemic inflammation, incorporating anti-inflammatory foods in your diet will be one of the best decisions you will make in your life. You will notice the difference when you start. Your energy levels will be much higher, your mood will be uplifted, and you will feel more alive, in general.

This book has a LOT of recipes, and not every recipe might work for you. For example, if you're allergic to dairy or gluten, the recipes containing those ingredients will cause more harm than good. However, substitutions are possible for all of these, so you will be fine following this book as long as you keep an eye on the ingredients and use a bit of creativity where you have to! Once you understand the fundamentals of the diet, you will be fully equipped to create your own recipes from scratch!

In this book, you will learn all about the ingredients that are alleviate inflammation, and those that aggravate it, so you can make an educated guess for what's the best recipe for you, and what's the worst, even if you're out eating at a restaurant.

CAUSES OF CHRONIC INFLAMMATION

Medical science is striving to pinpoint the causes of chronic inflammation, and according to the Autoimmunity Research Foundation, numerous possible causes have been identified. This knowledge has mainly been derived from observational studies in which researchers can find correlation, though correlation does not equate to causation. Which is to say that while causes are identified by the studies, there is no scientifically proven concrete link between causes and outcomes. This uncertainty is an integral part of epidemiological studies, but they can still provide some very useful information.

Suggested causes for widespread chronic inflammation include:

- Antibiotic overuse and misuse (including in the food supply and through prescribed medications)
- Dietary factors (processed foods, unbalanced essential fatty acids, and chemical additives, among others)
- Environmental factors (endocrine disrupters and pesticides, among others)
- Use of substances (medications) that suppress immune responses, such as anti-inflammatories, antibacterial agents, and corticosteroids

In addition, Medical News Today *(MNT) notes other factors that may play a role in chronic inflammation, including:*

- Autoimmune diseases
- Obesity
- Poor sleep quality and sleep deprivation

CHRONIC INFLAMMATORY DISEASES

The research goes on but quite a few diseases have been linked to chronic inflammation. In this section, we will take a look at some of these.

AUTOINFLAMMATORY DISEASE

According to the National Institutes of Health's (NIH) National Institute of Arthritis and Musculoskeletal and Skin Diseases (NIAMS), autoinflammatory disease is a rather new class that is quite unlike autoimmune disease, although the names are rather similar and they share some features. Autoimmune diseases are caused by the immune system attacking healthy tissue, leading to chronic inflammation. The reason for this is not fully understood by science just yet.

Autoinflammatory diseases can cause intense, chronic inflammation that can lead to symptoms such as fever and joint swelling. A few common diseases in this category are:

- Behçet's disease
- Chronic Atypical Neutrophilic Dermatosis with Lipodystrophy and Elevated Temperature (CANDLE)
- Deficiency of the Interleuken-1 Receptor Agonist (DIRA)
- Familial Mediterranean Fever (FMF)
- Neonatal Onset Multisystem Inflammatory Disease (NOMID)
- Tumor Necrosis Factor Receptor-Associated Periodic Syndrome (TRAP)

AUTOIMMUNE DISEASE

NIAMS says that autoimmune diseases also have a chronic inflammatory component to them. When your body sees its own healthy tissue as an intruder, it attacks it. Inflammation is one of the key signs of autoimmune disease, although, depending on the disease, other symptoms might be exhibited too.

More than 80 autoimmune diseases have been identified at the time of writing this book, and some of the most common ones are listed below:

- Addison's disease
- Ankylosing spondylitis
- Celiac disease
- Crohn's disease
- Endometriosis
- Fibromyalgia
- Grave's disease
- Hashimoto's disease
- Interstitial cystitis
- Juvenile (type 1) diabetes
- Juvenile arthritis
- Lupus
- Lyme disease (chronic)
- Multiple sclerosis
- Psoriasis
- Rheumatoid arthritis

- Scleroderma
- Ulcerative colitis
- Vitiligo

CARDIOVASCULAR DISEASE

The American Heart Association notes that while it isn't currently established that inflammation causes cardiovascular disease (diseases of the heart and blood vessels), it is usually present, particularly in arteries of people suffering from this kind of a disease. Multiple factors are associated with heart disease, such as tobacco use, high blood pressure, and high levels of "bad" cholesterol called low-density lipoprotein (LDL), etc., so managing these is key to preventing and managing cardiovascular diseases.

TYPE 2 DIABETES AND OBESITY

An article in the May 2, 2005 issue of the Journal of Clinical Investigation studied the link between type 2 (adult onset) diabetes, inflammation, and stress, and found a close correlation between inflammation and type 2 diabetes, mostly triggered by obesity. This research suggests that obesity activates multiple chemical responses in the body that result in extensive inflammation, and this inflammation further causes metabolic disorders like type 2 diabetes.

MANAGING CHRONIC INFLAMMATION

With advances in medical science, we have quite a few options for managing chronic inflammation. Some of the most popular options today are as follows.

NSAIDS

Nonsteroidal anti-inflammatory drugs (NSAIDs) such as ibuprofen or naproxen sodium (Aleve) are often recommended by health experts for managing and treating inflammation. However, these can potentially cause side effects, especially when used in the long term.

CORTICOSTEROIDS

These synthetic steroids are administered both orally and externally, and are great at suppressing the body's immune response. However, these too can cause side effects in the long run.

HERBAL REMEDIES

Minor inflammation can be managed by simple herbal remedies containing anti-inflammatory ingredients like turmeric and ginger. Combining turmeric with black pepper, coconut oil, or quercetin increases its bioavailability, thus making it easier for the body to absorb it.

LIFESTYLE CHANGES

Simple lifestyle changes such as exercise, yoga, meditation, better sleep, losing weight, stress reduction techniques, etc. can go a long way in managing inflammation.

ANTI-INFLAMMATORY DIET

The anti-inflammatory diet is a fairly new concept, and research is still going on. However, a review in the December 2010 issue of Nutrition in Clinical Practice notes an anti-inflammatory eating pattern which balances the ratio of essential fatty acids (omega-3 to omega-6 fatty acids) and consists mainly of fresh fruits, vegetables, legumes, and whole grains while reducing saturated fats (such as fats from meat) and maximizing monounsaturated fats (such as olive oil), is much better at managing inflammation than a typical western diet.

ANTI-INFLAMMATORY EATING HABITS

You are what you eat. Eat good, look good, feel good. Eat trash, look like trash, feel like trash.

FIGHTING INFLAMMATION THROUGH DIET

The anti-inflammatory diet has a very simple concept. When you plan your meals, you maximize the ingredients that reduce inflammation, and minimize/eliminate the ingredients that aggravate inflammation. Though, this is easier said than done.

We live in a world where everything, even food, is available at the flick of your finger. We are surrounded by delicious processed food with chemical additives, preservatives, and unhealthy fats. When such good taste comes with such high convenience, it is easy to give in.

However, if you do manage to overcome your urges, and decide to eat healthy, I'll tell you what you need to look for. Head to a nearby farmers' market and pick out fresh anti-inflammatory ingredients. Some of the most potent anti-inflammatory ingredients are listed under the next heading.

ANTI-INFLAMMATORY INGREDIENTS

Not all ingredients are created equal when it comes to the anti-inflammatory diet. Some are simply better and more potent than the others. I am a woman of science, and medical research has revealed some of the best ingredients for managing inflammation. If you're serious about this diet, you will do well to have all these ingredients on hand at all times.

BELL PEPPERS

Bell peppers—particularly red bell peppers—are a great source of antioxidants and capsaicin, both of which are exceptional at fighting inflammation. Add them to recipes containing turmeric for an anti-inflammatory bomb. They also contain quercetin, which enhances your body's absorption of anti-inflammatory curcumin. Be careful using these if you're sensitive to nightshades though.

BROCCOLI

High in fiber and immunity-boosting antioxidants like vitamin C, broccoli is a potent inti-inflammatory ingredient.

KALE

This vegetable is loaded with fiber and antioxidants.

SPINACH

Loaded with antioxidants like vitamin C and K, spinach is great at fighting inflammation.

TOMATOES

As long as you're not sensitive to nightshades, tomato is amazing at fighting inflammation, thanks to the lycopene contained within.

BLUEBERRIES

Blueberries are rich in antioxidants, and augment your immune system while fighting inflammation. Oh, and they taste absolutely amazing!

SALMON AND OTHER FATTY FISH

A good balance of essential fatty acids (omega-3 and omega-6 fatty acids) is absolutely vital to combat inflammation. Omega-3 fatty acids are anti-inflammatory, while omega-6 fatty acids are pro-inflammatory. Functional medicine specialist Chris Kresser notes that the perfect ratio of omega-6 fatty acids to omega-3 fatty acids is 1:1 or 2:1. The problem with the typical western diet is that this ratio is really unbalanced. The omega-6 fatty acid is so high in the western diet that the ratio can be as bad as 25:1! To counter this, supplemental fish oil rich in omega-3 fatty acids can be taken, or better yet, a diet rich in salmon and other fatty fish can be taken. These fish taste absolutely amazing, and are great anti-inflammatory ingredients!

NUTS

Nuts rich in omega-3 fatty acids are best. Some of these are: walnuts, cashews, almonds, pecans, etc. These have a high calorie density, so eat in moderation if you're looking to lose weight.

CINNAMON

Cinnamon contains cinnamaldehyde, which, according to an article in the January 2008 issue of Food and Chemical Toxicology, is a great at fighting inflammation.

GARLIC

One of the most potent anti-inflammatory ingredients, garlic has been used in home remedies since ancient times. Modern science too has now confirmed that garlic enhances the immune system, and is one of the best anti-inflammatory ingredients out there.

GINGER

Ginger adds an amazing flavor to whichever dish it is added, and boasts potent anti-inflammatory properties to boot!

ROSEMARY

This fragrant and flavorful herb is a potent anti-inflammatory ingredient. It goes especially well in a non-vegetarian dish.

TURMERIC

Turmeric contains curcumin, which many studies have concluded is great at fighting inflammation.

EXTRA-VIRGIN OLIVE OIL

EVOO is loaded with healthy fats, and contains oleocanthal, which is a potent anti-inflammatory compound.

GREEN TEA

Green tea is loaded with antioxidants, enhances the immune system, and has anti-inflammatory properties.

INGREDIENTS TO WATCH OUT FOR

While a certain ingredient might reduce inflammation in one person, it might do the exact opposite for another. Below is the list of a few ingredients that are common allergens, and if a certain recipe in this book doesn't help with inflammation, try eliminating these ingredients first.

The anti-inflammatory diet for every person will be a little different, and you are the only person who can find what ingredients suit you best. Below is the list of ingredients to watch out for:

- Dairy Products: A lot of people are allergic to casein, whey, and lactose. All three are contained in milk, and if you're allergic to even one of these, substitute dairy for nondairy alternatives such as almond milk or hemp milk.
- Eggs: This is an allergen that is hard to substitute in most cases. If you're baking, eggs can be replaced by flax eggs. Flax eggs can be made by mixing 1 tbsp ground flaxseed with 2½ tablespoons water and allowing to rest for 5 minutes until thick. This substitutes one egg in baking recipes.
- Fish: If you're allergic to fish, try shellfish instead. If you're allergic to that too, try chicken instead. Try tofu in fish recipes for a vegan dish. Soy sauce is a great alternative to fish sauce.
- Gluten: Gluten is one of the most common allergens out there. This protein is found in wheat, barley, etc. Two of my favorite gluten free grains are millet and quinoa.
- Nightshades: If you're sensitive to these, you should avoid eating tomatoes, tomatillos, goji berries, eggplant, bell peppers, chile peppers, and potatoes. Two alternatives are onions are garlic, but nightshades can never truly be substituted.
- Peanuts: Peanut allergy is quite common. It is a legume so substitute it with a nut you like and are not allergic to.
- Soy: If you're allergic to soy, you will need to read labels of all food items you buy. Tofu can be substituted by chicken, while soy sauce can be replaced by a spice blend of your choice.

- Tree Nuts: Tree such as almonds, walnuts, pecans, cashews, Brazil nuts, macadamia nuts, etc. are allergens to some. Try peanuts or a different nut you're not allergic to instead.
- Wheat: Another common allergen, wheat is easily replaced by buckwheat or rice flour.

THE COMPLETE ANTI-INFLAMMATORY FOOD LIST

BEVERAGES

POTENTIAL PRO-INFLAMMATORY INGREDIENTS (AVOID/MINIMIZE)

Soft drinks, sweetened (with sugar or artificial sweetener) || Soda, regular || Soda, diet || Milk, dairy || Liquor, hard || Liqueurs || Juice, sweetened || Energy drinks || Beer || Artificially or sugar sweetened drinks

INGREDIENTS THAT REDUCE INFLAMMATION (EAT THESE)

Wine (limit 4 oz.) || Kombucha || Coffee || Chai (with nondairy milk and no sugar)

POTENT ANTI-INFLAMMATORY FOODS (EAT A LOT)

Water || Tea (Particularly Green Tea)

CONDIMENTS

POTENTIAL PRO-INFLAMMATORY INGREDIENTS (AVOID/MINIMIZE)

Vinaigrette (store-bought) || Teriyaki sauce (store-bought) || Salsa, with sugar || Salad dressing || Mayonnaise (store-bought) || Ketchup || Cocktail sauce || Barbecue sauce

INGREDIENTS THAT REDUCE INFLAMMATION (EAT THESE)

Worcestershire sauce || Wasabi || Vinegar, all kinds || Vinaigrette (homemade) || Tomato paste || Teriyaki sauce, sugar-free (homemade) || Tamari || Tahini || Soy sauce || Salsa, sugar-free || Mustard, ground || Mustard, Dijon || Miso || Mayonnaise (homemade) || Hot sauce, sugar-free || Horseradish, prepared, sugar-free || Fish sauce, sugar-free || Anchovy paste

DAIRY AND DAIRY ALTERNATIVES

POTENTIAL PRO-INFLAMMATORY INGREDIENTS (AVOID/MINIMIZE)

Whipped cream || Sour cream || Nondairy creamer || Kefir, cow's milk || Ice cream || Heavy (whipping) cream || Half-and-half || Goat's milk || Cow's milk (all types) || Cheese, dairy (all types)

INGREDIENTS THAT REDUCE INFLAMMATION (EAT THESE)

Yogurt, Greek || Yogurt, dairy || Yogurt, coconut, plain, unsweetened || Yogurt, almond, plain, unsweetened || Soymilk, unsweetened || Kefir, water || Hemp milk, unsweetened || Coconut milk, lite, unsweetened || Coconut milk, full-fat, unsweetened || Almond milk, unsweetened

FATS AND OILS

POTENTIAL PRO-INFLAMMATORY INGREDIENTS (AVOID/MINIMIZE)

Vegetable oil || Sunflower oil || Soybean oil || Shortening || Sesame oil || Safflower oil || Peanut oil || Palm oil || Margarine || Lite olive oil || Hydrogenated oils || Corn oil || Canola oil || Butter

INGREDIENTS THAT REDUCE INFLAMMATION (EAT THESE)

Macadamia oil || Coconut oil || Avocado oil

POTENT ANTI-INFLAMMATORY FOODS (EAT A LOT)

Extra-Virgin Olive Oil

FRUITS

POTENTIAL PRO-INFLAMMATORY INGREDIENTS (AVOID/MINIMIZE)

Processed juices with added sugar || Canned fruit in syrup

INGREDIENTS THAT REDUCE INFLAMMATION (EAT THESE)

Yuzu || Watermelon || Ugli fruit || Tayberry || Tangerine || Tamarind || Strawberry || Star fruit || Satsuma || Santa Claus melon || Salmonberry || Red currant || Raspberry || Raisin || Quince || Prunes || Prickly pear || Pomelo || Pomegranate || Pluot || Plum || Plantain || Pineapple || Persimmon || Persian melon || Pear || Peach || Passionfruit || Papaya || Orange || Olives || Nectarine || Mulberry || Marionberry || Mangosteen || Mango || Mandarin || Lychee || Lime || Lemon || Kumquat || Kiwi || Jackfruit || Huckleberry || Horned melon || Honeydew || Guava || Grapefruit || Grape || Gooseberry || Goji berry || Galia (melon) || Fig || Elderberry || Durian || Dragon fruit || Date || Currant || Cranberry || Coconut || Clementine || Chokecherry || Cherry || Charentais (melon) || Casaba melon || Cantaloupe || Canary melon || Breadfruit || Boysenberry || Blood orange || Blackcurrant || Blackberry || Banana || Avocado || Asian pear || Apricot || Apple || Acai

POTENT ANTI-INFLAMMATORY FOODS (EAT A LOT)

Blueberries

GRAINS AND STARCHES

INGREDIENTS THAT MAY TRIGGER INFLAMMATION (AVOID/MINIMIZE)

Wheat, refined || Rice, white || Potato starch || Pasta || Oatmeal, instant, with sugar || Flour, white || Cereal || Bread, white || Baked goods (bread, cookies, donuts, pies, etc.)

INGREDIENTS THAT REDUCE INFLAMMATION (EAT THESE)

Wild rice || Wheat, whole || Wheat, cracked || Teff || Rye || Rice, brown || Quinoa || Oats, rolled || Millet || Kamut || Farro || Cornstarch || Corn || Bulgur || Buckwheat || Barley || Arrowroot || Amaranth

MEATS, POULTRY, FISH, AND PROTEINS

POTENTIAL PRO-INFLAMMATORY INGREDIENTS (AVOID/MINIMIZE)

Whey protein || Trout, fried || Shrimp, fried || Scallops, fried || Sausage || Salami || Pork, ground || Liver (all types) || Lamb, rib chops || Lamb, rack || Kidney (all types) || Hot dogs || Heart (all types) || Ham || Gizzards || Foie gras || Fish, fried || Farmed seafood || Deli meats || Cured meats || Chicken, fried || Catfish, fried || Brains (all types) || Bologna || Beef, rib eye || Beef, prime rib || Beef, New York strip || Beef, feedlot || Bacon

INGREDIENTS THAT REDUCE INFLAMMATION (EAT THESE)

Venison || Turkey, free-range, skinless || Tilapia, wild-caught || Sturgeon, wild-caught || Snapper || Skate || Shrimp || Scallops || Razor clams || Pork, top loin roast || Pork, tenderloin (preferably pastured) || Pork, sirloin roast || Pork, rib chop || Pork, center loin chop || Pork, boneless top loin chop || Orange roughy || Mussels || Lamb, very lean cuts || Halibut || Elk || Eggs || Duck, free-range, skinless || Cod || Clams || Chicken, free-range, skinless || Catfish, wild-caught || Bison, lean || Beef, lean or very lean || Bass, wild-caught || Anchovy

POTENT ANTI-INFLAMMATORY FOODS (EAT A LOT)

Salmon (and other fatty fish including tuna, mackerel, sardines, and trout)

NUTS, SEEDS, AND LEGUMES

INGREDIENTS THAT REDUCE INFLAMMATION (EAT THESE)

Walnuts, raw || Sunflower seeds || Soybeans || Sesame seeds || Poppy seeds || Pistachios, raw || Pinto beans || Pine nuts || Pecans, raw || Peas, sugar snap || Peas, split || Peas, snow || Peas, green || Peas, black-eyed || Peanuts, raw || Peanut butter || Macadamia nuts, raw || Lima beans || Lentils || Kidney beans || Hazelnuts, raw || Flaxseed || Fava beans || Cocoa beans (dark chocolate, cocoa powder) || Chickpeas (garbanzo beans) || Chia seeds || Cashews, raw || Brazil nuts, raw || Black beans || Almonds, raw || Almond butter || Adzuki beans

POTENT ANTI-INFLAMMATORY FOODS (EAT A LOT)

NUTS

SWEETENERS

POTENTIAL PRO-INFLAMMATORY INGREDIENTS (AVOID/MINIMIZE)

Xylitol || Syrup, brown rice, corn, high fructose corn, maple (artificial), simple || Sugar, brown and powdered || Sugar alcohols || Sucralose (Splenda) || Sorbitol || Saccharine || Molasses, refined || Mannitol || Erythritol || Aspartame (NutraSweet) || Agave nectar || Acesulfame-K (Acesulfame potassium)

INGREDIENTS THAT REDUCE INFLAMMATION (EAT THESE)

Stevia || Maple syrup, pure || Honey

VEGETABLES

POTENTIAL PRO-INFLAMMATORY INGREDIENTS (AVOID/MINIMIZE)

Zucchini || Yam || Watercress || Water chestnut || Wakame || Turnip greens || Turnip || Tomatoes, canned (sugar-free) || Tomato sauce (sugar-free) || Tomatillo || Swiss chard || Sweet potato || Sunchoke || Sprouts || Spinach || Spaghetti squash || Shallots || Scallions || Rutabaga || Rapini || Purslane || Pumpkin || Potatoes || Pea pods || Pattypan squash || Parsnip || Onions || Okra || Nori || Nopales || Mustard greens || Mushrooms || Lettuce (all types) || Kohlrabi Leeks || Jicama

INGREDIENTS THAT REDUCE INFLAMMATION (EAT THESE)

Hearts of palm || Grape leaves || Frisée || Fennel || Endive || Eggplant || Edamame || Dulse || Cucumber || Corn || Collard greens || Chayote || Celery || Celeriac (celery root) || Cauliflower || Carrots || Cabbage || Butternut squash || Brussels sprouts || Broccolini || Broccoli rabe || Bok choy || Beets || Beet greens || Beans, green || Asparagus || Arugula || Artichoke || Acorn squash

POTENT ANTI-INFLAMMATORY FOODS (EAT A LOT)

Tomatoes || spinach || kale || broccoli || bell peppers

HERBS, AND SPICES

POTENTIAL PRO-INFLAMMATORY INGREDIENTS (AVOID/MINIMIZE)

Table salt || Spice blends with sugar || Seasoning salt || Garlic salt

INGREDIENTS THAT REDUCE INFLAMMATION (EAT THESE)

Vanilla bean || Thyme || Tarragon || Sumac || Spearmint || Salt, Himalayan pink and sea || Sage || Saffron || Rhubarb || Red pepper flakes || Radish || Radicchio || Pepper (black) || Parsley || Paprika || Oregano || Orange zest || Onion powder || Nutmeg || Mustard seed || Mustard powder || Mint || Marjoram || Mace || Lime zest || Lemongrass || Lemon zest || Lemon pepper || Lavender || Juniper berry || Horseradish || Herbes de Provence || Garam masala || Galangal || Fenugreek || Fennel seed || Dill || Curry powder || Cumin || Coriander || Cilantro || Chives || Chipotle || Chinese five-spice powder || Chile peppers || Chamomile || Celery salt || Cayenne || Cassia || Caraway || Bay leaves || Basil || Asafoetida || Anise, star || Anise || Allspice

POTENT ANTI-INFLAMMATORY FOODS (EAT A LOT)

TURMERIC || ROSEMARY || GINGER || GARLIC || CINNAMON

PANTRY ESSENTIALS

If you're serious about the anti-inflammatory diet, you will do well to make the following ingredients a staple in your pantry:

CANNED ITEMS

- Tomatoes, crushed
- Tomatoes, chopped
- Red bell peppers, roasted, in oil
- Coconut milk, lite
- Broth, vegetable, no salt added
- Broth, chicken, no salt added

HERBS AND SPICES

- Turmeric, ground
- Thyme, dried
- Salt, Himalayan pink or sea
- Rosemary, dried
- Red pepper flakes
- Peppercorns
- Oregano, dried
- Onion powder
- Nutmeg, ground
- Ginger, ground
- Garlic powder
- Curry powder
- Cinnamon, ground
- Chili powder

NUTS, SEEDS, LEGUMES, AND GRAINS

- Sunflower seeds
- Sesame seeds, toasted
- Rice, brown, cooked
- Quinoa
- Peanut butter
- Lentils, canned
- Chickpeas, canned
- Beans, kidney, canned
- Beans, black, canned
- Almond butter

OILS, VINEGARS, AND CONDIMENTS

- Vinegar, apple cider
- Soy sauce, low-sodium (or gluten-free or tamari)
- Olive oil, extra-virgin
- Mustard, Dijon

SUGAR, BAKING INGREDIENTS, AND FLOURS

- Vanilla extract

- Sugar, brown
- Stevia
- Milk, almond, hemp, or rice, unsweetened
- Maple syrup, pure
- Honey
- Green tea
- Cocoa powder, unsweetened
- Arrowroot powder (or cornstarch)

TIPS AND TRICKS

Here are a few suggestions I give to my clients to make it easier for them to cook the food, and stick to the diet:

- Weekly Diet Plans Work. If you think too much ahead, things will be hard. Plan for a week, or even less. Make a meal plan using the recipes in this book, and make a shopping list. Shopping only for the ingredients you'll be using in the following week will ensure that they stay fresh, and your brain stays relatively stress-free.
- Cook in Large Batches. If you're lazy like me and wouldn't like to cook three times every day, try cooking a LOT. This only works for dishes that store well in the fridge. Take a serving size out of the fridge, heat using a microwave, eat, repeat.
- Have Fun With Leftovers. Leftovers are a great opportunity to let your imagination run wild and invent a new recipe tailored to your personal taste!
- Veggies are Love. Buy lots of fresh vegetables when you're at a grocery store. Better yet, take a stroll through a farmers' market near you.
- Try Different Cooking Methods. Depending on how much time you have, and when you want to eat, a different cooking method might make the work easier. Slow cooking, for example, is great for someone who has a day job and would like to come back home to a home cooked meal, without another home cook.
- Prepare and Shop on Weekends and Holidays. If you have a full time job, make sure you take care of some of the planning and shopping on the day off.
- Frozen veggies and fruits are Great. There is a misconception that frozen fruits and vegetables lose their nutrition. That is just not true. These are usually flash frozen while they are at their peak of ripeness, and due to being frozen, that peak is maintained for much longer!

- Machine Tools are Handy. Food processors are love, Food processors are life.
- Store Food Right. Different ingredients like to be stored in different ways. While an ingredient is best stored in the freezer, another might do stored at room temperature. If you're not sure about the best way to store a particular ingredient, google is your friend!
- Internet for The Win. If you can't find that pesky ingredient in a nearby store, check online on amazon. If you can't figure out a cooking procedure by words alone, watch a YouTube video.

ABOUT THE RECIPES

All right! I think we are done with the basics. Let us dive into the recipes! Make sure you read the ingredients and directions carefully before starting a recipe. This book calls for all kinds of tools ranging from slow cookers to instant pots. If you don't have the appliance required to cook a particular recipe, just skip to a different recipe, and return to it once you have invested in the appliance. Also, Make sure you're not allergic to any of the ingredients. Let's go!

POULTRY RECIPES

ADOBO LIME CHICKEN MIX

Time To Prepare: ten minutes

Time to Cook: forty minutes

Yield: Servings 6

Ingredients:

- 1 cup cut peach
- 1 tablespoon lime juice
- 1 tablespoon olive oil
- 1½ teaspoons chipotle peppers in adobo sauce
- 6 chicken thighs
- Salt and black pepper to the taste
- Zest of 1 lime

Directions:

1. Warm a pan with the oil on moderate to high heat and put in the chicken thighs. Sprinkle with salt and pepper, then brown for about four minutes on each side and bake in your oven at 375 degrees F for about twenty minutes.
2. In your food processor, combine the peaches with the chipotle, lime zest, and lime juice, then blend and pour over the chicken. Bake for about ten minutes more, split everything between plates before you serve.

Nutritional Info: Calories: 309 ‖ Fat: 6 ‖ Fiber: 4 ‖ Carbohydrates: 16 ‖ Protein: fifteen

ALMOND CHICKEN CUTLETS

Time To Prepare: ten minutes

Time to Cook: 15 minutes

Yield: Servings 4

Ingredients:

- ¼ cup good-quality olive oil

- ½ teaspoon garlic powder
- 1 cup almond flour
- 1 tablespoon chopped fresh oregano
- 2 eggs
- 2 tablespoons grass-fed butter
- 4 (4-ounce) boneless skinless chicken breasts, pounded to approximately ¼ inch thick

Directions:

1. Bread the chicken. Mix together the eggs, garlic powder in a moderate-sized container, and set it aside. Mix together the almond flour and oregano on a plate and set the plate next to the egg mixture. Pat the chicken breasts to dry using paper towels and immerse them into the egg mixture. Remove surplus egg then roll the chicken in the almond flour until they are coated.
2. Fry the chicken. In a big frying pan on moderate to high heat, warm the olive oil and butter. Put in the breaded chicken breasts and fry them, turning them once, until they are thoroughly cooked, very crunchy, and golden brown, and 14 to 16 minutes in total.
3. Serve. Put one cutlet on each of four plates and serve them instantly.

Nutritional Info: Calories: 328 Total fat: 23g Total carbs: 0g || Fiber: 0g Net carbs: 0g || Sodium: 75mg || Protein: 28g

APRICOT CHICKEN WINGS

Time To Prepare: 15 minutes

Time to Cook: 45-60 minutes

Yield: Servings 3-4

Ingredients:

- 1 medium bottle Russian dressing
- 1 medium jar apricot preserve
- 1 package Lipton onion dry soup mix
- 2 lbs. chicken wings

Directions:

1. Preheat your oven to 350°F.
2. Wash and pat dry the chicken wings.

3. Bring the chicken wings on a baking pan, single layer.
4. Bake for 45 – 60 minutes, turning midway.
5. In a moderate-sized container, mix the Lipton soup mix, apricot preserve, and Russian dressing.
6. Once the wings are cooked, toss with the sauce, until the pieces are coated.
7. Serve instantly with a side dish.

Nutritional Info: Calories: 162 || Fat:17 g || Carbohydrates:76 g || Protein:13 g Sugars:24 g Sodium:700 mg

ASIAN SAUCY CHICKEN

Time To Prepare: ten minutes

Time to Cook: 15 minutes

Yield: Servings 4

Ingredients:

- 1 tablespoon sesame oil
- 1/4 cup Shaoxing wine
- 1/4 cup spicy tomato sauce
- 2 tablespoons brown erythritol
- 4 chicken legs

Directions:

1. Heat the sesame oil in a wok at moderate to high heat. Fry the chicken until golden in color; reserve.
2. Put in Shaoxing wine to deglaze the pan.
3. Put in in erythritol and spicy tomato sauce, and bring the mixture to its boiling point. Next, instantly decrease the heat to moderate-low.
4. Allow it to simmer for approximately ten minutes until the sauce coats the back of a spoon. Put in the chicken back to the wok.
5. Continue to cook until the chicken is sticky and golden or approximately four minutes. Enjoy!

Nutritional Info: 367 Calories 14.7g || Fat: 3.5g || Carbs: 51.2g || Protein: 1.1g Fiber

AVOCADO-ORANGE GRILLED CHICKEN

Time To Prepare: ten minutes

Time to Cook: twelve minutes

Yield: Servings 4

Ingredients:

- ¼ c. fresh lime juice
- ¼ c. minced red onion
- 1 c. low-fat yogurt
- 1 deseeded avocado, peeled and chopped
- 1 tbsp. honey
- 1 thinly cut small red onion
- 2 peeled and sectioned oranges
- 2 tbsps. chopped cilantro
- 4 pieces of 4-6oz boneless, skinless chicken breasts
- Pepper
- Salt

Directions:

1. Set up a big mixing container and mix yogurt, minced red onion, cilantro and honey
2. Put in chicken into the mixture and marinate for half an hour
3. Grease grate and preheat the grill to moderate-high heat.
4. Position the chicken aside and put in seasonings
5. Grill for about six minutes on each side
6. Set the avocado in a container.
7. Put in lime juice and toss avocado to coat well.
8. Put in oranges, thinly cut onions, and cilantro into the container with avocado and mix well.
9. Serve avocado dressing alongside grilled chicken.

Nutritional Info: Calories: 216 kcal || Protein: 8.83 g || Fat: 11.48 g || Carbohydrates: 21.86 g

BACON-WRAPPED CHICKEN WITH CHEDDAR CHEESE

Time To Prepare: ten minutes

Time to Cook: 4 hours

Yield: Servings 6

Ingredients:

- ½ cup Cheddar cheese, grated
- 1 tablespoon olive oil
- 2 big chicken breasts, each cut into 6 pieces
- 4 garlic cloves, crushed
- 6 slices of streaky bacon, each cut in half widthways
- Freshly ground black pepper, to taste
- Salt, to taste

Directions:

1. Grease the insert of the slow cooker with olive oil.
2. Cover each piece of chicken breast with each half of the bacon slice, and place them in the slow cooker. Drizzle with garlic, salt, and black pepper.
3. Place the lid and then cook on LOW for 4 hours.
4. Set the oven to 350ºF (180ºC).
5. Move the cooked bacon-wrapped chicken to a baking dish, then sprinkle with cheese.
6. Cook in the preheated oven for five minutes or until the cheese melts.
7. Take it off from the oven and serve warm.

Nutritional Info: Calories: 308 Total fat: 20.8g Total carbs: 2.9g ‖ Fiber: 0g Net carbs: 2.9g ‖ Protein: 26.1g

---

BAKED CHICKEN MEATBALLS - HABANERO & GREEN CHILI

Time To Prepare: ten minutes

Time to Cook: twenty-five minutes

Yield: Servings fifteen

Ingredients:

- ½ cup cilantro
- 1 habanero pepper
- 1 jalapeno pepper

- 1 poblano pepper
- 1 pound ground chicken
- 1 tbsp. olive oil
- 1 tbsp. vinegar
- salt to taste

Directions:

1. Preheat broiler to 400 degrees Fahrenheit.
2. In an enormous blending container, join chicken, minced peppers, cilantro, salt, and vinegar with your hands. Structure 1-inch meatballs with the blend
3. Coat every meatball with olive oil, at that point, place on a rimmed heating sheet or meal dish.
4. Heat for about twenty-five minutes

Nutritional Info: Calories 54 || Fat: 3g || Carbs: 5g || Protein: 5g

BALSAMIC-GLAZED TURKEY WINGS

Time To Prepare: 15 minutes

Time to Cook: 7 to 8 hours

Yield: Servings 4

Ingredients:

- 1 teaspoon garlic powder
- 1¼ cups balsamic vinegar
- 2 pounds turkey wings
- 2 tablespoons raw honey

Directions:

1. In a container, put together the vinegar, honey, and garlic powder then mix.
2. Place the wings on the bottom of the slow cooker, and pour the vinegar sauce on top.
3. Secure the lid of your cooker and set to low. Cook for about eight hours.
4. Baste the wings with the sauce from the bottom of the slow cooker before you serve.

Nutritional Info: Calories: 501 || Total Fat: 25g || Sugar: 9g || Fiber: 0g || Protein: 47g || Sodium: 162mg

BASIC "ROTISSERIE" CHICKEN

Time To Prepare: 15 minutes

Time to Cook: six to eight hours

Yield: Servings 6

Ingredients:

- ½ medium onion, cut
- 1 (4-5 lb.) whole chicken, neck and giblets removed
- 1 teaspoon chili powder
- 1 teaspoon dried thyme leaves
- 1 teaspoon garlic powder
- 1 teaspoon paprika
- 1 teaspoon sea salt
- Freshly ground black pepper
- Pinch cayenne pepper

Directions:

1. In a small container, mix together the garlic powder, chili powder, paprika, thyme, salt, and cayenne. Flavor it with black pepper, and stir again to blend. Rub the spice mix all over the exterior of the chicken.
2. Put the chicken in the cooker with the cut onion sprinkled around it.
3. Secure the lid of your cooker and set to low. Cook for minimum six to eight hours, or until the internal temperature reaches 165ºF on a meat thermometer and the juices run clear, before you serve.

Nutritional Info: Calories: 862 || Total Fat: 59g || Total Carbohydrates: 7g || Sugar: 6g || Fiber: 0g || Protein: 86g || Sodium: 1,200mg

---

BASIL CHICKEN SAUTE

Time To Prepare: ten minutes

Time to Cook: 15 minutes

Yield: Servings 2

Ingredients:

- 1 chicken breast, minced or chopped minuscule
- 1 chili pepper, diced (not necessary)
- 1 cup) basil leaves, finely chopped
- 1 Tablespoon tamari sauce
- 2 cloves of garlic, minced
- 2 Tablespoons avocado or coconut oil to cook in
- Salt, to taste

Directions:

1. Put in oil to a frying pan and saute the garlic and pepper.
2. Then put in in the minced chicken and saute until the chicken is cooked.
3. Put in the tamari sauce and salt to taste. Put in in the basil leaves and mix it in.

Nutritional Info: Calories: 320 || Fat: 24 g || Net Carbohydrates: 2 g || Protein: 24 g

BBQ CHICKEN ZUCCHINI BOATS

Time To Prepare: ten minutes

Time to Cook: fifteen-twenty minutes

Yield: Servings 4

Ingredients:

- .25 cup Diced green onions
- .33 cup Shredded Mexican cheese
- .5 cup BBQ sauce
- .5 cup Halved cherry tomatoes
- 1 Avocado, cut
- 1 lb. cooked Chicken breast
- 3 tbsp. Keto-friendly ranch dressing
- 3 Zucchini halved
- Also Needed: 9x13 casserole dish

Directions:

1. Set the oven to reach 350° Fahrenheit.

2. Using a knife, chop the zucchini in half. Discard the seeds. Make the boat by carving out of the center. Put the zucchini flesh side up into the casserole dish.
3. Discard and chop the skin and bones from the chicken. Shred and put in the chicken in with the barbeque sauce. Toss to coat all the chicken fully.
4. Fill the zucchini boats with the mixture using about .25 to .33 cup each.
5. Drizzle with Mexican cheese on top.
6. Bake for roughly fifteen minutes. (If you would like it tenderer; bake for another 5 to ten minutes to reach the desired tenderness.)
7. Take out of the oven. Top it off with avocado, green onion, tomatoes, and a sprinkle of dressing and serve.

Nutritional Info: Calories: 212 ‖ Net Carbohydrates: 9 g ‖ Total Fat: Content: 11 g ‖ Protein: 19 g

---

BLUE CHEESE BUFFALO CHICKEN BALLS

Time To Prepare: ten minutes

Time to Cook: eighteen minutes

Yield: Servings 4-6

Ingredients:

- ¼ cup chopped celery
- ½ cup crumbled organic blue cheese
- ½ teaspoon freshly ground black pepper
- ½ teaspoon sea salt
- 1 big free-range egg, lightly beaten
- 1 cup shredded organic mozzarella cheese
- 1 pound free-range ground chicken
- 1 recipe Buffalo Sauce
- 1 teaspoon onion powder
- 2 tablespoons water

Directions:

1. Preheat your oven to 450°F.
2. Coat a baking pan using parchment paper.

3. In a big container, put and mix the chicken, egg, mozzarella, blue cheeses, celery, water, onion powder, salt, and pepper. Use your hands to combine the ingredients thoroughly.
4. Make 20 meatballs into a mixture then put them in the baking pan as you do.
5. Bake until the internal temperature reaches 165°F, approximately eighteen minutes.
6. On the other hand, warm the buffalo sauce in a moderate-sized deep cooking pan using low heat.
7. When the meatballs are done, toss them in the warm sauce before you serve.

Nutritional Info: Calories: 340 || Total Fat: 17g || Saturated Fat: 6g || Protein: 44g || Cholesterol: 157mg || Carbohydrates: 2g || Fiber: 0g || Net Carbohydrates: 2g

BOOZY GLAZED CHICKEN

Time To Prepare: five minutes

Time to Cook: 55 minutes

Yield: Servings 4

Ingredients:

- 1 tablespoon minced fresh ginger
- 1 teaspoon chile peppers, minced
- 1 teaspoon ground cardamom
- 1 teaspoon Mediterranean seasoning mix
- 2 pounds chicken drumettes
- 2 tablespoons fresh lemon juice, + wedges for serving
- 2 tablespoons ghee, at room temperature
- 2 vine-ripened tomatoes, pureed
- 3 tablespoons coconut aminos
- 3/4 cup rum
- A few drops of liquid Stevia
- Ground black pepper, to taste
- Sea salt, to taste

Directions:

1. Toss the chicken with the melted ghee, salt, black pepper, and Mediterranean seasoning stir until thoroughly coated on all sides.

2. In another container, meticulously mix the pureed tomato puree, rum, coconut aminos, Stevia, chile peppers, ginger, cardamom, and lemon juice.
3. Pour the tomato mixture over the chicken drumettes; allow it to marinate for about two hours. Bake in the preheated oven at 410 degrees F for approximately 45 minutes.
4. Put in in the reserved marinade and place under the preheated broiler for about ten minutes.

Nutritional Info: 307 Calories 12.1g || Fat: 2.7g || Carbs: 33.6g || Protein: 1.5g Fiber

BREADED CHICKEN FILLETS

Time To Prepare: five minutes

Time to Cook: 10-twenty-five minutes

Yield: Servings 4

Ingredients:

- 1 garlic clove, minced
- 1 pound chicken fillets
- 1/3 cup crushed pork rinds
- 1/3 cup Romano cheese
- 2 teaspoons olive oil
- 3 bell peppers, quartered along the length
- Ground black pepper, to taste
- Kosher salt, to taste

Directions:

1. Set oven to 410°F
2. Combine the crushed pork rinds, Romano cheese, olive oil, and minced garlic. Immerse the chicken into this mixture.
3. Bring the chicken into a mildly greased baking sheet. Drizzle with salt and black pepper to taste.
4. Spread the peppers around the chicken and bake in the preheated oven for twenty to twenty-five minutes or until meticulously cooked.

Nutritional Info: 367 Calories 16.9g || Fat: 6g || Carbs: 43g || Protein: 0.7g Fiber

BUFFALO BALLS

Time To Prepare: ten minutes

Time to Cook: forty minutes

Yield: Servings 18

Ingredients:

For the Meatballs:

- 1lb ground chicken or turkey
- 2 oz. cream cheese softened
- 1 egg
- 2 tbsp. chopped celery
- 3 tbsp. crumbled blue cheese
- 1/4 cup almond flour
- 1/4 tsp black pepper

For the Sauce:

- ½ cup Frank's Red Hot
- ½ stick (4 oz.) unsalted butter

Directions:

1. In a moderate-sized container, put all the meatballs ingredients then mix. Form into approximately 1 inch balls.
2. Set it on a greased cookie sheet (with sides) and bake at 350°F for minimum ten minutes.
3. To make the sauce: put the Frank's and butter in a small deep cooking pan on moderate heat, or put in a microwave-safe container for a couple of minutes on high.
4. After ten minutes, remove balls from the oven and dunk cautiously in the buffalo sauce.
5. Return onto the cookie sheet and bake for an additional twelve minutes. If you have a leftover sauce, you could pour it over the meatballs and bake for an additional three to four minutes if you wish them saucy.

Nutritional Info: Calories: 331 || Fat: 28g || Carbohydrates: 2g || Protein: 17g

BUFFALO CHICKEN LETTUCE WRAPS

Time To Prepare: 15 minutes

Time to Cook: 7 to 8 hours

Yield: Servings 4

Ingredients:

- ½ red onion, thinly cut
- 1 cup cherry tomatoes, halved
- 1 cup water
- 1 tablespoon extra-virgin olive oil
- 2 cups Vegan Buffalo Dip
- 2 pounds boneless, skinless chicken breast
- 8 to 10 romaine lettuce leaves

Directions:

1. Coat the bottom of the slow cooker with olive oil.
2. Put in the chicken, dip, and water, and stir until blended.
3. Secure the lid of your cooker and set to low. Cook for about eight hours, or until the internal temperature reaches 165°F on a meat thermometer and the juices run clear.
4. Shred the chicken using a fork, then mix it into the dip in the slow cooker.
5. Split the meat mixture among the lettuce leaves. Top with onion and tomato, before you serve.

Nutritional Info: Calories: 437 || Total Fat: 18g || Total Carbohydrates: 18g || Sugar: 8g || Fiber: 4g || Protein: 49g || Sodium: 993mg

BUFFALO PIZZA CHICKEN

Time To Prepare: five minutes

Time to Cook: 5-6 minutes

Yield: Servings 5

Ingredients:

- ¼ cup crumbled blue cheese
- ½ cup Buffalo-style hot sauce
- 1 (16-oz) package prebaked Italian pizza crust

- 1 cup (4 oz) shredded Provolone cheese
- 2 cups chopped deli-roasted whole chicken
- Vegetable cooking spray

Directions:

1. Coat the grill with the spray and put it on the grill. Preheat grill to 350° F (moderate heat).
2. Spread the hot sauce over the crust, and the next 3 ingredients surface.
3. Put the crust on the cooking grate directly. Grill at 350° F (moderate heat) for 4 min, covered with the grill lid.
4. Rotate 1-quarter turn pizza and grill, covered with grill top, for five to 6 min or until heated meticulously. Serve immediately.

Nutritional Info: Calories: 365 || Fat: 11g || Net Carbohydrates: 42g || Protein: 24g

CAJUN CHICKEN & PRAWN

Time To Prepare: five minutes

Time to Cook: thirty-five minutes

Yield: Servings 2

Ingredients:

- 1 can Tomatoes, chopped
- 1 cup Brown or wholegrain rice
- 1 Onion, chopped
- 1 Red pepper, chopped
- 1 tbsp. Extra Virgin olive oil
- 1 tsp. Cayenne powder
- 1 tsp. Chili powder
- 1 tsp. Dried oregano
- 1 tsp. Dried thyme
- 1 tsp. Paprika
- 1/4 tsp. Chili powder
- 10 Fresh or frozen prawn
- 2 cups Homemade chicken stock

- 2 Free-range Skinless Chicken breast, chopped
- 2 Garlic cloves, crushed

Directions:

1. In a container, put all the spices and herbs then mix to make your Cajun spice mix.
2. Grab a big pan and put in the olive oil, heating on moderate heat.
3. Put in the chicken and brown each side for about five minutes. Put to one side.
4. Put in the onion to the pan and fry until tender.
5. Put in the garlic, prawns, Cajun seasoning, and red pepper to the pan and cook for around five minutes or until prawns become opaque.
6. Put in the brown rice together with the chopped tomatoes, chicken, and chicken stock to the pan.
7. Cover the pan and let simmer for around twenty-five minutes or until the rice is tender.
8. Serve and enjoy!

Nutritional Info: Calories: 557 kcal || Protein: 18.96 g || Fat: 12.34 g || Carbohydrates: 93.28 g

CAPOCOLLO AND GARLIC CHICKEN

Time To Prepare: ten minutes

Time to Cook: forty minutes

Yield: Servings 5

Ingredients:

- ½ teaspoon smoked paprika
- 1 garlic clove, peeled and halved
- 10 fine slices of capocollo
- 2 pounds chicken drumsticks, skinless and boneless, butterflied
- Coarse sea salt, to taste
- Ground black pepper, to taste

Directions:

1. Rub garlic halves on the surface of chicken drumsticks. Flavor it with paprika, salt, and black pepper.
2. Put a slice of capocollo on each chicken drumsticks and roll them up; secure using a kitchen twine.

3. Bake using your oven at 410°F for half an hour until your chicken starts to brown. Enjoy!

Nutritional Info: 485 Calories 33.8g || Fat: 3.6g || Carbs: 39.2g || Protein: 1g Fiber

CELERY FRIES AND CHICKEN

Time To Prepare: 15 minutes

Time to Cook: 20 minutes

Yield: Servings 6

Ingredients:

Chicken

- 2 tbsp. Coconut oil
- 4 Chicken breasts
- Pepper (as required)
- Salt (as required)

Celery Fries

- .25 tsp. Pepper
- .5 tsp. Salt
- 1.5lbs. Root celery
- 2 tbsp. Coconut oil

Directions:

1. Ensure the oven is on and turn to 400F.
2. Cube the chicken before you put in it to a big mixing container before you put in in 2 T coconut oil and seasoning as required. Let the chicken marinate for minimum fifteen minutes.
3. Simultaneously, chop the root celery into strips and place it in a big container before you put in in the rest of the coconut oil and seasoning as required. Shake well to coat.
4. Put the celery strips and chicken on a baking sheet before placing the sheet in your oven to bake for about twenty minutes.

Nutritional Info: Calories: 623 kcal || Protein: 74.67 g || Fat: 32.46 g || Carbohydrates: 4.26 g

CHAMPION CHICKEN POCKETS

Time To Prepare: five minutes

Time to Cook: 0 minutes

Yield: Servings 4

Ingredients:

- ¼ c. bottled reduced-fat ranch salad dressing
- ¼ c. chopped pecans or walnuts
- ¼ c. plain low-fat yogurt
- ¼ c. shredded carrot
- ½ c. chopped broccoli
- 1 ½ c. chopped cooked chicken
- 2 halved whole wheat pita bread rounds

Directions:

1. In a container, put together yogurt and ranch salad dressing then mix.
2. In a moderate-sized container, put then mix chicken, broccoli, carrot, and, if you wish, nuts. Pour yogurt mixture over chicken; toss to coat.
3. Ladle chicken mixture into pita halves.

Nutritional Info: Calories: 384 ‖ Fat: 11.4 g ‖ Carbohydrates: 7.4 g ‖ Protein: 59.3 g ‖ Sugars: 1.3 g ‖ Sodium: 368.7 mg

CHEESY BACON-WRAPPED CHICKEN WITH ASPARAGUS SPEARS

Time To Prepare: 20 minutes

Time to Cook: thirty minutes

Yield: Servings 4

Ingredients:

- ½ cup Manchego cheese, grated
- 1 pound (454 g) asparagus spears
- 2 tablespoons fresh lemon juice
- 4 chicken breasts
- 4 tablespoons olive oil, divided

- 8 bacon slices
- Freshly ground black pepper, to taste
- Salt, to taste

Directions:

1. Set the oven to 400ºF. Coat a baking sheet using parchment paper, then grease with 1 tablespoon olive oil.
2. Place the chicken breasts in a big container, and drizzle with salt and black pepper. Toss to blend well.
3. Cover every chicken breast with 2 slices of bacon. Put the chicken on the baking sheet, then bake in the preheated oven for about twenty-five minutes or until the bacon is crunchy.
4. Preheat the grill to high, then brush with the rest of the olive oil.
5. Put the asparagus spears on the grill grate, and drizzle with salt. Grill for five minutes or until fork-soft. Flip the asparagus regularly during the grilling.
6. Move the bacon-wrapped chicken breasts to four plates, sprinkle with lemon juice, and sprinkle with Manchego cheese. Spread the hot asparagus spears on top to serve.

Nutritional Info: Calories: 455 Total fat: 38.1g Net carbs: 2g || Protein: 26.1g

CHEESY CHICKEN SUN-DRIED TOMATO PACKETS

Time To Prepare: 15 minutes

Time to Cook: forty minutes

Yield: Servings 4

Ingredients:

- ½ cup chopped oil-packed sun-dried tomatoes
- ½ teaspoon dried basil
- ½ teaspoon dried oregano
- 1 cup goat cheese
- 1 teaspoon minced garlic
- 3 tablespoons olive oil
- 4 (4-ounce) boneless chicken breasts
- Freshly ground black pepper, for seasoning
- Sea salt, for seasoning

Directions:

1. Preheat your oven. Set the oven temperature to 375°F.
2. Prepare the filling. In a moderate-sized container, put the goat cheese, sun-dried tomatoes, garlic, basil, and oregano then stir until everything is well mixed.
3. Fill the chicken. Make a horizontal slice in the center of each chicken breast to make a pocket, ensuring not to cut through the sides or ends. Ladle one-quarter of the filling into each breast, folding the skin and chicken meat over the slit to make packets. Secure the packets using a toothpick. Lightly flavor the breasts with salt and pepper.
4. Brown the chicken. In a big oven-safe frying pan on moderate heat, warm the olive oil. Put in the breasts and sear them, turning them once, until they are golden, approximately eight minutes in total.
5. Bake the chicken. Bring the frying pan into the oven and bake the chicken for thirty minutes or until it's thoroughly cooked.
6. Serve. Take away the toothpicks. Split the chicken into 4 plates and serve them instantly.

Nutritional Info: Calories: 388 Total fat: 29g Total carbs: 4g ‖ Fiber: 1g; Net carbs: 3g ‖ Sodium: 210mg ‖ Protein: 28g

CHEESY MEXICAN-STYLE CHICKEN

Time To Prepare: ten minutes

Time to Cook: twenty-five minutes

Yield: Servings 6

Ingredients:

- 1 ½ pounds chicken breasts, cut into bite-sized cubes
- 1 Mexican chili pepper, finely chopped
- 2 ripe tomatoes, pureed
- 4 ounces sour cream
- 6 ounces Cotija cheese, crumbled

Directions:

1. Preheat the oven to 390 degrees F.

2. In a deep cooking pan, heat 2 tablespoons of olive oil on moderate to high heat. Cook the chicken breasts for approximately ten minutes, regularly stirring to make sure even cooking.
3. Next, put in in Mexican chili pepper and cook until it has tenderized.
4. Put in in the pureed tomatoes and carry on cooking, partly covered, for four to five minutes—flavor with the Mexican spice mix. Move the mixture to a mildly greased baking dish.
5. Top with the sour cream and Cotija cheese. Bake in the preheated oven for approximately fifteen minutes or until hot and bubbly. Enjoy!

Nutritional Info: 354 Calories 23.2g || Fat: 6g || Carbs: 29.3g || Protein: 0.6g Fiber

CHEESY PINWHEELS WITH CHICKEN

Time To Prepare: ten minutes

Time to Cook: thirty minutes

Yield: Servings 2

Ingredients:

- ¼ cup fresh cilantro, chopped
- ¼ cup whipping cream
- ½ cup chicken stock
- ½ cup mozzarella cheese, grated
- 1 garlic, minced
- 1 tomato, chopped
- 1 tsp creole seasoning
- 1/3 pound chicken breasts, cubed
- 1/3 red onion, chopped
- 2 tbsp. ghee
- 4 ounces cream cheese
- 5 eggs
- A pinch of garlic powder
- Salt and black pepper, to taste

Directions:

1. Flavour the chicken with creole seasoning. Heat a pan at moderate heat and warm 1 tbsp. ghee. Put chicken and cook per side for a couple of minutes; transfer to a plate.
2. Melt the remaining ghee and mix in garlic and tomato; cook for about four minutes. Put the chicken back into the pan and pour in stock; cook for fifteen minutes. Put in whipping cream, red onion, salt, mozzarella cheese, and black pepper; cook for a couple of minutes.
3. In a blender, combine the cream cheese with garlic powder, salt, eggs, and black pepper, and pulse well. Put the mixture into a lined baking sheet, and then bake for about ten minutes in your oven at 320 F. Allow the cheese sheet to cool down, place on a cutting board, roll, and slice into moderate slices.
4. Organize the slices on a serving plate and top with chicken mixture. Drizzle with cilantro to serve.

Nutritional Info: Calories 463 ‖ Fat: 36.4g Net ‖ Carbs: 6.3g ‖ Protein: 35.2g

CHEESY RANCH CHICKEN

Time To Prepare: ten minutes

Time to Cook: 20 minutes

Yield: Servings 4

Ingredients:

- ½ cup Monterey-Jack cheese, grated
- ½ tablespoon ranch seasoning mix
- 2 chicken breasts
- 4 ounces Ricotta cheese, room temperature
- 4 slices bacon, chopped

Directions:

1. Preheat the oven to 360 degrees F.
2. Rub the chicken with ranch seasoning mix.
3. Heat a deep cooking pan over moderate to high flame. Now, sear the chicken for approximately 8 minutes. Lower the chicken into a mildly greased casserole dish.
4. Top with cheese and bacon and bake in the preheated oven for approximately ten minutes until hot and bubbly. Serve with freshly snipped scallions, if you wish.

Nutritional Info: 295 Calories 19.5g || Fat: 2.9g || Carbs: 25.5g || Protein: 0.4g Fiber

CHICKEN & CHEESE FILLED AVOCADOS

Time To Prepare: ten minutes

Time to Cook: 0 minutes

Yield: Servings 2

Ingredients:

- ¼ cup mayonnaise
- ¼ tsp cayenne pepper
- ½ tsp garlic powder
- ½ tsp onion powder
- 1 ½ cups chicken, cooked and shredded
- 1 tsp dried thyme
- 1 tsp paprika
- 2 avocados
- 2 tbsp. cream cheese
- 2 tbsp. lemon juice
- Salt and black pepper, to taste

Directions:

1. Halve the avocados and scoop the insides.
2. Place the flesh in a container, then put in in the chicken; mix in the rest of the ingredients.
3. Fill the avocado cups with chicken mixture before you serve.

Nutritional Info: Calories 518 || Fat: 41.6 Net || Carbs: 5.3g || Protein: 23.2g

CHICKEN AND SNAP PEAS STIR FRY

Time To Prepare: ten minutes

Time to Cook: 20 minutes

Yield: Servings 8

Ingredients:

- 1/3 cup fresh cilantro, chopped
- 2 ½ cups chicken breast, skinless, boneless, thinly cut
- 2 bunches scallions, thinly cut
- 2 red bell peppers, thinly cut
- 4 cloves garlic, peeled, minced
- 4 tablespoons rice vinegar
- 4 tablespoons sesame seeds
- 4 tablespoons vegetable oil
- 4 teaspoons Sriracha sauce (not necessary)
- 5 cups snap peas
- 6 tablespoons soy sauce
- Freshly ground pepper to taste
- Salt to taste

Directions:

1. Put a big frying pan on moderate heat. Put in oil. Once the oil is heated, put the garlic and onion and cook until aromatic.
2. Mix in the bell peppers and snap peas and cook for about four minutes until slightly soft.
3. Mix in the chicken and cook until brown and thoroughly cooked.
4. Mix in the soy sauce, sesame seeds, sriracha, and vinegar. Mix thoroughly. Allow it to cook for three to five minutes.
5. Put in most of the cilantro and mix thoroughly.
6. Decorate using remaining cilantro before you serve.

Nutritional Info: Calories: 296 kcal || Protein: 21.79 g || Fat: 20.62 g || Carbohydrates: 5.36 g

CHICKEN BURRITO

Time To Prepare: 15 minutes

Time to Cook: thirty minutes

Yield: Servings 6-8

Ingredients:

- ½ teaspoon dried basil

- 1 teaspoon chili flakes
- 1 teaspoon cumin powder
- 2 bell peppers (any 2 colors), cut
- 2 cans (fifteen ounces each) diced tomatoes
- 2 carrots, peeled, grated
- 2 onions, chopped
- 2 tablespoons olive oil or ghee
- 2 teaspoons gram masala
- 2 zucchinis, grated
- Iceberg lettuce leaves, as needed
- pounds chicken thighs, diced

Directions:

1. Put in tomatoes and basil into a pan. Put the pan on moderate heat. Heat meticulously. Remove the heat.
2. Put a wok or big pan on moderate heat. Put in ½ tablespoon oil. When the oil is heated, put the onion and sauté until light brown.
3. Put in garam masala, chili flakes, cumin, and basil and sauté for a few seconds until aromatic. Move into a container and save for later.
4. Put the pan back overheat. Put in remaining oil. When the oil is heated, put the chicken and sauté until brown.
5. Put in the onions back into the pan and sauté until chicken is soft.
6. Split chicken into bowls. Top with tomato mixture. Top lettuce leaves with carrot, zucchini, and bell pepper and serve.

Nutritional Info: Calories: 346 kcal || Protein: 22.58 g || Fat: 25.16 g || Carbohydrates: 6.96 g

CHICKEN CACCIATORE WITH SPAGHETTI SQUASH

Time To Prepare: 60 minutes

Time to Cook: thirty minutes

Yield: Servings 6

Ingredients:

- .5 tsp. Dried basil
- .5 tsp. Dried oregano

- .5 tsp. Dried thyme
- .5 Yellow squash, diced
- 1 (28 oz.) can diced tomatoes
- 1 (8 oz.) can Tomato sauce
- 1 cup Chicken stock
- 1 Large Bell peppers (bite-sized)
- 1 medium Onion, diced
- 1 small Spaghetti squash
- 2 cloves Garlic, minced
- 4 Chicken thighs, boneless, skinless, bite-size
- Pepper (as you wish)
- Salt (as you wish)

Directions:

1. Dice the veggies. Set them aside.
2. Chop the chicken up. Season it as you wish.
3. Bring the chicken in a Dutch oven and allow it to brown for approximately 8 minutes.
4. Put in in the onion, garlic, and bell pepper and cook for roughly five minutes or until the onions become tender.
5. Put in the chicken tomato sauce, tomatoes, and chicken stock.
6. Season as you wish and mix thoroughly before letting everything boil.
7. Reduce the heat then cook for minimum 30 minutes.
8. Put in the yellow squash. Cook between fifteen and 30 more minutes.

Nutritional Info: Calories: 524 kcal || Protein: 57.01 g || Fat: 27.23 g || Carbohydrates: 11.31 g

CHICKEN CHEESE STEAK

Time To Prepare: 20 minutes

Time to Cook: 5 hours

Yield: Servings 4

Ingredients:

- 1 lb. Chicken breasts
- 1 Onion, cut

- 2 Garlic cloves, chopped
- 2 Green peppers, thinly cut
- 2 tbsp. Light Coconut oil
- 2 tbsp. Steak seasoning
- 6 Oopsie Bread, slices
- 6 Provolone cheese, cut
- Black pepper (as you wish)
- Sea salt (as you wish)

Directions:

1. Thinly slice the chicken into strips before you put in it to a container and seasoning with steak seasoning, pepper, and salt as required.
2. Put in the coconut oil to the slow cooker before you put in in the green peppers and the onions and then top it all with the chick.
3. Cover the slow cooker and allow it to cook on low heat for around five hours.
4. Split the results into 6 servings and put in the results to each roll before topping with the cheese and toasting for a couple of minutes prior to serving.

Nutritional Info: Calories: 532 kcal || Protein: 39.63 g || Fat: 31.06 g || Carbohydrates: 22.1 g

CHICKEN DIVAN

Time To Prepare: 15 minutes

Time to Cook: thirty minutes

Yield: Servings 4

Ingredients:

- ½ c. water
- ½ lb. de-boned and skinless cooked chicken pieces
- 1 c. cooked and diced broccoli pieces
- 1 c. croutons
- 1 c. grated extra sharp cheddar cheese
- 1 can mushroom soup

Directions:

1. Preheat your oven to 350°F

2. In a big pot, heat the soup and water. Put in the chicken, broccoli, and cheese. Mix meticulously.
3. Pour into a greased baking dish.
4. Put the croutons over the mixture.
5. Bake for thirty minutes or until the casserole is bubbling, and the croutons are golden brown.

Nutritional Info: Calories: 380 || Fat: 22 g || Carbohydrates: 10 g || Protein: 25 g || Sugars: 2 g || Sodium: 475 mg

CHICKEN FRITTATA WITH ASIAGO CHEESE AND HERBS

Time To Prepare: ten minutes

Time to Cook: thirty minutes

Yield: Servings 4

Ingredients:

- ½ cup yogurt
- 1 cup Asiago cheese, shredded
- 1 pound chicken breasts, chopped into little strips
- 4 slices of bacon
- 6 eggs

Directions:

1. Preheat an oven-proof frying pan. Next, fry the bacon until crunchy and save for later. Next, in the pan drippings, cook the chicken for approximately 8 minutes or until no longer pink.
2. Put in the reserved bacon back to the frying pan.
3. In a mixing dish, meticulously mix the eggs and yogurt; flavor with Italian spice mix.
4. Pour the egg mixture over the chicken and bacon. Top with cheese , preheat your oven and bake at 380 degrees F for 22 minutes until hot and bubbly.
5. Allow it to sit for a couple of minutes before cutting and serving. Enjoy!

Nutritional Info: 484 Calories 31.8g || Fat: 5.8g || Carbs: 41.9g || Protein: 0.7g Fiber

CHICKEN IN PITA BREAD

Time To Prepare: ten minutes

Time to Cook: ten minutes

Yield: Servings 4

Ingredients:

- ½ c. chopped green onions
- ½ c. diced tomato
- ½ c. plain low-fat yogurt
- ½ tsp. crudely ground black pepper
- 1 ½ tsps. chopped fresh oregano
- 1 lb. Ground chicken
- 1 tbsp. Greek seasoning blend
- 1 tbsp. olive oil
- 2 c. shredded lettuce
- 2 tsp. Divided grated lemon rind
- 4 pieces of 6-inch halved pitas
- Two lightly beaten big egg whites

Directions:

1. Mix egg whites, Greek seasoning, a tablespoon lemon rind, green onions, and black pepper. Separate into 8 parts and mold each into ¼ inch thick patty.
2. Adjust your heat to moderate-high. Set a non-stick frying pan in place and fry patties until browned.
3. Reduce the heat to moderate. Next, cover the frying pan to cook for 4 more minutes.
4. Set up a small container and mix yogurt, oregano, and a tablespoon of lemon rind.
5. Spread the mixture on the pita and put in ¼ cup lettuce and a tablespoon of tomato.

Nutritional Info:

|| Calories: 421 kcal || Protein: 29.72 g || Fat: 23.37 g || Carbohydrates: 23.26 g

CHICKEN KORMA

Time To Prepare: 15 minutes

Time to Cook: thirty minutes

Yield: **Servings 3**

Ingredients:

- .5 tbsp. Curry
- .5 tsp. Salt
- 1 Onion
- 1 stick Cinnamon
- 100 milliliters 35 percent || Fat: Cooking cream
- 16 oz. Chicken breast, grilled
- 2 cloves Garlic, chopped
- 2 leaves bay
- 2 tbsp. Ginger, grated
- 3 tbsp. Water
- 30 grams Coconut oil
- 5 tbsp. Coconut oil
- 7 pods Cardamom
- Cayenne pepper (as you wish)

Directions:

1. Chop the onion so that one half is chopped, and the other is thinly cut.
2. Put the coconut oil and coconut oil together into a frying pan before you put in a moderate heat.
3. Once the mixture is heated, put in in the cardamom pods, bay leaves, and cinnamon sticks and sizzle for just a few seconds.
4. Put in the onion slices into the mixture and let them become light brown.
5. Combine the salt, curry, cayenne pepper, garlic, ginger, and chopped onion together well before you put in in the cooking cream.
6. Put in the results to the chicken and mix thoroughly.
7. Put in the water to the pan before letting it simmer for about ten minutes.

Nutritional Info: Calories: 6290 kcal || Protein: 132.39 g || Fat: 47.08 g || Carbohydrates: 1287.37 g

CHICKEN PARMIGIANA

Time To Prepare: 15 minutes

Time to Cook: 26 minutes

Yield: Servings 4

Ingredients:

- ¼ cup olive oil
- ¼ cup Parmesan cheese, grated
- ½ cup of superfine blanched almond flour
- ½ teaspoon dried parsley
- ½ teaspoon garlic powder
- ½ teaspoon paprika
- 1 big organic egg, beaten
- 1½ cups marinara sauce
- 2 tablespoons fresh parsley, chopped
- 4 -6-ounces grass-fed skinless, boneless chicken breasts, pounded into a ½-inch thickness
- 4 ounces mozzarella cheese, thinly cut
- Salt and ground black pepper, as needed

Directions:

1. Preheat your oven to 375 degrees F.
2. Put in the beaten egg into a shallow dish.
3. Put the almond flour, Parmesan, parsley, spices, salt, and black pepper in a different shallow dish and mix thoroughly.
4. Immerse each chicken breast into the beaten egg and then coat with the flour mixture.
5. Heat the oil in a deep frying pan on moderate to high heat and fry the chicken breasts for approximately 3 minutes per side.
6. Use a slotted spoon to moved the chicken breasts onto a paper towel-lined plate to drain.
7. At the bottom of a casserole, put about ½ cup of marinara sauce and spread uniformly.
8. Position the chicken breasts over marinara sauce in a single layer.
9. Top with the rest of the marinara sauce, followed by mozzarella cheese slices.
10. Bake for approximately minimum 20 minutes or until done completely.
11. Remove from the oven and serve hot with the garnishing of fresh parsley.

Nutritional Info: Calories: 542 || Net Carbohydrates: 5.7g || Carbohydrates: 9g || Fiber: 3.3g || Protein: 54.2g || Fat: 33.2g || Sugar: 3.8g || Sodium: 609mg

CHICKEN PICCATA

Time To Prepare: 15 minutes

Time to Cook: thirty minutes

Yield: Servings 4

Ingredients:

- ½ cup organic, gluten-free chicken broth
- ½ teaspoon Dijon mustard
- ½ teaspoon ground black pepper
- 1 cup ground almond meal
- 1 teaspoon of sea salt
- 1 yellow onion, chopped
- 1/4 cup fresh parsley, chopped
- 1/4 cup grated Parmesan cheese
- 2 tablespoons capers
- 3 tablespoons lemon juice
- 3 tablespoons organic butter
- 4 boneless, skinless chicken breast
- 4 tablespoons olive oil
- 4 tablespoons organic unsalted butter

Directions:

1. Mix the almond meal, cheese, mustard, salt, and pepper spread the mixture on a shallow dish.
2. Rinse the pounded chicken breasts in water and shake off the surplus. Immerse the chicken in the flour mixture.
3. Put in tablespoons of butter in a big deep cooking pan using high heat; put in the olive oil.
4. Cook chicken in butter and oil for roughly 3-4 minutes on each side until a golden-brown color is achieved.
5. Put the cooked chicken on a serving dish and cover to keep warm.
6. Mix in the chicken broth, lemon juice, and capers, scraping up any brown bits in the pan.

7. Put in the chicken broth, lemon juice, and capers to the frying pan, stirring and scraping up any brown bits in the frying pan. Simmer until the sauce is reduced and reaches a light syrup consistency. Decrease the heat to low and mix in remaining butter.
8. Ladle the sauce over the chicken breasts and top with chopped parsley. Serve with lemon slices or wedges.

Nutritional Info: Calories: 357 kcal || Protein: 4.51 g || Fat: 35.73 g || Carbohydrates: 6.16 g

CHICKEN PIE WITH BACON

Time To Prepare: 20 minutes

Time to Cook: thirty-five minutes

Yield: Servings 24

Ingredients:

- ½ cup chicken stock
- ¾ cup cheddar cheese, shredded
- ¾ cup crème fraîche
- 1 carrot, chopped
- 1 onion, chopped
- 1 pound chicken breasts, cubed
- 2 tbsp. yellow mustard
- 3 garlic cloves, minced
- 3 tbsp. butter
- 4 oz. bacon, cut
- Salt and black pepper, to taste

Dough

- ¾ cup almond flour
- 1 ½ cups mozzarella cheese, shredded
- 1 egg
- 1 tsp garlic powder
- 1 tsp onion powder
- 3 tbsp. cream cheese
- Salt and black pepper, to taste

Directions:

1. Sauté the onion, garlic, black pepper, bacon, and carrot in melted butter for five minutes. Put in in the chicken and cook for about three minutes. Mix in the crème fraîche, salt, mustard, black pepper, and stock, and cook for seven minutes. Put in in the cheddar cheese and save for later.
2. In a container, mix the mozzarella cheese with the cream cheese and heat in a microwave for a minute. Mix in the garlic powder, salt, flour, black pepper, onion powder, and egg. Knead the dough well, split into 4 pieces, and flatten each into a circle.
3. Position the chicken mixture into 4 ramekins, top each with a dough circle, and cook in your oven at 370 F for about twenty-five minutes.

Nutritional Info: Calories 563 || Fat: 44.6g Net || Carbs: 7.7g || Protein: 36g

---

CHICKEN QUICHE

Time To Prepare: 15 minutes

Time to Cook: 50 minutes

Yield: Servings 6

Ingredients:

- ½ cup heavy cream
- 1 lb. ground chicken
- 1 tsp dried oregano
- 1 tsp fennel seeds
- 16 oz. almond flour
- 2 small zucchini, grated
- 2 tbsp. coconut oil
- 7 medium eggs
- Salt and ground black pepper to taste

Directions:

1. Put almond flour, 1 egg, salt, and coconut oil in blender or food processor and blend.
2. Grease pie pan and pour the dough in it. Push well on the bottom.

3. Preheat pan on moderate heat and toss ground chicken, cook for a couple of minutes, set aside.
4. In a moderate-sized container, whisk together 6 eggs, zucchini, oregano, salt, pepper, fennel seeds, and heavy cream.
5. Put in chicken to egg mixture and stir thoroughly.
6. Preheat your oven to 350 F.
7. Pour egg mixture into pie pan and place in oven. Cook for forty minutes.
8. Allow it to cool and slice and serve.

Nutritional Info: Calories 295 || Carbs: 3.95g || Fat: 24g || Protein: 19g

---

CHICKEN SCARPARIELLO WITH SPICY SAUSAGE

Time To Prepare: ten minutes

Time to Cook: forty-five minutes

Yield: Servings 6

Ingredients:

- ¼ cup dry white wine
- ½ pound Italian sausage (sweet or hot)
- 1 cup chicken stock
- 1 pimiento, chopped
- 1 pound boneless chicken thighs
- 1 tablespoon minced garlic
- 2 tablespoons chopped fresh parsley
- 3 tablespoons good-quality olive oil, divided
- Freshly ground black pepper, for seasoning
- Sea salt, for seasoning

Directions:

1. Preheat your oven. Set the oven temperature to 425°F.
2. Brown the chicken and sausage. Pat the chicken thighs to dry using paper towels and flavor them lightly with salt and pepper. In a big oven-safe frying pan on moderate to high heat, warm 2 tablespoons of the olive oil. Put in the chicken thighs and sausage to the frying pan and brown them on all sides, turning them cautiously, approximately ten minutes.

3. Bake the chicken and sausage. Bring the frying pan into the oven and bake for about twenty-five minutes or until the chicken is thoroughly cooked. Take the frying pan out of the oven, move the chicken and sausage to a plate, and put the frying pan on moderate heat on the stovetop.
4. Make the sauce. Warm the rest of the 1 tablespoon of olive oil, put in the garlic and pimiento and sauté for about three minutes. Pour the white wine and deglaze the frying pan by using a spoon to scrape up any browned bits from the bottom of the frying pan. Pour in the chicken stock and bring it to its boiling point, then decrease the heat to low and simmer until the sauce reduces by about half, approximately 6 minutes.
5. Finish before you serve. Put back the chicken and sausage to the frying pan, toss it to coat it with the sauce, and serve it topped with the parsley.

Nutritional Info: Calories: 370 Total fat: 30g Total carbs: 3g || Fiber: 0g Net carbs: 3g || Sodium: 314mg || Protein: 19g

---

CHICKEN WITH FENNEL

Time To Prepare: ten minutes

Time to Cook: 8 minutes

Yield: Servings 4

Ingredients:

- ¾ cup fennel fronds
- 1 ¼ pounds chicken cutlets
- 1 ½ teaspoon smoked paprika
- 1 avocado, peeled, pitted and cut
- 1 fennel bulb, cut
- 1/3 cup red onion, cut
- 2 tablespoons lemon juice
- 3 tablespoons olive oil
- A pinch of salt and black pepper

Directions:

1. Warm a pan with 1 tbsp. Olive oil on moderate to high heat temperature, then put in the chicken, sprinkle with salt, pepper, and smoked paprika and cook for about four minutes on each side.

2. Split between plates. In a container, mix the remaining oil with the fennel, fennel fronds, onion, avocado, and lemon juice. Toss the salad and place next to the chicken then serve.

Nutritional Info: Calories: 288 || Fat: 4 || Fiber: 6 || Carbohydrates: 12 || Protein: 7

CHICKEN-BELL PEPPER SAUTÉ

Time To Prepare: ten minutes

Time to Cook: thirty minutes

Yield: Servings 6

Ingredients:

- ¼ tsp. Freshly ground black pepper
- ½ tsp. salt
- 1 cut big red bell pepper
- 1 cut big yellow bell pepper
- 1 tbsp. olive oil
- 1 tsp. chopped fresh oregano
- 2 1/3 c. crudely chopped tomato
- 2 tbsps. finely chopped fresh flat-leaf parsley
- 20 Kalamata olives
- 3 c. onion cut crosswise
- 6 4-oz skinless, boneless chicken breast halves
- Cooking spray

Directions:

1. Adjust your heat to moderate-high and set non-stick frying in place. Heat the oil. Sauté the onions for eight minutes once the oil is hot.
2. Put in bell pepper and sauté for ten more minutes.
3. Put in tomato, salt, and black pepper to cook for approximately seven minutes until the tomato juice has vaporized.
4. Put in parsley, oregano, and olives to cook for a couple of minutes until heated. Set into a container and keep warm.

5. Use a paper towel to wipe the pam and grease with cooking spray. Set back to heat and put in chicken breasts. Cook for 3 more minutes on each of the sides. If you want you can cook the chicken in batches
6. When cooking the final batch, put in back the previous batch of chicken and onion-bell pepper mixture then cook for one minute as you toss.
7. Serve warm and enjoy.

Nutritional Info: Calories: 223 kcal || Protein: 28.13 g || Fat: 7.82 g || Carbohydrates: 9.5 g

CHILI & LEMON MARINATED CHICKEN WINGS

Time To Prepare: five minutes

Time to Cook: twelve minutes

Yield: Servings 2-4

Ingredients:

- ½ cup fresh parsley, chopped
- ½ tsp cilantro
- 1 pound wings
- 1 red chili pepper, chopped
- 1 tsp coriander seeds
- 1 tsp xylitol
- 2 garlic cloves, minced
- 3 tbsp. olive oil
- Juice from 1 lemon
- Lemon wedges, for serving
- Salt and black pepper, to taste

Directions:

1. Using a container, mix together lemon juice, xylitol, garlic, salt, red chili pepper, cilantro, olive oil, and black pepper. Put in the chicken wings and toss thoroughly to coat. Place in your fridge for about two hours.
2. Preheat grill using high heat. Put in the chicken wings, and grill each side for about six minutes. Serve the chicken wings with lemon wedges.

Nutritional Info: Calories 223 || Fat: 12g Net || Carbs: 5.1g || Protein: 16.8g

CHILI CHICKEN KEBAB WITH GARLIC DRESSING

Time To Prepare: seven minutes

Time to Cook: ten minutes

Yield: Servings 2-4

Ingredients:

Skewers

- 1 tbsp. ginger paste
- 2 chicken breasts, cut into cubes
- 2 tbsp. olive oil
- 2 tbsp. swerve brown sugar
- 3 tbsp. soy sauce, sugar-free
- Chili pepper to taste

Dressing

- ¼ cup warm water
- ½ cup tahini
- 1 garlic clove, minced
- 1 tbsp. parsley, chopped
- Salt and black pepper to taste

Directions:

1. To prepare the marinade:
2. In a small container, place and mix the soy sauce, ginger paste, brown sugar, chili pepper, and olive oil. Place the chicken in a zipper bag, pour the marinade over, seal, and shake for a uniform coat. Marinate in your refrigerator for about two hours.
3. Preheat a grill to high heat. Thread the chicken on skewers and cook for about ten minutes, with three to four turnings to be golden brown. Move to a plate.
4. Combine the tahini, garlic, salt, parsley, and warm water in a container. Serve the chicken skewers topped with the tahini dressing.

Nutritional Info: Calories 410 || Fat: 32g Net || Carbs: 4.8g || Protein: 23.5g

CHIMICHURRI TURKEY & GREEN BEANS

Time To Prepare: **15 minutes**

Time to Cook: **7 to 8 hours**

Yield: **Servings 4**

Ingredients:

- ½ cup broth of choice
- 1 (2-to 3-pound) whole, boneless turkey breast
- 1 pound green beans
- 2 cups Chimichurri Sauce (double the recipe)

Directions:

1. Place the green beans in the slow cooker. Place the turkey on top. Pour on the sauce and broth.
2. Secure the lid of your cooker and set to low. Cook for 6 to 7 hours, or until the internal temperature of the turkey reaches 165°F on a meat thermometer and the juices run clear, before you serve.

Nutritional Info: Calories: 776 || Total Fat: 59g || Total Carbohydrates: 14g || Sugar: 4g || Fiber: 6 || Protein: 60g || Sodium: 1,128mg

CHINESE-ORANGE SPICED DUCK BREASTS

Time To Prepare: **4 minutes**

Time to Cook: **20 minutes**

Yield: **Servings 2**

Ingredients:

- 1 Orange-Zest and Juice (Reserved the wedges)
- 1 tsp. Cinnamon
- 1 tsp. Cloves
- 1 tsp. EXTRA Virgin olive oil
- 1 White onion, cut
- 2 Bok or Pak Choy plants leaves separated
- 2 Duck breasts, skin removed
- 2 tsp. Ginger, grated

- 3 Cloves garlic, minced

Directions:

1. Cut the duck breasts into strips and put in to a dry, hot pan, cooking for five to seven minutes on each side or until thoroughly cooked to your preference.
2. Remove to one side.
3. Put in olive oil to a clean pan and sauté the onions with the ginger, garlic, and the remaining spices for a minute.
4. Place the juice and zest of the orange and continue to sauté for three to five minutes.
5. Put in the duck and bok choi and heat through until wilted and duck is piping hot.
6. Serve and decorate with the orange segments.

Nutritional Info: Calories: 267 kcal || Protein: 36.58 g || Fat: 11.1 g || Carbohydrates: 3.31 g

CILANTRO-LIME CHICKEN DRUMSTICKS

Time To Prepare: 15 minutes

Time to Cook: two to three hours

Yield: Servings 4

Ingredients:

- ¼ cup fresh cilantro, chopped
- ¼ teaspoon ground cumin
- ½ teaspoon garlic powder
- ½ teaspoon sea salt
- 3 pounds chicken drumsticks
- 3 tablespoons freshly squeezed lime juice

Directions:

1. In a container, combine the cilantro, lime juice, garlic powder, salt, and cumin to make a paste.
2. Place the drumsticks in the slow cooker. Spread the cilantro paste uniformly on each drumstick.
3. Secure the lid of your cooker and set to high. Cook for two to three hours, or until the internal temperature of the chicken reaches 165°F on a meat thermometer and the juices run clear, and serve (see Tip).

Nutritional Info: Calories: 417 || Total Fat: 12g || Total Carbohydrates: 1g || Sugar: 1g || Fiber: 1g || Protein: 71g || Sodium: 591mg

CIPOLLINI & BELL PEPPER CHICKEN SOUVLAKI

Time To Prepare: five minutes

Time to Cook: twelve minutes

Yield: Servings 2-4

Ingredients:

- ½ cup lemon juice
- 1 red bell pepper, cut into chunks
- 1 tsp rosemary leaves to decorate
- 2 chicken breasts, cubed
- 2 cloves garlic, minced
- 2 tbsp. olive oil
- 2 to 4 lemon wedges to decorate
- 8 oz. small cipollini
- Salt and black pepper to taste

Directions:

1. Thread the chicken, bell pepper, and cipollini onto skewers and save for later. In a container, mix half of the oil, garlic, salt, black pepper, and lemon juice, and put in the chicken skewers. Cover the container and let the chicken marinate for minimum 2 hours in your fridge.
2. Preheat a grill to high heat and grill the skewers for about six minutes on each side. Remove and serve decorated with rosemary leaves and lemons wedges.

Nutritional Info: Calories 363 || Fat: 14.2g Net || Carbs: 4.2g || Protein: 32.5g

COCONUT-CURRY-CASHEW CHICKEN

Time To Prepare: 15 minutes

Time to Cook: 7 to 8 hours

Yield: Servings 4

Ingredients:

- ½ cup diced white onion
- ½ teaspoon coconut sugar
- ½ teaspoon freshly ground black pepper
- 1 (14-ounce) can full-fat coconut milk
- 1 tablespoon red curry paste
- 1 teaspoon garlic powder
- 1 teaspoon sea salt
- 1½ cup unsalted cashews
- 1½ cups Chicken Bone Broth
- 2 pounds boneless, skinless chicken breasts

Directions:

1. In a container, mix the broth, coconut milk, garlic powder, red curry paste, salt, pepper, and coconut sugar. Stir thoroughly.
2. Place the chicken, cashews, and onion in the slow cooker. Pour the coconut milk, mixture on top.
3. Secure the lid of your cooker and set to low. Cook for about eight hours, or until the internal temperature of the chicken reaches 165°F on a meat thermometer and the juices run clear.
4. Shred the chicken using a fork, then mix it into the cooking liquid. You can also remove the chicken from the broth and cut it using a knife into bite-size pieces before returning it to the slow cooker and serve.

Nutritional Info: Calories: 714 || Total Fat: 43g || Total Carbohydrates: 21g || Sugar: 5g || Fiber: 3g || Protein: 57g || Sodium: 1,606mg

CREAMY CHICKEN & GREENS

Time To Prepare: ten minutes

Time to Cook: 20 minutes

Yield: Servings 4

Ingredients:

- 1 cup. Chicken stock

- 1 cup. Cream
- 1 lb. Chicken thighs – skins on
- 1 tsp. Italian herbs
- 2 cups Dark leafy greens
- 2 tbsp. Coconut flour
- 2 tbsp. Coconut oil
- 2 tbsp. Melted butter
- Pepper & Salt (your preference)

Directions:

1. On the stovetop, put in oil in a frying pan using the med-high temperature setting.
2. Take away the bones from the chicken and dust using salt and pepper. Fry the chicken until done.
3. Make the sauce by putting in the butter to a deep cooking pan. Whisk in the flour to make a thick paste. Slowly, whisk in the cream. Once it boils, mix in the herbs.
4. Move the chicken to the counter and put in the stock.
5. Deglaze the pan, and whisk the cream sauce. Throw in the greens until meticulously covered with the sauce.
6. Position the thighs on the greens, warm up, before you serve.

Nutritional Info: Calories: 446 ‖ Net Carbohydrates: 3 g ‖ Total Fat: Content: 38 g ‖ Protein: 18 g

CURRY CHICKEN LETTUCE WRAPS

Time To Prepare: 15 minutes

Time to Cook: ten minutes

Yield: Servings 5

Ingredients:

- .25 cups Minced onion
- 1 cup Riced cauliflower
- 1 lb. Chicken thighs – skinless & boneless
- 1 tsp. Black pepper
- 2 Minced garlic cloves

- 2 tbsp. Ghee
- 2 tsp. Curry powder
- 5-6 Lettuce leaves
- Keto-friendly sour cream (as you wish - count the carbs)
- Salt to taste

Directions:

1. Mince the garlic and onions. Set on the side for later.
2. Pull out the bones and skin from the chicken and dice into one-inch pieces.
3. On the stovetop, put in 2 tbsp. of ghee to a frying pan and melt. Toss in the onion and sauté until browned. Fold in the chicken and drizzle with the garlic, pepper, and salt.
4. Cook for 8 minutes. Mix in the rest of the ghee, riced cauliflower, and curry. Stir until thoroughly combined.
5. Prepare the lettuce leaves and put in the mixture.
6. Serve with a spoonful of cream.

Nutritional Info: Calories: 554 || Net Carbohydrates: 7 g || Total Fat: Content: 36 g || Protein: 50 g

DELICIOUS ROASTED DUCK

Time To Prepare: ten minutes

Time to Cook: 4 hours and 50 minutes

Yield: Servings 4

Ingredients:

- ¼ cup parsley, chopped
- 1 celery stalk, chopped
- 1 medium duck
- 2 bay leaves
- 2 teaspoons thyme, dried
- 2 yellow onions, chopped
- 8 garlic cloves, minced
- A pinch of salt and black pepper
- One teaspoon herbs de Provence

For the sauce:

- ¼ teaspoon herbs de Provence
- ½ cup white wine
- ½ teaspoon sugar
- 1 and ½ cups black olives, pitted and chopped
- 1 cup chicken stock
- 1 tablespoon tomato paste
- 1 yellow onion, chopped
- 3 cups water

Directions:

1. In a baking dish, position thyme, parsley, garlic, and 2 onions.
2. Put in duck, sprinkle with salt, 1 teaspoon herbs de Provence and pepper.
3. Put in your oven at 475 degrees F and roast for about ten minutes.
4. Cover the dish, decrease the heat to 275 degrees F, and roast duck for around three hours and thirty minutes.
5. In the meantime, heat a pan on moderate heat, put in 1 yellow onion, stir and cook for about ten minutes.
6. Put in tomato paste, stock, sugar, ¼ teaspoon herbs de Provence, olives and water, cover, decrease the heat to low, and cook for an hour.
7. Move duck to a work surface, carve, discard bones, and split between plates.
8. Sprinkle the sauce all over and serve immediately.

Nutritional Info: Calories: 254 || Fat: 3 || Fiber: 3 || Carbohydrates: 8 || Protein: 13

DELIGHTFUL TERIYAKI CHICKEN UNDER PRESSURE

Time To Prepare: five minutes

Time to Cook: 20 minutes

Yield: Servings 8

Ingredients:

- ¼ cup Apple Cider Vinegar
- ¾ cup Brown Sugar
- ¾ cup low-sodium Soy Sauce

- 1 cup Chicken Broth
- 1 tsp Pepper
- 2 tbsp. Garlic Powder
- 2 tbsp. ground Ginger
- 20 ounces canned Pineapple, crushed
- 3 pounds Boneless and Skinless Chicken Thighs

Directions:

1. Mix all of the ingredients, excluding the chicken. Put in the chicken meat and turn to coat.
2. Secure the lid, press POULTRY, and cook for about twenty minutes at High. Do a quick pressure release by turning the valve to an "open" position.

Nutritional Info: Calories 352 || Carbs: 31g || Fat: 11g || Protein: 31g

DOUBLE CHEESE ITALIAN CHICKEN

Time To Prepare: ten minutes

Time to Cook: 20 minutes

Yield: Servings 2

Ingredients:

- ½ cup cream cheese
- 1 cup Asiago cheese, grated
- 1 teaspoon Italian spice mix
- 2 chicken drumsticks
- 2 cups baby spinach

Directions:

1. In a deep cooking pan, heat 1 tbsp. of oil on moderate to high heat. Sear the chicken drumsticks for seven to eight minutes or until well browned on all sides; reserve.
2. Pour in ½ cup of chicken bone broth; put in in spinach and carry on cooking for five minutes more until spinach has wilted.
3. Put in in Italian spice mix, cream cheese, Asiago cheese, and reserved chicken drumsticks; partly cover and carry on cooking for 5 more minutes. Serve warm.

Nutritional Info: 589 Calories 46g || Fat: 5.8g || Carbs: 37.5g || Protein: 2g Fiber

DUCK BREAST AND BLACKBERRIES MIX

Time To Prepare: ten minutes

Time to Cook: twenty-five minutes

Yield: Servings 4

Ingredients:

- ¼ cup chicken stock
- 1 ½ cups water
- 1 tablespoon butter
- 2 tablespoons balsamic vinegar
- 2 teaspoons cornflour
- 3 tablespoons sugar
- 4 duck breasts
- 4 ounces blackberries
- Salt and black pepper to taste

Directions:

1. Pat dry duck breasts using paper towels score the skin, sprinkle with salt and pepper to taste, and set aside for half an hour
2. Put breasts skin side down in a pan, heat on moderate heat, and cook for eight minutes.
3. Flip breasts and cook for another half a minute.
4. Move duck breasts to a baking dish skin side up, place in your oven at 425 degrees F, and bake for fifteen minutes.
5. Pull out the meat from the oven and leave aside to cool down for about ten minutes before you cut them.
6. In the meantime, put sugar in a pan, heat on moderate heat, and melt it, stirring all the time.
7. Take the pan off the heat, put in the water, stock, balsamic vinegar, and the blackberries.
8. Heat this mix to moderate temperature and cook until sauce is reduced to half.
9. Move sauce to another pan, put in cornflour mixed with water, heat again, and cook for about four minutes until it becomes thick.

10. Put in salt and pepper, the butter, and mix thoroughly. Cut the duck breasts, split between plates and serve with the berries sauce on top.

Nutritional Info: Calories: 320 || Fat: fifteen || Fiber: fifteen || Carbohydrates: 16 || Protein: 11

DUCK BREAST SALAD

Time To Prepare: ten minutes

Time to Cook: 20 minutes

Yield: Servings 4

Ingredients:

- 1 head of frisee, torn
- 1 tablespoon lemon juice
- 1 teaspoon lemon zest, grated
- 1 teaspoon orange zest, grated
- 2 duck breasts, boneless but the skin on, cut into 4 pieces
- 2 oranges, peeled and slice into segments
- 2 small lettuce heads washed, torn into little pieces
- 2 tablespoons chives, chopped
- 2 tablespoons sugar
- 3 tablespoons shallot, minced
- 3 tablespoons white wine vinegar
- Salt and black pepper to taste
- tablespoons canola oil

Directions:

1. Warm a small deep cooking pan on moderate to high heat, put in vinegar and sugar, stir and boil for five minutes and take off the heat.
2. Put in orange zest, lemon zest and lemon juice, stir and leave aside for a few minutes.
3. Put in shallot, salt, and pepper to taste and the oil, mix thoroughly and leave aside.
4. Pat dry duck pieces score skin, trim, and sprinkle with salt and pepper.
5. Warm a pan on moderate to high heat for a minute, position duck breast pieces skin side down, brown for eight minutes, decrease the heat to moderate and cook for 4 more minutes.

6. Flip pieces, cook for about three minutes, move to a cutting board and cover them using foil.
7. Put frisee and lettuce in a container, stir and split between plates.
8. Slice duck, position on top, put in orange segments, drizzle chives, and sprinkle the vinaigrette.

Nutritional Info: Calories: 320 || Fat: 4 || Fiber: 4 || Carbohydrates: 6 || Protein: 14

DUCK BREAST WITH APRICOT SAUCE

Time To Prepare: ten minutes

Time to Cook: 20 minutes

Yield: Servings 4

Ingredients:

- ¼ teaspoon cinnamon, ground
- ¼ teaspoon coriander, ground
- ¾ cup blackberries
- 1 cup apricots, chopped
- 2 tablespoons parsley, chopped
- 2 tablespoons red onions, chopped
- 3 tablespoons apple cider vinegar
- 3 tablespoons chives, chopped
- 4 duck breasts, boneless
- 5 tablespoons apricot preserving
- A sprinkle of olive oil
- Salt and black pepper to taste

Directions:

1. Season duck breasts with salt, pepper, coriander, and cinnamon, put them on a preheated grill pan on moderate to high heat, cook for a couple of minutes, flip them and cook for about three minutes more.
2. Flip duck breasts again, put in 3 tablespoons apricot preServings, cook for a minute, move them to a cutting board, leave aside for at least two minutes and slice.
3. Heat a pan on moderate heat, put in vinegar, onion, 2 tablespoons apricot preServings, apricots, blackberries, and chives, stir and cook for about three minutes.

4. Split cut duck breasts between plates and serve with apricot sauce sprinkled on top.

Nutritional Info: Calories: 275 || Fat: 4 || Fiber: 4 || Carbohydrates: 7 || Protein: 12

DUCK LEGS AND WINE SAUCE

Time To Prepare: ten minutes

Time to Cook: 1 hour and thirty minutes

Yield: Servings 4

Ingredients:

- ½ cup chicken stock
- 1 and ½ cups red wine
- 1 carrot, chopped
- 1 tablespoon balsamic vinegar
- 1 teaspoon olive oil
- 1 teaspoon rosemary, dried
- 2 shallots, chopped
- 2 tablespoons sugar
- 2 teaspoons tomato paste
- 4 duck legs, trimmed
- Salt and black pepper

Directions:

1. Warm a pan with the oil on moderate to high heat.
2. Put in duck legs, sprinkle with salt and pepper, brown for five minutes on all sides and move to a plate.
3. Heat the same pan on moderate heat, put in the shallots and carrots, stir and cook for a couple of minutes.
4. Put in the wine, tomato paste, stock, sugar, vinegar, rosemary, stir and simmer for five minutes.
5. Return the duck legs, toss, cook everything for an hour and 30 on moderate to low heat stirring frequently, split everything between plates before you serve.

Nutritional Info: Calories: 257 || Fat: 14 || Fiber: 6 || Carbohydrates: 14 || Protein: 8

DUCK STEW OLLA TAPADA

Time To Prepare: 15 minutes

Time to Cook: thirty minutes

Yield: Servings 3

Ingredients:

- ½ cup chayote, peeled and cubed
- 1 pound duck breasts, boneless, skinless, and chopped into little chunks
- 1 red bell pepper, deveined and chopped
- 1 shallot, chopped
- 1 teaspoon Mexican spice mix

Directions:

1. In a clay pot, heat 2 teaspoons of canola oil over a moderate to high flame. Sauté the peppers and shallot until tender approximately four minutes.
2. Put in in the rest of the ingredients; pour in 1 ½ cups of water or chicken bone broth. Once your mixture begins boiling, decrease the heat to moderate-low.
3. Allow it to simmer, partly covered, for eighteen to 22 minutes, until thoroughly cooked. Enjoy!

Nutritional Info: 228 Calorie 9.5g || Fat: 3.3g || Carbs: 30.6g || Protein: 1g Fiber

EASY CHICKEN TACOS

Time To Prepare: five minutes

Time to Cook: 2seven minutes

Yield: Servings 4

Ingredients:

- ½ cup salsa
- 1 ½ cups Mexican cheese blend
- 1 clove garlic, minced
- 1 cup tomato puree
- 1 pound ground chicken
- 1 tablespoon Mexican seasoning blend

- 2 slices bacon, chopped
- 2 small-sized shallots, peeled and finely chopped
- 2 teaspoons butter, room temperature

Directions:

1. In a deep cooking pan, put butter then melt in over a moderately high flame. Now, cook the shallots until soft and aromatic.
2. Next, sauté the garlic, chicken, and bacon for approximately five minutes, stirring constantly and crumbling using a fork. Put in the in Mexican seasoning blend.
3. Fold in the tomato puree and salsa; carry on simmering for five to seven minutes on moderate to low heat; reserve.
4. Coat a baking pan with wax paper. Put 4 piles of the shredded cheese on the baking pan and softly push them down with a wide spatula to make "taco shells."
5. Bake in the preheated oven at 365 degrees F for six to seven minutes or until melted. Allow these taco shells to cool for approximately ten minutes.

Nutritional Info: 535 Calories 33.3g || Fat: 4.8g || Carbs: 47.9g || Protein: 1.9g Fiber

EXQUISITE PEAR AND ONION GOOSE

Time To Prepare: 15 minutes

Time to Cook: 20 minutes

Yield: Servings 8

Ingredients:

- ¼ tsp Garlic Powder
- ½ cup slice Onions
- ½ tsp Pepper
- 1 ½ pounds Goose, chopped into big pieces
- 1 tbsp. Butter
- 1 tsp Cayenne Pepper
- 2 cups Chicken Broth
- 2 tbsp. Balsamic Vinegar
- 3 Pears, peeled and cut

Directions:

1. Melt the butter on SAUTÉ. Put in the goose and cook until it becomes golden on all sides. Move to a plate. Put in the onions and cook for a couple of minutes. Return the goose to the cooker.
2. Put in the remaining ingredients, stir thoroughly to blend and secure the lid. Select PRESSURE COOK/MANUAL mode, and set the timer to eighteen minutes at High Pressure. Do a quick pressure release. Serve and enjoy!

Nutritional Info: Calories 313 || Carbs: 14g || Fat: 8g || Protein: 38g

FETA & BACON CHICKEN

Time To Prepare: 20 minutes

Time to Cook: 10minutes

Yield: Servings 2-4

Ingredients:

- 1 pound chicken breasts
- 1 tbsp. parsley
- 2 tbsp. coconut oil
- 3 green onions, chopped
- 4 oz. bacon, chopped
- 4 oz. feta cheese, crumbled

Directions:

1. Put a pan on moderate heat and coat with cooking spray. Put in in the bacon and cook until crunchy. Remove to paper towels, drain the grease and crumble.
2. To the same pan, put in in the oil and cook the chicken breasts for 4-5 minutes, then flip to the other side; cook for another 4-5 minutes. Put the chicken breasts to a baking dish. Put the green onions, set in your oven, turn on the broiler, and cook for five minutes at high temperature. Remove to serving plates and serve topped with bacon, feta cheese, and parsley.

Nutritional Info: Calories 459 || Fat: 35g Net || Carbs: 3.1g || Protein: 31.5g

FLYING JACOB CASSEROLE

Time To Prepare: 15 minutes

Time to Cook: 20-twenty-five minutes

Yield: Servings 6

Ingredients:

- 1 pc Grilled Chicken
- 1 tsp. Seasoning curry
- 125 g Peanuts
- 125 ml hot chili sauce
- 2 tbsp. Butter
- 225 g Diced bacon
- 250 g Mushrooms
- 475 ml Cream
- Salt and black pepper to taste

Salad

- 175 g Spinach
- 2 pcs Tomato

Directions:

1. Preheat your oven to 400 ° F.
2. Cut the mushrooms into little pieces then fry in oil with bacon. Salt and pepper to taste.
3. Separate the chicken meat from the bones and cut it into little pieces.
4. Place these pieces of chicken in a mold for baking, oiled. Put in mushrooms and bacon.
5. Beat the cream until tender peaks. Put chili sauce, curry, and salt and pepper to taste.
6. Pour the chicken into the resulting mixture.
7. Bake using your oven for minimum 20-twenty-five minutes until the dish will get a pleasant golden color. Drizzle toasted and chopped nuts on top. Serve with salad.

Nutritional Info: Carbohydrates: 11 g || Fat: 80 g || Protein: 40 g || Calories: 912

GREEK CHICKEN STIFADO

Time To Prepare: ten minutes

Time to Cook: thirty-five minutes

Yield: Servings 2

Ingredients:

- ½ moderate-sized leek, chopped
- 1 teaspoon poultry seasoning mix
- 2 ounces bacon, diced
- 2 vine-ripe tomatoes, pureed
- 3/4 pound whole chicken, boneless and chopped

Directions:

1. Cook the bacon in the preheated frying pan on moderate to high heat. Fold in the chicken and carry on cooking for five minutes more until it is no longer pink; set aside.
2. In the same frying pan, sauté the leek until it has tenderized or approximately four minutes. Mix in the poultry seasoning mix and 2 cups of water or chicken broth.
3. Now, decrease the heat to moderate-low and carry on simmering for fifteen to twenty minutes.
4. Put in in tomatoes together with the reserved meat. Continue to cook for another 13 minutes or until thoroughly cooked. Enjoy!

Nutritional Info: 352 Calories 14.3g || Fat: 5.9g || Carbs: 44.2g || Protein: 2.4g Fiber

GRILLED CHICKEN WITH BLACK BEAN MANGO SALSA

Time To Prepare: ten minutes

Time to Cook: seven minutes

Yield: Servings 2

Ingredients:

- ½ cup black beans
- ½ red bell pepper, diced
- ½ teaspoon salt
- 1 big ripe mango
- 1 clove garlic, minced
- 1 tablespoon dried parsley flakes
- 1 tablespoon fresh cilantro, chopped
- 1 tablespoon lemon juice

- 1 tablespoon orange juice
- 1 teaspoon dried basil
- 1 teaspoon ground black pepper
- 1 teaspoon ground cumin
- 1/3 cup extra-virgin olive oil
- 1/4 teaspoon ground black pepper
- 2 Chicken Breast
- 2 tablespoons lemon juice
- 2 tablespoons red onion, minced

Directions:

1. In a mixing container, mix all the salsa ingredients and place in your fridge until serving.
2. Put chicken in a big dish.
3. Mix together the garlic, parsley, basil, lemon juice, olive oil, salt, and pepper in a container. Pour marinade onto chicken and turn sides to coat. Put in your refrigerator for an hour.
4. Preheat a mildly oiled grill to moderate-high.
5. Discard tilapia marinade and grill the chicken seven minutes each side.

Nutritional Info: Calories: 876 kcal ǁ Protein: 75.37 g ǁ Fat: 46.56 g ǁ Carbohydrates: 37.2 g

HEALTHY TURKEY GUMBO

Time To Prepare: five minutes

Time to Cook: 2 hours

Yield: Servings 1

Ingredients:

- ½ cup Okra
- 1 can chopped tomatoes
- 1 Onion, quartered
- 1 tbsp. Extra virgin olive oils
- 1 Whole Turkey
- 1-2 Bay leaves
- 3 Cloves garlic, chopped

- Black pepper to taste
- Stalk of Celery, chopped

Directions:

1. Take the first four ingredients and put in 2 cups of water in a stockpot, heating on a high heat until boiling.
2. Reduce the heat and simmer for about fifty minutes or until turkey is thoroughly cooked.
3. Take away the turkey and strain the broth.
4. Grab a frying pan and then heat the oil on moderate heat and brown the remaining vegetables for five to ten minutes.
5. Stir until soft, and then put in to the broth.
6. Put in the tomatoes and turkey meat to the broth and stir.
7. Put in the bay leaves and carry on cooking for about 1 hour or until the sauce has become thick.
8. Flavor it with black pepper and enjoy.

Nutritional Info: Calories: 261 kcal || Protein: 11.72 g || Fat: 12.91 g || Carbohydrates: 28.33 g

HIDDEN VALLEY CHICKEN DRUMMIES

Time To Prepare: 15 minutes

Time to Cook: thirty minutes

Yield: Servings 4

Ingredients:

- ½ c. melted butter
- 12 chicken drumsticks
- 2 packages Hidden Valley dressing dry mix
- 2 tbsps. Hot sauce
- 3 tbsps. Vinegar
- Celery sticks
- Paprika

Directions:

1. Preheat your oven to 350 0F.

2. Wash and pat dry the chicken.
3. In a container, blend the dry dressing, melted butter, vinegar, and hot sauce. Stir until blended.
4. Put the drumsticks in a big plastic baggie, pour the sauce over drumsticks. Massage the sauce until the drumsticks are coated.
5. Put the chicken in a single layer on a baking dish. Drizzle with paprika.
6. Bake for thirty minutes, turning midway.
7. Serve with crudité or salad.

Nutritional Info: Calories: 155 || Fat: 18 g || Carbohydrates: 96 g || Protein: 15 g || Sugars: 0.7 g || Sodium: 340 mg

HOME-STYLE CHICKEN KEBAB

Time To Prepare: ten minutes

Time to Cook: ten minutes

Yield: Servings 2

Ingredients:

- ½ cup Greek-style yogurt
- 1 ½ ounce Swiss cheese, cut
- 1 pound chicken thighs, boneless, skinless and halved
- 2 Roma tomatoes, chopped
- 2 tablespoons olive oil

Directions:

1. Put the chicken thighs, yogurt, tomatoes, and olive oil in a glass storage container. You can put in in mustard seeds, cinnamon, and sumac if you wish.
2. Cover then store in the refrigerator to marinate for three to four hours.
3. Thread the chicken thighs onto skewers, making a thick log shape. Grill the kebabs on moderate to high heat for three to four minutes on each side.
4. Use an instant-read thermometer to check the doneness of meat; it should read approximately 165 degrees F.
5. Top with the cheese; carry on cooking for about four minutes or until cheesy is melted. Enjoy!

Nutritional Info: 498 Calories 23.2g || Fat: 6.2g || Carbs: 61g || Protein: 1.7g Fiber

HONEY CHICKEN TAGINE

Time To Prepare: 60 minutes

Time to Cook: twenty-five minutes

Yield: Servings 12

Ingredients:

- ½ tsp. ground pepper
- ½ tsp. salt
- ¾ tsp. ground cinnamon
- 1 ½ tbsps. honey
- 1 tbsp. extra virgin olive oil
- 1 tbsp. Minced fresh ginger
- 1 tsp. ground coriander
- 1 tsp. ground cumin
- 1/8 tsp. Ground cloves
- 12-oz. seeded and roughly chopped kumquats
- 14-oz. vegetable broth
- 2 lbs. boneless, skinless chicken thighs
- 2 thinly cut onions
- 4 slivered garlic cloves
- fifteen-oz washed chickpeas

Directions:

1. Preheat your oven to approximately 3750F.
2. Place a heatproof casserole on moderate heat and heat the oil.
3. Put in onions to sauté for about four minutes
4. Put in garlic and ginger to sauté for a minute
5. Put in coriander, cumin, cloves, salt, pepper, and cloves seasonings. Sauté for one minute.
6. Put in kumquats, broth, chickpeas, and honey, then bring to its boiling point before turning off the heat.

7. Set the casserole in your oven while covered. Bake for fifteen minutes as you stir at a fifteen-minute interval.
8. Serve and enjoy

Nutritional Info: Calories: 586 kcal || Protein: 15.5 g || Fat: 40.82 g || Carbohydrates: 43.56 g

---

HONEY-MUSTARD LEMON MARINATED CHICKEN

Time To Prepare: ten minutes

Time to Cook: 20 minutes

Yield: Servings 4

Ingredients:

- 1 pound lean chicken breast
- 1 tablespoon olive oil
- 1 lemon, zested and juiced
- 1 tablespoon cayenne pepper
- ½ teaspoon ground black pepper
- ½ teaspoon sea salt
- 1/4 cup Dijon mustard
- 1/4 cup rosemary leaves, chopped

Directions:

1. Put chicken breasts in a 7 x 11-inch baking dish.
2. Mix together all ingredients apart from the chicken in a moderate-sized container.
3. Pour prepared marinade over chicken; turn sides to coat. Cover, store in the refrigerator and marinate for about 1 hour or overnight for the best flavor.
4. Bake at 350°F for about twenty minutes.
5. Use the additional sauce over the top before you serve.

Nutritional Info: Calories: 265 kcal || Protein: 26.12 g || Fat: 16.27 g || Carbohydrates: 3.08 g

---

HOT CHICKEN MEATBALLS

Time To Prepare: five minutes

Time to Cook: 21 minutes

Yield: Servings 2

Ingredients:

- ¼ cup hot sauce
- ¼ cup mozzarella cheese, grated
- ½ cup almond flour
- 1 egg
- 1 pound ground chicken
- 2 tablespoons yellow mustard
- Salt and black pepper, to taste

Directions:

1. Preheat your oven to 4000F and line a baking tray using parchment paper.
2. In a container, mix the chicken, black pepper, mustard, flour, mozzarella cheese, salt, and egg. Form meatballs and place them on the baking tray.
3. Cook for 16 minutes, then pour over the hot sauce and bake for 5 more minutes.

Nutritional Info: Calories: 487 || Fat: 35g || Net Carbohydrates: 4.3g || Protein: 31.5g

KETO CHICKEN ENCHALADAS

Time To Prepare: ten minutes

Time to Cook: twenty-five minutes

Yield: Servings 6

Ingredients:

- 2 cups gluten-free enchilada sauce

Chicken

- ¼ cup Chicken broth
- ¼ cup fresh cilantro (chopped)
- 1 tablespoon Avocado oil
- 3 cups Shredded chicken (cooked)
- 4 cloves Garlic (minced)

Assembly

- 12 Coconut tortillas
- ¼ cup Green onions (chopped)
- 3/4 cup Colby jack cheese (shredded)

Directions:

1. Warm oil at moderate-high heat in a big pan. Put in the chopped garlic and cook until aromatic for approximately one minute.
2. Put in rice, 1 cup enchilada sauce (half the total), chicken, and coriander. Simmer for five minutes.
3. Meanwhile, heat the oven to 3750 F. Grease a 9x13 baking dish.
4. In the center of each tortilla, place ¼ cup chicken mixture. Roll up and place seam side down in the baking dish.
5. Pour the rest of the cup enchilada sauce over the enchiladas. Drizzle with shredded cheese.
6. Bake for ten to twelve minutes Drizzle with green onions.

Nutritional Info: Calories: 349 || Fat: 19g || Net Carbohydrates: 9g || Protein: 31g

LEBANESE CHICKEN KEBABS AND HUMMUS

Time To Prepare: ten minutes + 1 hour marinate

Time to Cook: thirty-five minutes

Yield: Servings 4

Ingredients:

For the Chicken:

- 1 cup Lemon Juice
- 1 tbsp. Paprika
- 1 tbsp. Thyme, finely chopped
- 1 tsp. Cayenne pepper
- 2 tsp. ground cumin
- 4 Free-range skinless chicken breasts, cubed
- 4 Metal kebabs skewers
- 8 Garlic cloves, minced
- Lemon wedges to decorate

For the Hummus:

- 1 can Chickpeas/ 1 cup dried (soaked overnight)
- 1 Lemon juice
- 1 tsp. Black pepper
- 1 tsp. Turmeric
- 2 tbsp. Olive oil
- 2 tbsp. Tahini paste

Directions:

1. Whisk the lemon juice, garlic, thyme, paprika, cumin, and cayenne pepper in a container.
2. Skewer the chicken cubes using kebab sticks (metal).
3. Baste the chicken per side with the marinade, covering for as long as you can in your refrigerator (the lemon juice will tenderize the meat and means it will be more suitable for the anti-inflammatory diet).
4. When ready to cook, set the oven to 400°F/200 °C/Gas Mark 6 and bake for about twenty minutes or until chicken is meticulously thoroughly cooked.
5. Prepare the hummus by putting the ingredients to a blender and whizzing up until the desired smoothness is achieved. If it is a little thick and lumpy, put in a little water to loosen the mix.
6. Serve the chicken kebabs, decorated with the lemon wedges and the hummus on the side.

Nutritional Info: Calories: 576 kcal ‖ Protein: 61.66 g ‖ Fat: 18.55 g ‖ Carbohydrates: 42.07 g

LEMON & GARLIC CHICKEN THIGHS

Time To Prepare: 15 minutes

Time to Cook: 7 to 8 hours

Yield: Servings 4

Ingredients:

- 1 teaspoon sea salt
- 1½ teaspoons garlic powder
- 2 cups chicken broth

- 2 pounds boneless skinless chicken thighs
- Juice and zest of 1 big lemon

Directions:

1. Pour the broth into the slow cooker.
2. In a small container, put the garlic powder, salt, lemon juice, and lemon zest then stir. Baste each chicken thigh with a uniform coating of the mixture. Put the thighs along the bottom of the slow cooker.
3. Secure the lid of your cooker and set to low. Cook for about eight hours, or until the internal temperature of the chicken reaches 165°F on a meat thermometer and the juices run clear, before you serve.

Nutritional Info: Calories: 29 || Total Fat: 14g || Total Carbohydrates: 3g || Sugar: 0g || Fiber: 0g || Protein: 43g || Sodium: 1,017mg

LEMON AND HERB CRUSTED CHICKEN FILLETS

Time To Prepare: ten minutes

Time to Cook: 20 minutes

Yield: Servings 4

Ingredients:

- ½ teaspoon garlic powder
- ½ teaspoon onion
- 1 cup gluten-free breadcrumbs
- 1 teaspoon Dijon mustard
- 1 teaspoon ginger, grated
- 1 teaspoon ground black pepper
- 1 teaspoon lemon peel
- 1/4 cup lemon juice
- 2 tablespoons chives
- 2 tablespoons fresh thyme, finely chopped
- 2 tablespoons parsley
- 2 teaspoons salt
- 4 Chicken Fillets

Directions:

1. Preheat your oven to 400 degrees F.
2. Coat a baking tray with parchment.
3. Season both sides of chicken fillets. Put skin side down on the
4. readied baking sheet.
5. Mix the breadcrumbs, chives, thy me, parsley, mustard, ginger, garlic powder, onion powder, and lemon peel in a moderate-sized container.
6. Drizzle chicken with lemon juice and press the breadcrumb mixture on top of the chicken fillets.
7. Cook for about twenty minutes.

Nutritional Info: Calories: 1123 kcal || Protein: 196.72 g || Fat: 27.62 g || Carbohydrates: 9.99 g

---

LEMON-GARLIC CHICKEN AND GREEN BEANS WITH CARAMELIZED ONIONS

Time To Prepare: ten minutes

Time to Cook: 65 minutes

Yield: Servings 2

Ingredients:

- ⅛ tsp. red pepper flakes
- ¼ cup Golden Ghee, melted
- ¼ tsp. paprika
- ¼ tsp. freshly ground black pepper
- 1 tsp. sea salt, plus additional for seasoning
- 1 yellow onion, quartered
- 2 big boneless, skinless free-range chicken breasts
- 2 cups trimmed green beans
- 2 tbsp. minced garlic
- 3 tbsp. extra-virgin olive oil
- 3 tbsp. freshly squeezed lemon juice

Directions:

1. In .a medium container or a zipper-top plastic bag, mix the olive oil, lemon juice, garlic, salt, black pepper, paprika, and red pepper flakes.

2. Place the chicken then coat it in the marinade.
3. Cover the container or seal the bag then marinate the chicken in your refrigerator for minimum 1 hour, or overnight if possible.
4. Preheat your oven to 350°F.
5. Dice 1 of the onion quarters, and chop the remaining 3 quarters into big chunks.
6. Place the bigger chunks of onion across the bottom of a cast iron or ovenproof frying pan.
7. Place the green beans, then sprinkle the diced onion above. Put on the top the green beans and onion with the ghee. Place the marinated chicken breasts on the green beans then spoon the rest of the marinade at the chicken. Flavour the dish with a drizzle of sea salt.
8. Bake the chicken until its internal temperature reaches minimum 165°F, approximately 65 minutes. Serve hot.

Nutritional Info: Calories: 803 || Total Fat: 61g || Saturated Fat: 23g || Protein: 53g || Cholesterol: 217mg || Carbohydrates: 14g || Fiber: 5g || Net Carbohydrates: 9g

MANGO & LIME BBQ TURKEY

Time To Prepare: ten minutes

Time to Cook: ten minutes

Yield: Servings 4

Ingredients:

- ½ tsp. black pepper
- 1 medium mango, chopped
- 4 boneless, skinless turkey breasts (approximately 1.5-lbs.)
- Juice of 2 limes
- Zest of 2 limes

Directions:

1. Mix the lime juice, lime zest, and black pepper in a sealable Ziploc bag. Put in in the turkey, seal bag, and toss to coat.
2. Set the grill to moderate-high and spray grates with a high heat cooking spray. Grill turkey for five to seven minutes each side or until an internal temperature of approximately 165°F is reached.

3. While the turkey is grilling, cut up mango.
4. Remove turkey from grill and place each breast on a serving dish. Top each turkey breast with chopped mango, to decorate. Sprinkle with a little lime juice, if you want. Serve and enjoy!

Nutritional Info: Calories: 2110 kcal || Protein: 427.56 g || Fat: 30.95 g || Carbohydrates: 3.94 g

MIDDLE EASTERN SHISH KEBAB

Time To Prepare: ten minutes

Time to Cook: 20 minutes

Yield: Servings 5

Ingredients:

- ½ cup ajran
- ½ cup tomato sauce
- 1 tablespoon mustard
- 2 pounds chicken tenders, cut into bite-sized cubes
- Turkish spice mix

Directions:

1. Put chicken tenders with the rest of the ingredients in a ceramic dish. Cover and allow it to marinate for 4 hours in your fridge.
2. Thread chicken tenders onto skewers and put them on the preheated grill until a golden-brown color is achieved on all sides roughly fifteen minutes.
3. Serve instantly and enjoy!

Nutritional Info: 274 Calories 10.7g || Fat: 3.3g || Carbs: 39.3g || Protein: 0.8g Fiber

MOROCCAN TURKEY TAGINE

Time To Prepare: 15 minutes

Time to Cook: 7 to 8 hours

Yield: Servings 4

Ingredients:

- ¼ teaspoon ground coriander
- ¼ teaspoon ground ginger
- ¼ teaspoon paprika
- ½ cup dried apricots
- ½ cup water
- ½ red onion, chopped
- ½ teaspoon sea salt
- 1 (14 oz.) can chickpeas, drained
- 1 (14 oz.) can diced tomatoes
- 1 tablespoon tomato paste
- 1 teaspoon garlic powder
- 1 teaspoon ground turmeric
- 2 big carrots, finely chopped
- 2 cups broth of choice
- 2 tablespoons raw honey
- 4 cups boneless, skinless turkey breast chunks
- Freshly ground black pepper

Directions:

1. In your slow cooker, mix the turkey, tomatoes, chickpeas, carrots, apricots, onion, honey, tomato paste, garlic powder, turmeric, salt, ginger, coriander, paprika, water, and broth, and flavor with pepper. Lightly stir to combine the ingredients.
2. Secure the lid of your cooker and set to low. Cook for about eight hours before you serve.

Nutritional Info: Calories: 428 || Total Fat: 5g || Total Carbohydrates: 46g || Sugar: 25g || Fiber: 8g || Protein: 49g || Sodium: 983mg

NACHO CHICKEN CASSEROLE

Time To Prepare: 15 minutes

Time to Cook: twenty-five minutes

Yield: Servings 6

Ingredients:

- .25 cup Sour cream
- 1 cup Green chilies and tomatoes
- 1 medium Jalapeño pepper
- 1 pkg. Frozen cauliflower
- 1.5tsp. Chili seasoning
- 1.75lb. Chicken thighs
- 2 tbsp. Olive oil
- 3 tbsp. Parmesan cheese
- 4 oz. Cheddar cheese
- 4 oz. Cream cheese
- NEEDED: Immersion blender
- Pepper and salt (to taste)

Directions:

1. Preheat your oven to 375º Fahrenheit.
2. Cut the jalapeño into pieces and save for later.
3. Cutaway the skin and bones from the chicken. Chop it and drizzle using the pepper and salt. Prepare in a frying pan using a portion of olive oil on the med-high temperature setting until browned.
4. Stir in the sour cream, cream cheese, and ¾ of the cheddar cheese. Stir until melted and blended well. Put in the tomatoes and chilies. Stir then put it all to a baking dish.
5. Cook the cauliflower in the microwave. Mix in the rest of the cheese with the immersion blender until it looks like mashed potatoes. Season as you wish.
6. Spread the cauliflower concoction over the casserole and drizzle with the peppers. Bake roughly fifteen to twenty minutes.

Nutritional Info: Calories: 426 || Net Carbohydrates: 4.3 g || Total Fat: Content: 32.2 g || Protein: 31 g

NUTTY PESTO CHICKEN SUPREME

Time To Prepare: ten minutes

Time to Cook: thirty minutes

Yield: Servings 2

Ingredients:

- ½ cup low-fat hard cheese (not necessary)
- ½ cup raw spinach
- 1 bunch of fresh basil
- 1 cup Crashed macadamias/almonds/walnuts or a combination
- 2 Free ranges skinless chicken/ turkey breasts
- 2 tbsp. Extra virgin olive oil

Directions:

1. Set the oven to 350°F.
2. Get the chicken breasts and use a meat pounder to 'thin' each breast into a 1cm thick escalope.
3. Reserve a handful of the nuts before you put in the remaining ingredients and a little black pepper to a blender or pestle and mortar and blend until the desired smoothness is achieved (you can leave this a little lumpy for a rustic feel if you prefer).
4. Put in a little water if the pesto needs loosening.
5. Coat the chicken in the pesto.
6. Bake for minimum 30 minutes in your oven, or until chicken is completely thoroughly cooked.
7. Top each chicken escalope with the rest of the nuts and place under the broiler for five minutes for a crunchy topping to complete.

Nutritional Info: Calories: 2539 kcal || Protein: 444.61 g || Fat: 71.66 g || Carbohydrates: 5.99 g

ORANGE CHICKEN LEGS

Time To Prepare: ten minutes

Time to Cook: 8 hours

Yield: Servings 4

Ingredients:

- ¼ cup red vinegar
- ½ cup chopped parsley
- 1 red onion, cut into wedges
- 4 chicken legs
- 5 garlic cloves, minced
- 7 ounces canned peaches, halved

- A pinch of salt and black pepper
- Juice of 1 orange
- Zest of 1 orange

Directions:

1. In a slow cooker, combine the orange zest with the orange juice, vinegar, salt, pepper, garlic, onion, peaches, and parsley. Put in the chicken, toss, cover, and cook on Low for eight hours. Split between plates before you serve.
2. Enjoy!

Nutritional Info:

Calories:251 || Fat: 4 || Fiber: 8 || Carbohydrates: 14 || Protein: 8

PANCETTA & CHEESE STUFFED CHICKEN

Time To Prepare: 15 minutes

Time to Cook: twenty-five minutes

Yield: Servings 2

Ingredients:

- 1 garlic clove, minced
- 1 lemon, zested
- 1 shallot, finely chopped
- 2 chicken breasts
- 2 tbsp. dried oregano
- 2 tbsp. olive oil
- 4 oz. mascarpone cheese
- 4 slices pancetta
- Salt and black pepper to taste

Directions:

1. Warm the oil in a small frying pan, then sauté the garlic and shallots for about three minutes. Mix in salt, black pepper, and lemon zest. Move to a container and allow it to cool. Mix in the mascarpone cheese and oregano.

2. Score a pocket in each chicken's breast, fill the holes with the cheese mixture and cover it with the cut-out chicken. Cover each breast with two pancetta slices and secure the ends using a toothpick.
3. Position the chicken on a greased baking sheet and cook in your oven for about twenty minutes at 380 F.

Nutritional Info: Calories 643 || Fat: 44.5g Net || Carbs: 6.2g || Protein: 52.8g

PANCETTA AND CHICKEN RISOTTO

Time To Prepare: 15 minutes

Time to Cook: 15 minutes

Yield: Servings 2

Ingredients:

- ½ onion; chopped
- 1 tablespoon lemon zest
- 1 tablespoon olive oil
- 1 tablespoon unsalted butter
- 1 teaspoon fresh thyme
- 1/3 cup white wine
- 2 garlic cloves; chopped
- 2 tablespoon parmesan; grated
- 2 to 3 slices pancetta; diced
- 3 ½ cups chicken stock
- 3/4 cup risotto or Arborio rice
- 3/4-pound. Chicken meat, diced
- Salt and Pepper to taste

Directions:

1. Put oil and butter to Instant Pot and press the "Sauté" button (*Normal* preset), wait till you see Hot on display.
2. Put in onion, cook for one to two minutes. Put in pancetta, chicken, and garlic. Cook for another two to three minutes.

3. Put in rice and mix thoroughly, the rice must be covered with oil-butter mixture. Pour the wine and scrape the sides of the pot. Cook for two to three minutes, stirring continuously. Push *Cancel* button.
4. Put in chicken stock, thyme, lemon zest, salt, and pepper. Secure the lid and turn the vent to *Sealed*. Push *Pressure Cook* (Manual) button, use *+* or *-* button to set the timer for about six minutes. Use *Pressure level* button to set Pressure to *HIGH*.
5. When the timer is up, press *Cancel* button and allow the pressure to be released naturally; until the float valve drops down.
6. Open the lid; Put in parmesan cheese to the pot and stir thoroughly until it melts. Serve topped with extra parmesan and lemon zest.

Nutritional Info: Calories: 586 g || Total Fat: 22.5 g Total || Carbohydrates: 23.6 g || Protein: 45

PAN-FRIED CHORIZO SAUSAGE

Time To Prepare: five minutes

Time to Cook: 15 minutes

Yield: Servings 4

Ingredients:

- 1 ½ cups Asiago cheese, grated
- 1 cup tomato puree
- 1 tablespoon dry sherry
- 1 tablespoon extra-virgin olive oil
- 1 teaspoon basil
- 1 teaspoon garlic paste
- 1 teaspoon oregano
- 16 ounces smoked turkey chorizo
- 2 tablespoons fresh coriander, roughly chopped
- 4 scallion stalks, chopped
- Ground black pepper, to taste
- Sea salt, to taste

Directions:

1. In a frying pan, put oil and heat it over moderately high heat. Now, brown the turkey chorizo, crumbling using a fork for approximately five minutes.

2. Put in in the other ingredients, apart from for cheese; carry on cooking for about ten minutes more or until thoroughly cooked.

Nutritional Info: 330 Calories 17.2g || Fat: 4.5g || Carbs: 34.4g || Protein: 1.6g Fiber

PAPRIKA CHICKEN & PANCETTA IN A SKILLET

Time To Prepare: 20 minutes

Time to Cook: ten minutes

Yield: Servings 2

Ingredients:

- ¼ tsp sweet paprika
- 1 cup chicken stock
- 1 onion, chopped
- 1 tbsp. olive oil
- 1/3 cup Dijon mustard
- 2 chicken breasts, skinless and boneless
- 2 tbsp. oregano, chopped
- 5 pancetta strips, chopped
- Salt and black pepper, to taste

Directions:

1. In a container, mix the paprika, black pepper, salt, and mustard. Drizzle this mixture the chicken breasts and massage.
2. Heat a frying pan on moderate heat, mix in the pancetta, cook until it browns, for approximately 3-4 minutes, and transfer to a plate.
3. To the pancetta fat, put in olive oil and cook the chicken breasts for a couple of minutes per side. Put in the stock, black pepper, pancetta, salt, and onion. Drizzle with oregano before you serve.

Nutritional Info: Calories 323 || Fat: 21g Net || Carbs: 4.8g || Protein: 24.5g

PEANUT-CRUSTED CHICKEN

Time To Prepare: 15 minutes

Time to Cook: 15 minutes

Yield: Servings 2

Ingredients:

- 1 ½ cups peanuts, ground
- 1 egg
- 2 chicken breast halves, boneless and skinless
- 3 tbsp. canola oil
- Lemon slices for decoration
- Salt and black pepper, to taste

Directions:

1. Whisk egg in one container and pour the peanuts in a different one. Flavour the chicken, dip in the egg, and then in peanuts. Warm oil in a pan on moderate heat and brown the chicken for a couple of minutes per side.
2. Take away the chicken pieces to a baking sheet, set in your oven, and bake for about ten minutes at 360 F. Serve topped with lemon slices.

Nutritional Info: Calories 634 || Fat: 51g Net || Carbs: 4.7g || Protein: 43.6g

PESTO & MOZZARELLA CHICKEN CASSEROLE

Time To Prepare: ten minutes

Time to Cook: 25-30 minutes

Yield: Servings 8

Ingredients:

- .25 cup Pesto
- .25 to .5 cup Heavy cream
- 2 lb. Grilled & cubed chicken breasts
- 8 oz. Cream cheese
- 8 oz. Cubed mozzarella
- 8 oz. Shredded mozzarella
- Cooking oil (as required)

Directions:

1. Warm the oven to 400º Fahrenheit. Spritz a casserole dish with a spritz of cooking oil spray.
2. Mix the pesto, heavy cream, and softened cream cheese.
3. Put in the chicken and cubed mozzarella into the greased dish.
4. Drizzle the chicken using the shredded mozzarella. Bake for around half an hour.

Nutritional Info: Calories: 451 || Net Carbohydrates: 3 g || Total Fat: Content: 30 g || Protein: 38 g

PULLED BUFFALO CHICKEN SALAD WITH BLUE CHEESE

Time To Prepare: ten minutes

Time to Cook: thirty minutes

Yield: Servings 2

Ingredients:

- ¼ cup Buffalo Sauce
- ¼ cup chopped red onion, divided
- ½ cup blue cheese dressing, divided
- ½ cup crumbled organic blue cheese, divided
- 2 boneless, skinless free-range chicken breasts
- 4 cups chopped romaine lettuce, divided
- 4 uncured center-cut bacon strips

Directions:

1. Put a big pot of water to its boiling point using high heat.
2. Place the chicken breasts to the water, reduce the heat then simmer the breasts until their internal temperature reaches 180°F, approximately 30 minutes.
3. Take the chicken to a container and allow it to cool for approximately ten minutes.
4. On the other hand, crisp the bacon strips in a frying pan on moderate heat, approximately 3 minutes per side. Drain the bacon on a paper towel.
5. Shred the chicken using a fork and toss it with the buffalo sauce.
6. Split the lettuce into 2 bowls. Top each with half of the pulled chicken, half of the blue cheese dressing, blue cheese crumbles, and chopped red onion. Crush the bacon over the salads before you serve.

Nutritional Info: Calories: 843 || Total Fat: 65g || Saturated Fat: 14g || Protein: 59g || Cholesterol: 156mg || Carbohydrates: 6g || Fiber: 1g || Net Carbohydrates: 5g

RED PEPPER AND MOZARELLA-STUFFED CHICKEN CAPRESE

Time To Prepare: ten minutes

Time to Cook: forty minutes

Yield: Servings 2

Ingredients:

- 1 (8-ounce) ball mozzarella cheese, cut into 4 pieces
- 1 cup Roasted Red Peppers
- 10 fresh basil leaves
- 2 chicken breasts, butterflied
- 2 tablespoons extra-virgin olive oil
- 2 tablespoons Italian seasoning
- Freshly ground black pepper
- Sea salt

Directions:

1. Preheat your oven to 400°F.
2. Coat a rimmed baking sheet using a parchment paper.
3. Put 5 basil leaves inside each chicken breast.
4. Put 2 mozzarella slices inside each breast.
5. Split the roasted red peppers into 2 breasts. Drizzle the Italian seasoning liberally over each breast and flavor them with salt and pepper. Close each breast to envelop the filling.
6. Place the breasts on the baking sheet and bake until thoroughly cooked about forty minutes. Serve hot.

Nutritional Info: Calories: 539 || Total Fat: 30g || Saturated Fat: 5g || Protein: 63g || Cholesterol: 152mg || Carbohydrates: 4g || Fiber: 1g || Net Carbohydrates: 3g

ROASTED CHICKEN

Time To Prepare: 60 minutes

Time to Cook: 60 minutes

Yield: Servings 8

Ingredients:

- ½ tbsp. salt
- ½ tsp. Black pepper
- ½ tsp. thyme
- 1 bay leaf
- 3 garlic cloves
- 3 lbs. whole chicken
- 4 tbsps. Coarsely chopped orange peel

Directions:

1. Place the chicken under room temperature for approximately 1 hour.
2. Using paper towels, pat dry the inside and outside of the chicken.
3. Preheat your oven to 4500F the moment you start preparing the chicken seasoning.
4. Mix thyme, salt, and pepper in a small container.
5. Wipe inside the using 1/3 of the seasoning. Inside the chicken, put the garlic, citrus peel, and bay leaf.
6. Tuck the tips of the wing and tie the legs together. Spread the remaining seasoning all over the chicken and put on a roasting pan.
7. Put in your oven to bake for 60 minutes at 1600F.
8. Set aside to rest for fifteen minutes.
9. Cut up the roasted chicken before you serve.
10. Enjoy.

Nutritional Info: Calories: 201 kcal || Protein: 35.48 g || Fat: 5.36 g || Carbohydrates: 0.5 g

ROASTED WHOLE CHICKEN

Time To Prepare: 20 minutes

Time to Cook: 1 and 32 minutes

Yield: Servings 6

Ingredients:

- 1 (3-pounds) grass-fed whole chicken, neck, and giblets removed
- 10 tablespoons unsalted butter
- 3 garlic cloves, minced
- Salt and ground black pepper, as needed

Directions:

1. Preheat your oven to 4000F. Position an oven rack into the lower portion of the oven.
2. Grease a big baking dish.
3. Put the butter and garlic in a small pan on moderate heat and cook for approximately 1-2 minutes.
4. Take away the pan from heat and allow it to cool for approximately 2 minutes.
5. Flavour the inside and outside of chicken uniformly with salt and black pepper.
6. Position the chicken into a readied baking dish, breast side up.
7. Pour the garlic butter over and inside of the chicken.
8. Bake for approximately 1-1½ hours, coating with the pan juices every twenty minutes.
9. Take out of the oven and put the chicken onto a cutting board for approximately 5-ten minutes before carving.
10. Cut into desired size pieces before you serve.

Nutritional Info: Calories: 772 || Fat: 39.1g || Net Carbohydrates: 0.7g || Protein: 99g

ROTISSERIE CHICKEN & CABBAGE SHREDS

Time To Prepare: ten minutes

Time to Cook: 0 minutes

Yield: Servings 2

Ingredients:

- .5 cup Keto-friendly mayo
- .5 of 1 Red onion
- 1 lb. Precooked rotisserie chicken
- 1 tbsp. Olive oil
- 7 oz. Fresh green cabbage
- Pepper & Salt

Directions::

1. Using a sharp kitchen knife, shred the cabbage and slice the onion into fine slices.
2. Put the chicken on a platter, put in the mayo, and a sprinkle of oil. Dust using salt and pepper and serve.

Nutritional Info: Calories: 423 || Net Carbohydrates: 6 g || Total Fat: Content: 35 g || Protein: 17 g

SALSA VERDE CHICKEN

Time To Prepare: 15 minutes

Time to Cook: six to eight hours

Yield: Servings 4

Ingredients:

- 1 cup chicken broth
- 1 teaspoon chili powder
- 1 teaspoon sea salt
- 2 cups green salsa
- 2 tablespoons freshly squeezed lime juice
- 4 to 5 boneless, skinless chicken breasts (about 2 pounds)

Directions:

1. In your slow cooker, mix the chicken, salsa, broth, lime juice, salt, and chili powder. Stir to blend.
2. Secure the lid of your cooker and set to low. Cook for at roughly six to eight hours, or until the internal temperature of the chicken reaches 165°F on a meat thermometer and the juices run clear.
3. Shred the chicken using a fork, mix it into the sauce, before you serve.

Nutritional Info: Calories: 318 || Total Fat: 8g || Total Carbohydrates: 6g || Sugar: 2g || Fiber: 1g || Protein: 52g || Sodium: 1,510mg

SIMPLE TURKEY GOULASH

Time To Prepare: 15 minutes

Time to Cook: forty-five minutes

Yield: Servings 4

Ingredients:

- 1 large-sized leek, chopped
- 2 celery stalks, chopped
- 2 cloves garlic, minced
- 2 pounds turkey thighs, skinless, boneless and chopped
- 2 tablespoons olive oil

Directions:

1. In a clay pot, heat 2 olive oil over a moderate to high flame. Next, cook the leeks until soft and translucent.
2. Next, continue to sauté the garlic for half a minute to one minute.
3. Mix in the turkey, celery, and 4 cups of water. Once your mixture begins boiling, allow it to simmer, partly covered, for approximately forty minutes.

Enjoy!

Nutritional Info: 220 Calories 7.4g || Fat: 2.7g || Carbs: 35.5g || Protein: 1g Fiber

---

SKILLET CHICKEN WITH BRUSSELS SPROUTS MIX

Time To Prepare: ten minutes

Time to Cook: 15 minutes

Yield: Servings 4

Ingredients:

- ¼ cup walnuts, chopped
- ½ red onion, cut
- 1 apple, cored and cut
- 1 garlic clove, minced
- 1 tablespoon olive oil
- 1½ pounds chicken thighs, skinless and boneless
- 12 ounces Brussel sprouts, shredded
- 2 tablespoons balsamic vinegar
- 2 teaspoons chopped thyme

- A pinch of salt and black pepper

Directions:

1. Warm a pan with the oil on moderate to high heat, then put in the chicken thighs, sprinkle with salt, pepper, and thyme.
2. Cook for five minutes on each side and move to a container.
3. Heat the pan again on moderate heat, put in the onion, apple, sprouts, and garlic. Toss the mix and cook for five minutes. Put in vinegar to the pan and return the chicken too. Put in the walnuts, toss, cook for a couple of minutes more then split between plates before you serve.
4. Enjoy!

Nutritional Info: Calories: 211 || Fat: 4 || Fiber: 7 || Carbohydrates:13 || Protein: 8

SLOW COOKER CHICKEN CACCIATORE

Time To Prepare: 15 minutes

Time to Cook: ten minutes

Yield: Servings 4

Ingredients:

- ⅛ teaspoon red pepper flakes
- ¼ cup good-quality olive oil
- ½ cup red wine
- ½ cup tomato paste
- 1 (28-ounce) can sodium-free diced tomatoes
- 1 cup cut mushrooms
- 1 onion, chopped
- 1 tablespoon dried basil
- 1 teaspoon dried oregano
- 2 celery stalks, chopped
- 2 tablespoons minced garlic
- 4 (4-ounce) boneless chicken breasts, each cut into three pieces

Directions:

1. Brown the chicken. In a frying pan at moderate to high heat, warm the olive oil. Put in the chicken breasts and brown them, turning them once, approximately ten minutes in total.
2. Cook in the slow cooker. Put the chicken in the slow cooker and mix in the onion, celery, mushrooms, garlic, tomatoes, red wine, tomato paste, basil, oregano, and red pepper flakes. Cook it on high for roughly three to four hours or on low for six to eight hours, until the chicken is fully cooked and soft.
3. Serve. Split the chicken and sauce between four bowls and serve it instantly.

Nutritional Info: Calories: 383 Total fat: 26g Total carbs: 11g ‖ Fiber: 4g Net carbs: 7g ‖ Sodium: 116mg ‖ Protein: 26g

SLOW COOKER CHICKEN FAJITAS

Time To Prepare: 15 minutes

Time to Cook: 7 to 8 hours

Yield: Servings 4

Ingredients:

- 1 (14.5-ounce) can diced tomatoes
- 1 (4-ounce) can Hatch green chiles
- 1 big onion, cut
- 1 green bell pepper, seeded and cut
- 1 red bell pepper, seeded and cut
- 1 teaspoon paprika
- 1 teaspoon sea salt
- 1 yellow bell pepper, seeded and cut
- 1½ teaspoons garlic powder
- 1½ teaspoons ground cumin
- 2 pounds boneless, skinless chicken breast
- 2 teaspoons chili powder
- Freshly ground black pepper
- Juice of 1 lime
- Pinch cayenne pepper

Directions:

1. In a moderate-sized container, put together the diced tomatoes, chiles, garlic powder, chili powder, cumin, paprika, salt, lime juice, and cayenne, and flavor with black pepper then mix. Pour half the diced tomato mixture into the bottom of your slow cooker.
2. Layer half the red, green, and yellow bell peppers and half the onion over the tomatoes in the cooker.
3. Put the chicken on top of the peppers and onions.
4. Cover the chicken with the rest of the red, green, and yellow bell peppers and onions. Pour the rest of the tomato mixture on top.
5. Secure the lid of your cooker and set to low. Cook for about eight hours, or until the internal temperature of the chicken reaches 165°F on a meat thermometer and the juices run clear, before you serve.

Nutritional Info: Calories: 310 || Total Fat: 5g || Total Carbohydrates: 19g || Sugar: 7g || Fiber: 4g || Protein: 46gb || Sodium: 1,541mg

SLOW COOKER JERK CHICKEN

Time To Prepare: ten minutes

Time to Cook: 5 hours

Yield: Servings 4

Ingredients:

- 1 teaspoon (2 g) black pepper
- 1 teaspoon (2 g) cayenne pepper
- 2 teaspoons (3 g) dried thyme
- 2 teaspoons (4 g) white pepper
- 2 teaspoons (5 g) onion powder
- 2 teaspoons (6 g) garlic powder
- 4 teaspoons (20 g) salt
- 4 teaspoons (9 g) paprika
- chicken drumsticks and 8 chicken wings

Directions:

1. Put all the spices in a container, then mix to make a rub for the chicken.

2. Rinse the chicken meat in cold water for a short period of time. Put the washed chicken meat into the container with the rub, and rub the spices onto the meat meticulously, including under the skin.
3. Put each piece of chicken covered with the spices into the slow cooker (no liquid required).
4. Set the slow cooker on moderate heat, and cook for around five hours or until the chicken meat falls off the bone.

Nutritional Info: Calories: 480 || Fat: 30 g || Net Carbohydrates: 4 g || Protein: 45 g

SPICY ALMOND CHICKEN STRIPS WITH GARLIC LIME TARTAR SAUCE

Time To Prepare: ten minutes

Time to Cook: ten minutes

Yield: Servings 4

Ingredients:

Chicken sticks:

- ½ cup blanched almond flour
- ½ cup coconut oil
- ½ teaspoon ground cayenne pepper
- 1 ½ pounds chicken breast, cut into 1x5-inch pieces
- 1 teaspoon salt
- 1/4 cup dried basil
- 1/4 teaspoon freshly ground black pepper
- 2 organic free-range eggs, whisked
- 3 cloves garlic, finely chopped

Garlic Lime Tartar Sauce:

- ½ teaspoon salt
- 1 ½ tablespoon dill pickle relish
- 1 cup mayonnaise
- 1 tablespoon dried onion flakes
- 1 teaspoon garlic powder
- 2 tablespoons lime juice

Directions:

1. Mix together all the ingredients for the tartar sauce until well-blended. Chill for minimum 30 minutes until serving.
2. Whisk eggs in a moderate-sized container. In another container, mix almond flour, cayenne pepper, basil, garlic, salt, and pepper.
3. Immerse chicken strips in egg, then flour mixture; coat well and place sticks in a plate.
4. Heat some coconut oil in a deep cooking pan on moderate to high heat. Put in half of the chicken strips and cook for at least two minutes on each side until well-browned. Leave enough room around chicken strips so that they aren't overcrowded.
5. Drain sticks using paper towels on a plate. Heat another 1/4 cup coconut oil and cook the rest of the half of the chicken strips. Serve with the prepared Garlic Lime Tartar Sauce.

Nutritional Info: Calories: 1092 kcal || Protein: 94.15 g || Fat: 75.01 g || Carbohydrates: 7.5 g

---

SPICY CHIPOTLE CHICKEN

Time To Prepare: ten minutes

Time to Cook: twelve minutes

Yield: Servings 4

Ingredients:

- 1 cup halved mushrooms
- 1 pound chicken breasts, skinless, boneless and slice into strips
- 1 red bell pepper, cut
- 1 tablespoon chopped chipotles in adobo
- 1 tablespoon olive oil
- 1 teaspoon chili powder
- 1 teaspoon ground cumin
- 1 yellow onion, chopped
- 1½ tablespoons lime juice
- 3 garlic cloves, minced
- A pinch of salt and black pepper

Directions:

1. Warm a pan with the oil on moderate to high heat and put in the chicken.
2. Mix and cook for about four minutes. Put in the chili powder, the cumin, salt, pepper, bell pepper, mushrooms, onion, garlic, chipotles, and lime juice.
3. Mix and cook for seven minutes more, split into bowls before you serve.
4. Enjoy!

Nutritional Info: Calories: 241 ‖ Fat: 4 ‖ Fiber: 7 ‖ Carbohydrates: 14 ‖ Protein: 7

SPICY PULLED CHICKEN WRAPS

Time To Prepare: 15 minutes

Time to Cook: six to eight hours

Yield: Servings 4

Ingredients:

- 1 head romaine lettuce
- 1 lb. skinless, deboned chicken breasts
- 1 tsp. garlic powder
- 1 tsp. paprika
- 1½ c. low-fat, low-sodium chicken broth
- 1½ tsp. ground cumin
- 2 tsp. Chili powder

Directions:

1. In a slow cooker, put all together the ingredients apart from lettuce and gently stir until blended.
2. Set the slow cooker on low.
3. Cover and cook for approximately 6-8 hours.
4. Uncover the slow cooker and move the breasts into a big plate.
5. Use a fork to shred the breasts.
6. Serve the shredded beef over lettuce leaves.

Nutritional Info: Calories: 150 ‖ Fat: 3.4 g ‖ Carbohydrates: 12 g ‖ Protein: 14 g ‖ Sugars: 7 g ‖ Sodium: 900 mg

SPINACH CHICKEN CHEESY BAKE

Time To Prepare: twenty-five minutes

Time to Cook: 20 minutes

Yield: Servings 6

Ingredients:

- 1 ¼ cups shredded mozzarella cheese
- 1 teaspoon mixed spice seasoning
- 2 loose cups baby spinach
- 3 teaspoons olive oil
- 4 oz cream cheese, cubed
- 4 tablespoons water
- 6 chicken breasts, skinless and boneless
- Pink salt and black pepper to season

Directions:

1. Preheat your oven to 3700F.
2. Season chicken with spice mix, salt, and black pepper. Pat with your hands to have the seasoning stick on the chicken.
3. Put in the casserole dish and layer spinach over the chicken.
4. Combine the oil with cream cheese, mozzarella, salt, and black pepper and mix in water a tablespoon at a time.
5. Pour the mixture over the chicken and cover the pot with aluminium foil.
6. Bake for minimum twenty minutes, take off the foil and carry on cooking for fifteen minutes until a nice golden brown color is formed on top. Take out and allow sitting for five minutes. Serve warm with braised asparagus.

Nutritional Info: Calories: 340 || Fat: 30.2g || Net Carbohydrates: 3.1g || Protein: 15g

STUFFED CHICKEN WITH SAUERKRAUT AND CHEESE

Time To Prepare: ten minutes

Time to Cook: thirty-five minutes

Yield: Servings 4

Ingredients:

- 1 cup Romano cheese, shredded
- 2 garlic cloves, minced
- 5 chicken cutlets
- 5 Italian peppers, deveined and chopped
- 5 tablespoons sauerkraut, for serving

Directions:

1. Spritz a baking pan with 1 tablespoon of the olive oil. Brush the chicken with another tablespoon of olive oil.
2. Flavour the chicken with Italian spice mix. You can spread Dijon mustard on one side of each chicken cutlet if you wish.
3. Split the garlic, peppers and Romano cheese between chicken cutlets; roll them up.
4. Bake at 360°F for around half an hour until nicely brown on all sides. Serve with the sauerkraut before you serve. Enjoy!

Nutritional Info: 376 Calories 16.7g || Fat: 5.8g || Carbs: 47g || Protein: 1g Fiber

SUPER SESAME CHICKEN NOODLES

Time To Prepare: ten minutes

Time to Cook: ten minutes

Yield: Servings 2

Ingredients:

- ½ cup || Sugar: snap peas
- ½ orange juiced
- 1 Carrot, chopped
- 1 cup Rice/Buckwheat noodles such as Japanese Udon
- 1 Thumb size piece of ginger, minced
- 1 tsp. Sesame Seed
- 2 Free-range skinless chicken breasts, chopped
- 2 tsp. Coconut Oil

Directions:

1. Warm 1 tsp oil on moderate heat in a frying pan.

2. Sauté the chopped chicken breast for approximately 10-fifteen minutes or until thoroughly cooked.
3. While cooking the chicken, put the noodles, carrots, and peas in a pot of boiling water for approximately five minutes. Drain.
4. In a container, combine the ginger, sesame seeds, 1 tsp oil, and orange juice to make your dressing.
5. Once the chicken is cooked and noodles are cooked and drained, put in the chicken, noodles, carrots, and peas to the dressing and toss.
6. Serve warm or chilled.

Nutritional Info: Calories: 168 kcal ‖ Protein: 5.31 g ‖ Fat: 8.66 g ‖ Carbohydrates: 19.34 g

TANGY BARBECUE CHICKEN

Time To Prepare: 15 minutes

Time to Cook: 3-4 hours

Yield: Servings 4

Ingredients:

- 2 cups Tangy Barbecue Sauce with Apple Cider Vinegar
- 4- 5 (2 lb.)boneless, skinless chicken breasts

Directions:

1. In your slow cooker, mix the chicken and barbecue sauce. Stir until the chicken breasts are thoroughly coated in the sauce.
2. Secure the lid of your cooker and set to high. Cook for three to four hours, or until the internal temperature of the chicken reaches 165°F on a meat thermometer and the juices run clear.
3. Shred the chicken using a fork, mix it into the sauce, before you serve.

Nutritional Info: Calories: 412 ‖ Total Fat: 13g ‖ Total Carbohydrates: 22g ‖ Sugar: 19g ‖ Fiber: 0g ‖ Protein: 51g ‖ Sodium: 766mg

TANGY CHICKEN WITH SCALLIONS

Time To Prepare: ten minutes

Time to Cook: forty minutes

Yield: Servings 4

Ingredients:

- 1 garlic clove, cut
- 1 pound chicken drumettes
- 1 tablespoon fresh scallions, chopped
- 2 tablespoons white wine
- 3 tablespoons butter, melted

Directions:

1. Position the chicken drumettes on a foil-lined baking pan. Brush with melted butter.
2. Put in in the garlic and wine. Spice with salt and black pepper to taste. Bake in the preheated oven at 400 degrees F for approximately 30 minutes or until internal temperature reaches approximately 165 degrees F.
3. Serve decorated with scallions and enjoy!

Nutritional Info: 209 Calories 12.2g || Fat: 0.4g || Carbs: 23.2g || Protein: 1.9g Fiber

---

TARRAGON CHICKEN WITH ROASTED BALSAMIC TURNIPS

Time To Prepare: ten minutes

Time to Cook: 50 minutes

Yield: Servings 2-4

Ingredients:

- 1 pound chicken thighs
- 1 tbsp. balsamic vinegar
- 1 tbsp. tarragon
- 2 lb. turnips, cut into wedges
- 2 tbsp. olive oil
- Salt and black pepper, to taste

Directions:

1. Set the oven to 400°F then grease a baking dish with olive oil. Cook turnips in boiling water for about ten minutes, drain and save for later. Put in the chicken and turnips to the baking dish.
2. Drizzle with tarragon, black pepper, and salt. Roast for a little more than half an hour. Take away the baking dish, sprinkle the turnip wedges with balsamic vinegar and put back into the oven for another five minutes.

Nutritional Info: Calories: 383 || Fat: 26g || Net Carbohydrates: 9.5g || Protein: 21.3g

TERIYAKI CHICKEN

Time To Prepare: 2 hours and twenty-five minutes

Time to Cook: 20 minutes

Yield: Servings 3

Ingredients:

- .5 cup Soy sauce
- 1 tbsp. Powdered garlic
- 1 tbsp. Powdered ginger
- 1 tbsp. White vinegar
- 1 tbsp. Worcestershire sauce
- 3 tbsp. Coconut oil
- Black pepper (as required)
- lbs. Chicken breast
- Salt (as required)
- Sweetener (as you wish)

Directions:

1. Mix the Worcestershire sauce, coconut oil, sweetener, soy sauce, pepper, salt, ginger, garlic, and vinegar together using a big container.
2. Put in in the chicken, cover the container and let the chicken marinate for about two hours.
3. Put in the chicken to a frying pan before placing the pan on the stove over a burner turned to moderate heat.
4. Cook the chicken until the marinate has nearly completely vaporized, and the internal temperature has reached 165 degrees F.

Nutritional Info: **Calories:** 675 kcal || **Protein:** 52.97 g || **Fat:** 44.35 g || **Carbohydrates:** 14.43 g

THREE-CHEESE CHICKEN CORDON BLEU

Time To Prepare: 10 minutes

Time to Cook: 50 minutes

Yield: Servings 2

Ingredients:

- ⅛ teaspoon ground nutmeg
- ¼ cup shredded organic Appenzeller cheese
- ½ cup grated organic Parmesan cheese
- ½ cup shredded organic Emmentaler (Swiss) cheese
- ½ cup shredded organic Gruyère cheese
- ½ teaspoon Seasoned Salt
- 1 tablespoon extra-virgin olive oil
- 2 big boneless, skinless, free-range chicken breasts, butterflied and pounded thin
- 2 teaspoons Dijon mustard (not necessary)
- 4 slices nitrate-free ham

Directions:

1. Preheat your oven to 375°F.
2. Coat a rimmed baking sheet using parchment paper.
3. In a small container, mix the Gruyère, Emmentaler, and Appenzeller cheeses with the nutmeg.
4. Place the butterflied chicken breasts flat on a work surface and split the cheese mixture between the two breasts.
5. Then place 2 slices of ham on top of the cheese on each breast, followed by 1 teaspoon of Dijon mustard in the center (if using). Fold the chicken breast over to enclose the filling.
6. Brush the olive oil into a chicken, and drizzle it with the Parmesan cheese and seasoned salt.
7. Put the stuffed chicken breasts on the baking sheet and bake until the internal temperature reaches minimum 165°F, approximately 50 minutes. Serve hot.

Nutritional Info: Calories: 848 || Total Fat: 52g || Saturated Fat: 23g || Protein: 88g || Cholesterol: 278mg || Carbohydrates: 4g || Fiber: 1g || Net Carbohydrates: 3g

TOMATO & CHEESE CHICKEN CHILI

Time To Prepare: five minutes

Time to Cook: twenty-five minutes

Yield: Servings 2-4

Ingredients:

- ½ cup mozzarella cheese, shredded
- ½ onion, chopped
- 1 garlic clove, minced
- 1 habanero pepper, minced
- 1 pound chicken breasts, skinless, boneless, cubed
- 1 tbsp. butter
- 1 tbsp. chili powder
- 1 tbsp. cumin
- 1 tbsp. olive oil
- 2 cups chicken broth
- 2 cups tomatoes, chopped
- 2 oz. tomato puree
- Salt and black pepper to taste

Directions:

1. Flavour the chicken using salt and pepper. Set a big pan at moderate heat and put in the chicken; cover it with water, and bring it to its boiling point. Cook until no longer pink, for about ten minutes.
2. Move the chicken to a flat surface to shred with forks. In a pot, pour in the butter and olive oil and set on moderate heat. Sauté onion and garlic until transparent for five minutes.
3. Mix in the chicken, tomatoes, cumin, habanero pepper, tomato puree, broth, and chili powder. Tweak the seasoning and allow the mixture to boil.
4. Decrease the heat to simmer for approximately ten minutes. Top with shredded cheese to serve.

Nutritional Info: Calories: 322 || Fat: 16.6g || Net Carbohydrates: 6.2g || Protein: 29g

TRADITIONAL HUNGARIAN GULYÁS

Time To Prepare: ten minutes

Time to Cook: 1 hour and ten minutes

Yield: Servings 4

Ingredients:

- ½ cup celery ribs, chopped
- ½ pound duck legs, skinless and boneless
- 1 ripe tomato, pureed
- 1 tablespoon spice mix for goulash
- 2 (1-ounce) slices bacon, chopped

Directions:

1. Heat a heavy-bottomed pot over the moderate to high flame; then, fry the bacon for approximately 3 minutes. Mix in the duck legs and carry on cooking until they are well browned on all sides.
2. Shred the meat and discard the bones. Set aside.
3. In the pan drippings, sauté the celery for approximately 3 minutes, stirring with a wide spatula. Put in in pureed tomatoes and spice mix for goulash; put in in the reserved bacon and meat.
4. Pour 2 cups of water or chicken broth into the pot.
5. Put heat to moderate-low, cover, and simmer for about fifty minutes more or until everything is cooked meticulously. Serve warm and enjoy!

Nutritional Info: 363 Calories 22.3g || Fat: 5.1g || Carbs: 33.2g || Protein: 1.4g Fiber

TURKEY & SWEET POTATO CHILI

Time To Prepare: 15 minutes

Time to Cook: four to 6 hours

Yield: Servings 4

Ingredients:

- ½ medium red onion, diced
- ½ teaspoon ground cinnamon
- 1 (28-ounce) can diced tomatoes
- 1 (4-ounce) can Hatch green chiles
- 1 pound ground turkey
- 1 red bell pepper, diced
- 1 tablespoon chili powder
- 1 tablespoon extra-virgin olive oil
- 1 tablespoon freshly squeezed lime juice
- 1 teaspoon cocoa powder
- 1 teaspoon garlic powder
- 1 teaspoon ground cumin
- 1 teaspoon sea salt
- 2 cups broth of choice
- 3 cups sweet potato cubes
- Pinch cayenne pepper

Directions:

1. In your slow cooker, mix the olive oil, turkey, sweet potato cubes, tomatoes, bell pepper, chiles, onion, broth, lime juice, chili powder, garlic powder, cocoa powder, cumin, salt, cinnamon, and cayenne. Using a big spoon, break up the turkey into smaller chunks as it blends with the other ingredients.
2. Secure the lid of your cooker and set to low. Cook for four to 6 hours.
3. Mix the chili well, continuing to break up the remaining turkey, before you serve.

Nutritional Info: Calories: 380 || Total Fat: 12g || Total Carbohydrates: 38g || Sugar: 12g || Fiber: 6g || Protein: 30g || Sodium: 1,268mg

TURKEY AND POTATOES WITH BUFFALO SAUCE

Time To Prepare: ten minutes

Time to Cook: 20 minutes

Yield: Servings 2

Ingredients:

- ½ cup Water
- ½ tsp Garlic Powder
- 1 ½ pound Turkey Breast, cut into pieces
- 1 Onion, diced
- 1 pound Sweet Potatoes, cut into cubes
- 3 tbsps. Olive Oil
- 4 tbsp. Buffalo Sauce

Directions:

1. Heat 1 tbsp. Of olive oil on SAUTÉ mode at High. Stir-fry onion in hot oil for approximately 3 minutes. Mix in the rest of the ingredients. Secure the lid, set to PRESSURE COOK/MANUAL mode for about twenty minutes at high pressure.
2. When done cooking, do a quick pressure release by turning the valve to an "open" position.

Nutritional Info: Calories 377 || Carbs: 32g || Fat: 9g || Protein: 14g

TURKEY BACON MELT SANDWICH

Time To Prepare: ten minutes

Time to Cook: ten minutes

Yield: Servings 2

Ingredients:

- 2 sprouted whole-grain English muffin
- 4 slices of organic cheese
- 4 thick slices of organic tomato
- 6 strips organic/natural turkey bacon, cut in half

Directions:

1. Preheat your oven to 400°F.
2. Prepare turkey bacon in accordance with package directions.
3. Split the muffins in half then put the muffin halves face-up on a baking sheet.
4. Layer only two of the halves with 3 half-slices of bacon, followed by a slice of cheese, followed by 3 half-slices of bacon, followed by the rest of the second slice of cheese. Put

the baking sheet in the preheated oven and bake for three to five minutes or until the muffins are toasted and the cheese melted.
5. Take off the baking sheet from the oven and place one to 2 thick slices of tomato on the top of two of the muffin halves. If you want, put the baking sheet back in your oven and carry on baking for another 3-4 minutes or until the tomato slices are warm.
6. Take out of the oven and move the layered half of the English muffins onto two separate breakfast plates. Top each layered-half of muffin with the rest of the non-layered halves to complete the sandwich. Serve instantly.

Nutritional Info: Calories: 431 kcal || Protein: 23.05 g || Fat: 23.22 g || Carbohydrates: 32.92 g

TURKEY BREAST WITH FENNEL AND CELERY

Time To Prepare: ten minutes

Time to Cook: 15 minutes

Yield: Servings 3

Ingredients:

- ¼ tsp Garlic Powder
- ¼ tsp Pepper
- 1 cup celery with leaves, chopped
- 1 cup Fennel Bulb, chopped
- 2 ¼ cups Chicken Stock
- 2 pounds Boneless and Skinless Turkey Breast

Directions:

1. Throw all ingredients in your pressure cooker. Give it a good stir and secure the lid.
2. Push PRESSURE COOK/MANUAL, and cook for fifteen minutes at High. Do a quick pressure release. Shred the turkey using two forks.

Nutritional Info: Calories 272 || Carbs: 7g || Fat: 4g || Protein: 48g

TURKEY CHILI

Time To Prepare: five minutes

Time to Cook: thirty minutes

Yield: Servings 2

Ingredients:

- ¼ teaspoon ground cumin (not necessary)
- ¼ teaspoon pepper
- 1 ½ ounces cauliflower rice
- 1 ½ tablespoon olive oil
- 1 ½ tablespoons sour cream
- 1 cup water or as required
- 1 ounce jalapeno pepper
- 1 ounce red bell pepper (or other colors)
- 1 teaspoon paprika
- 1/3 teaspoon onion powder or garlic powder (not necessary)
- 3 ounces zucchini
- 4 tablespoons shredded cheddar cheese
- 5 ounces ground turkey
- Salt to taste

Directions:

1. Cut the red bell pepper, jalapeno pepper, and zucchini into smaller, bite-sized pieces. Feel free to slice jalapeno pepper into bigger pieces if you wish to avoid them and control the spiciness in your mouth later on.
2. Take a big stewing pot, put in the olive oil, and put it on moderate heat. Place the ground turkey and cook it until it becomes brown. Use a spatula to break it up.
3. Mix bell pepper, jalapeno, and zucchini with turkey. Place a cover on your pot and let your mixture cook on a low heat for roughly five minutes or until you see that vegetables became a little bit softer.
4. Season everything and put in water. Mix the chili.
5. Cover your pot once again and bring your mixture to a simmer. Continue to stir it for approximately 10 more minutes.
6. Put in the cauliflower rice. Take away the cover and keep cooking at the low heat.
7. Fill roughly ½ of a cup with the liquid you take out of the pot. Put it into a clean container and mix it with the sour cream.
8. Bring the thickened liquid back to the pot. Stir your ingredients once again and let your chili simmer for 5 more minutes for it to become thick a little bit more.

9. While serving this meal, fill 2 bowls and top each of those with 2 tablespoons of cheddar cheese.

Nutritional Info: Calories: 378 || Total Carbohydrates: 6,3g || Fiber: 2g || Net Carbohydrates: 4,3g || Fat: 30g || Protein: 23g

TURKEY CLUB WRAPS

Time To Prepare: five minutes

Time to Cook: five minutes

Yield: Servings 1

Ingredients:

- ½ slice sharp American cheese (cut deli-thin)
- 1 flatbread wrap or whole wheat tortilla
- 1 tbsp. ranch yogurt dressing
- 2 slices cooked bacon
- 2 tomato slices
- 2-ounce of smoked turkey (cut deli-thin)
- romaine lettuce (or baby spinach)

Directions:

1. Start by spreading ranch dressing out over the center of the wrap or tortilla.
2. After this, layer on the turkey, cheese, bacon, tomato, and lettuce (or spinach).
3. To finish, fold in each side of wrap or tortilla and then roll up and enjoy!

Nutritional Info: Calories: 791 kcal || Protein: 31.84 g || Fat: 63.37 g || Carbohydrates: 22.53 g

TURKEY CRUST MEATZA

Time To Prepare: 15 minutes

Time to Cook: thirty-five minutes

Yield: Servings 4

Ingredients:

- ½ pound ground turkey

- 1 cup Mozzarella cheese, grated
- 1 tablespoon pizza spice mix
- 1 tomato, chopped
- 2 slices Canadian bacon

Directions:

1. Combine the ground turkey and cheese; sprinkle with salt and black pepper and stir until everything is well blended.
2. Push the mixture into a foil-lined baking pan. Bake in the preheated oven at 380 degrees F for about twenty-five minutes.
3. Top the crust with Canadian bacon, tomato, and pizza spice mix. Carry on baking for another 8 minutes.
4. Allow it to rest for a few minutes before cutting and serving. Enjoy!

Nutritional Info: 360 Calories 22.7g || Fat: 5.9g || Carbs: 32.6g || Protein: 0.7g Fiber

TURKEY HAM AND MOZZARELLA PATE

Time To Prepare: ten minutes

Time to Cook: 0 minutes

Yield: Servings 6

Ingredients:

- 2 tablespoons flaxseed meal
- 2 tablespoons fresh parsley, roughly chopped
- 2 tablespoons sunflower seeds
- 4 ounces mozzarella cheese, crumbled
- 4 ounces turkey ham, chopped

Directions:

1. Thoroughly mix the ingredients, apart from for the sunflower seeds, in a food processor.
2. Ladle the mixture into a serving container and sprinkle the sunflower seeds over the top.

Nutritional Info: 212 Calories 18.8g || Fat: 2g || Carbs: 10.6g || Protein: 1.6g Fiber

TURKEY MEATBALLS WITH SPAGHETTI SQUASH

Time To Prepare: 15 minutes

Time to Cook: 7 to 8 hours

Yield: Servings 4

Ingredients:

- ½ small white onion, minced
- ½ teaspoon dried basil leaves
- ½ teaspoon dried oregano
- ½ teaspoon garlic powder
- ½ teaspoon sea salt
- 1 (fifteen-ounce) can diced tomatoes
- 1 big egg, whisked
- 1 pound ground turkey
- 1 spaghetti squash, halved along the length and seeded
- 1 teaspoon garlic powder
- For the Meatballs:
- For the Sauce:
- Freshly ground black pepper

Directions:

1. Put the squash halves on the bottom of your slow cooker, cut-side down.

To make the Sauce:

1. Pour the diced tomatoes around the squash on the bottom of the slow cooker.
2. Drizzle in the garlic powder, oregano, and salt.

To make the meatballs:

1. In a moderate-sized container, combine the turkey, egg, onion, garlic powder, salt, oregano, and basil, and flavor with pepper. Form the turkey mixture into 12 balls, and put them in the slow cooker around the spaghetti squash.
2. Secure the lid of your cooker and set to low. Cook for 6 to 7 hours.

3. Move the squash to a work surface, and use a fork to shred it into spaghetti-like strands. Mix the strands with the tomato sauce, top with the meatballs, before you serve.

Nutritional Info: Calories: 253 || Total Fat: 8g || Total Carbohydrates: 22g || Sugar: 4g || Fiber: 1g || Protein: 24g || Sodium: 948mg

---

TURKEY SLOPPY JOES

Time To Prepare: 15 minutes

Time to Cook: four to 6 hours

Yield: Servings 4

Ingredients:

- ½ medium sweet onion, diced
- ½ red bell pepper, finely chopped
- ½ teaspoon dried oregano
- ½ teaspoon garlic powder
- ½ teaspoon sea salt
- 1 carrot, minced
- 1 celery stalk, minced
- 1 pound ground turkey
- 1 tablespoon extra-virgin olive oil
- 1 tablespoon maple syrup
- 1 teaspoon chili powder
- 1 teaspoon Dijon mustard
- 2 tablespoons apple cider vinegar
- 6 tablespoons tomato paste

Directions:

1. In your slow cooker, mix the olive oil, turkey, celery, carrot, onion, red bell pepper, tomato paste, vinegar, maple syrup, mustard, chili powder, garlic powder, salt, and oregano. Using a big spoon, break up the turkey into smaller chunks as it blends with the other ingredients.

2. Secure the lid of your cooker and set to low. Cook for four to 6 hours, stir meticulously before you serve.

Nutritional Info: Calories: 251 || Total Fat: 12g || Total Carbohydrates: 14g || Sugar: 9g || Fiber: 3g || Protein: 24g || Sodium: 690mg

---

TURMERIC CHICKEN WINGS WITH GINGER SAUCE

Time To Prepare: five minutes

Time to Cook: 20 minutes

Yield: Servings 2-4

Ingredients:

- ¾ cup cilantro, chopped
- 1 cup thyme leaves
- 1 jalapeño pepper
- 1 pound chicken wings, cut in half
- 1 tbsp. cumin
- 1 tbsp. turmeric
- 1 tbsp. water
- 2 tbsp. olive oil
- 3 tbsp. fresh ginger, grated
- Juice of ½ lime
- Salt and black pepper, to taste

Directions:

1. In a container, mix together 1 tbsp. ginger, cumin, salt, half of the olive oil, black pepper, turmeric, and cilantro. Put in the chicken wings pieces, toss to coat, and place in your fridge for about twenty minutes.
2. Heat the grill to high heat. Take away the wings from the marinade, drain, and grill for about twenty minutes, turning occasionally, then set aside.
3. Using a blender, mix thyme, remaining ginger, salt, jalapeno pepper, black pepper, lime juice, the rest of the olive oil, and water, and blend thoroughly. Serve the chicken wings topped with the sauce.

Nutritional Info: Calories 253 || Fat: 16.1g Net || Carbs: 4.1g || Protein: 21.7g

TURNIP GREENS & ARTICHOKE CHICKEN

Time To Prepare: five minutes

Time to Cook: thirty minutes

Yield: Servings 2

Ingredients:

- ¼ cup Pecorino cheese, grated
- ½ tbsp. garlic powder
- ½ tbsp. onion powder
- 1 cup turnip greens
- 2 chicken breasts
- 2 ounces Monterrey Jack cheese, shredded
- 4 ounces cream cheese
- 4 oz. canned artichoke hearts, chopped
- Salt and black pepper, to taste

Directions:

1. Coat a baking dish using parchment paper and place it in the chicken breasts. Flavor it with black pepper and salt. Set in your oven at 350 F and bake for a little more than half an hour.
2. In a container, mix the artichokes with onion powder, Pecorino cheese, salt, turnip greens, cream cheese, garlic powder, and black pepper.
3. Take off the chicken from the oven, cut each piece in half, split artichokes mixture on top, spread with Monterrey cheese, and bake for 5 more minutes.

Nutritional Info: Calories 443 || Fat: 24.5g Net || Carbs: 4.2g || Protein: 35.4g

TUSCAN CHICKEN SAUTE

Time To Prepare: ten minutes

Time to Cook: thirty-five minutes

Yield: Servings 4

Ingredients:

- ¼ cup cut Kalamata olives

- ½ cup heavy (whipping) cream
- ½ cup shredded Asiago cheese
- ½ teaspoon dried basil
- ¾ cup chicken stock
- 1 cup fresh spinach
- 1 pound boneless chicken breasts, each cut into three pieces
- 1 tablespoon minced garlic
- 1 teaspoon dried oregano
- 3 tablespoons olive oil
- Freshly ground black pepper, for seasoning
- Sea salt, for seasoning

Directions:

1. Prepare the chicken. Pat, the chicken, breasts dry and lightly flavor them with salt and pepper.
2. Sauté the chicken. In a big frying pan on moderate to high heat, warm the olive oil. Put in the chicken and sauté until it is golden brown and just thoroughly cooked, approximately fifteen minutes in total. Move the chicken to a plate and set it aside.
3. Make the sauce. Place the garlic to the frying pan, then sauté until it's softened about two minutes. Mix in the chicken stock, oregano, and basil, scraping up any browned bits in the frying pan. Bring to its boiling point, then decrease the heat to low and simmer until the sauce is reduced by about one-quarter, approximately ten minutes.
4. Finish the dish. Mix in the cream, Asiago, and simmer while stirring the sauce regularly, until it has become thick about five minutes. Put back the chicken to the frying pan together with any collected juices. Mix in the spinach and olives and simmer until the spinach is wilted about two minutes.
5. Serve. Split the chicken and sauce between four plates and serve it instantly.

Nutritional Info: Calories: 483 Total fat: 38g Total carbs: 5g || Fiber: 1g; Net carbs: 3g || Sodium: 332mg || Protein: 31g

VODKA DUCK FILLETS

Time To Prepare: five minutes

Time to Cook: 15 minutes

Yield: Servings 4

Ingredients:

- ½ cup sour cream
- ½ teaspoon ground bay leaf
- 1 ½ cups turkey stock
- 1 tablespoon lard, room temperature
- 1 teaspoon mixed peppercorns
- 2 ounces vodka
- 3 tablespoons Worcestershire sauce
- 4 duck fillets
- 4 green onions, chopped
- Salt and cayenne pepper, to taste

Directions:

1. Melt the lard in a frying pan that is preheated on moderate to high heat. Sear the duck fillets, flipping over once, for four to six minutes.
2. Now, put in the rest of the ingredients, apart from for the sour cream, to the frying pan. Cook, partly covered, for another seven minutes.
3. Serve warm, decorated with sour cream. Enjoy!

Nutritional Info: 351 Calories 24.7g || Fat: 6.6g || Carbs: 22.1g Protein

WHITE BEAN AND CHICKEN CHILI BLANCA

Time To Prepare: ten minutes

Time to Cook: thirty minutes

Yield: Servings 4-5

Ingredients:

- ½ cup corn kernels, fresh or frozen
- ½ pound chicken tenders or boneless chicken breasts, skinless
- 1 ½ cups water
- 1 can (fifteen ounces) white or Great Northern beans, drained, washed
- 1 clove garlic, peeled, minced
- 1 cup Monterey Jack cheese, grated

- 1 small onion, chopped
- 1 tablespoon extra-virgin olive oil
- 1 tablespoon fresh cilantro, chopped
- 1 teaspoon chili powder
- 1 teaspoon cumin powder
- 2 ounces canned green chilies
- A pinch cayenne pepper
- Pepper to taste
- Salt to taste

Directions:

1. Drizzle salt and pepper over the chicken.
2. Put a frying pan using high heat. Put in oil. When the oil is heated, place chicken and sauté until brown.
3. Reduce the heat to moderate heat. Mix in the garlic and onion and sauté until tender.
4. Mix in corn, beans, green chilies, water, cumin powder, chili powder, salt, and cayenne pepper. Simmer for about twenty minutes.
5. Ladle into bowls. Decorate using cheese and cilantro before you serve.

Nutritional Info: Calories: 243 kcal || Protein: 20.57 g || Fat: 13.94 g || Carbohydrates: 11.96 g

WHITE BEAN, CHICKEN & APPLE CIDER CHILI

Time To Prepare: 15 minutes

Time to Cook: 7 to 8 hours

Yield: Servings 4

Ingredients:

- ¼ cup apple cider vinegar
- ¼ teaspoon ground cinnamon
- ½ teaspoon ground cumin
- 1 (fifteen-ounce) can diced tomatoes
- 1 cup apple cider
- 1 medium onion, chopped
- 1 tablespoon extra-virgin olive oil

- 1 teaspoon chili powder
- 1 teaspoon sea salt
- 2 (fifteen-ounce) cans white navy beans, washed well and drained
- 2 bay leaves
- 2 teaspoons garlic powder
- 3 cups Chicken Bone Broth or store-bought chicken broth
- 3 cups chopped cooked chicken (see Basic "Rotisserie" Chicken)
- Freshly ground black pepper
- Pinch cayenne pepper

Directions:

1. In your slow cooker, mix the chicken, beans, onion, tomatoes, broth, cider, bay leaves, olive oil, garlic powder, chili powder, salt, cumin, cinnamon cayenne, and flavor with black pepper.
2. Secure the lid of your cooker and set to low. Cook for about eight hours.
3. Remove and discard the bay leaves. Mix in the apple cider vinegar until well mixed before you serve.

Nutritional Info: Calories: 469 || Total Fat: 8g || Total Carbohydrates: 46g || Sugar: 13g || Fiber: 9g || Protein: 51g || Sodium: 1,047mg

WINTER CHICKEN WITH VEGETABLES

Time To Prepare: five minutes

Time to Cook: thirty minutes

Yield: Servings 2

Ingredients:

- 1 bay leaf
- 1 carrot, chopped
- 1 cup green beans, chopped
- 1 onion, chopped
- 1 parsnip, chopped
- 1 pound chicken breasts, chopped
- 1 turnip, chopped

- 2 cups chicken stock
- 2 cups whipping cream
- 2 tbsp. olive oil
- 2 tsp fresh thyme, chopped
- Salt and black pepper, to taste

Directions:

1. Heat a pan at moderate heat and warm the olive oil. Sauté the onion for about three minutes, pour in the stock, carrot, turnip, parsnip, chicken, and bay leaf. Put to its boiling point, and simmer for about twenty minutes.
2. Put in in the asparagus and cook for seven minutes. Discard the bay leaf, mix in the whipping cream, tweak the seasoning, and sprinkle it with fresh thyme to serve.

Nutritional Info: Calories 483 || Fat: 32.5g Net || Carbs: 6.9g || Protein: 33g

SIDES

BEET HUMMUS

Time To Prepare: five minutes

Time to Cook: 0 minutes

Yield: Servings 2

Ingredients:

- ¼ tsp of chili flakes
- ½ cup of olive oil
- ½ tsp of oregano
- ½ tsp of salt
- 1 ½ tsp of cumin
- 1 ¾ cup of chickpeas
- 1 clove of garlic
- 1 nub of fresh ginger
- 1 skinless roasted beet
- 1 tsp of curry
- 1 tsp of maple syrup
- 2 tbsp. of sunflower seeds
- Juice of one lemon

Directions:

1. Blend all together the ingredients in a food processor until they're smooth and decorate them with sunflower seeds.
2. Enjoy!

Nutritional Info: || Calories: 423 kcal || Protein: 13.98 g || Fat: 24.26 g || Carbohydrates: 40.13 g

BROCCOLI AND BLACK BEANS STIR FRY

Time To Prepare: ten minutes

Time to Cook: fifteen minutes

Yield: Servings 4

Ingredients:

- 1 tablespoon sesame oil
- 2 cloves garlic, thoroughly minced
- 2 cups cooked black beans
- 2 teaspoons ginger, finely chopped
- 4 cups broccoli florets
- 4 teaspoons sesame seeds
- A big pinch red chili flakes
- A pinch turmeric powder
- Lime juice to taste (not necessary)
- Salt to taste

Directions:

1. Pour enough water to immerse the bottom of the deep cooking pan by an inch. Put a strainer on the deep cooking pan. Put broccoli florets on the strainer. Steam the broccoli for about six minutes.
2. Put a big frying pan on moderate heat. Put in sesame oil. When the oil is just warm, put in sesame seeds, chili flakes, ginger, garlic, turmeric powder and salt. Sauté for about 2 minutes until aromatic.
3. Put in steamed broccoli and black beans and sauté until meticulously heated.
4. Put in lime juice and stir.
5. Serve hot.

Nutritional Info: || Calories: 196 kcal || Protein: 11.2 g || Fat: 7.25 g || Carbohydrates: 23.45 g

CARAMELIZED PEARS AND ONIONS

Time To Prepare: five minutes

Time to Cook: thirty-five minutes

Yield: Servings 4

Ingredients:

- 1 tablespoon olive oil
- 2 firm red pears, cored and quartered

- 2 red onion, cut into wedges
- Salt and pepper, to taste

Directions:

1. Preheat the oven to 425 degrees F
2. Put the pears and onion on a baking tray
3. Sprinkle with olive oil
4. Sprinkle with salt and pepper
5. Bake using your oven for a little more than half an hour
6. Serve and enjoy!

Nutritional Info: || Calories: 101 || Fat: 4g || Carbohydrates: 17g || Protein: 1g

CAULIFLOWER BROCCOLI MASH

Time To Prepare: five minutes

Time to Cook: ten minutes

Yield: Servings 6

Ingredients:

- 1 big head cauliflower, cut into chunks
- 1 small head broccoli, cut into florets
- 1 teaspoon salt
- 3 tablespoons extra virgin olive oil
- Pepper, to taste

Directions:

1. Take a pot and put in oil then heat it
2. Put in the cauliflower and broccoli
3. Sprinkle with salt and pepper to taste
4. Keep stirring to make vegetable soft
5. Put in water if required
6. When is already cooked, use a food processor or a potato masher to puree the vegetables
7. Serve and enjoy!

Nutritional Info: || Calories: 39 || Fat: 3g || Carbohydrates: 2g || Protein: 0.89g

CILANTRO AND AVOCADO PLATTER

Time To Prepare: ten minutes

Time to Cook: 0 minutes

Yield: Servings 6

Ingredients:

- ¼ cup of fresh cilantro, chopped
- ½ a lime, juiced
- 1 big ripe tomato, chopped
- 1 green bell pepper, chopped
- 1 sweet onion, chopped
- 2 avocados, peeled, pitted and diced
- Salt and pepper as required

Directions:

1. Take a moderate-sized container and put in onion, bell pepper, tomato, avocados, lime and cilantro
2. Mix thoroughly and give it a toss
3. Sprinkle with salt and pepper in accordance with your taste
4. Serve and enjoy!

Nutritional Info: || Calories: 126 || Fat: 10g || Carbohydrates: 10g || Protein: 2g

CITRUS COUSCOUS WITH HERB

Time To Prepare: five minutes

Time to Cook: fifteen minutes

Yield: Servings 2

Ingredients:

- ¼ cup of water
- ¼ orange, chopped

- ½ teaspoon butter
- 1 teaspoon Italian seasonings
- 1/3 cup couscous
- 1/3 teaspoon salt
- 4 tablespoons orange juice

Directions:

1. Pour water and orange juice in the pan.
2. Put in orange, Italian seasoning, and salt.
3. Bring the liquid to boil and take it off the heat.
4. Put in butter and couscous. Stir thoroughly and close the lid.
5. Leave the couscous rest for about ten minutes.

Nutritional Info: Calories 149 || Fat: 1.9 || Fiber: 2.1 || Carbs: 28.5 || Protein: 4.1

COOL GARBANZO AND SPINACH BEANS

Time To Prepare: 5-ten minutes

Time to Cook: 0 minute

Yield: Servings 4

Ingredients:

- ½ onion, diced
- ½ teaspoon cumin
- 1 tablespoon olive oil
- 10 ounces spinach, chopped
- 12 ounces garbanzo beans

Directions:

1. Take a frying pan and put in olive oil
2. Put it on moderate to low heat
3. Put in onions, garbanzo and cook for five minutes
4. Mix in cumin, garbanzo beans, spinach and flavor with sunflower seeds
5. Use a spoon to smash gently
6. Cook meticulously
7. Serve and enjoy!

Nutritional Info: || Calories: 90 || Fat: 4g || Carbohydrates:11g || Protein:4g

---

COUSCOUS SALAD

Time To Prepare: ten minutes

Time to Cook: six minutes

Yield: Servings 4

Ingredients:

- ¼ teaspoon ground black pepper
- ¾ teaspoon ground coriander
- ½ teaspoon salt
- ¼ teaspoon paprika
- ¼ teaspoon turmeric
- 1 tablespoon butter
- 2 oz. chickpeas, canned, drained
- 1 cup fresh arugula, chopped
- 2 oz. sun-dried tomatoes, chopped
- 1 oz. Feta cheese, crumbled
- 1 tablespoon canola oil
- 1/3 cup couscous
- 1/3 cup chicken stock

Directions:

1. Bring the chicken stock to boil.
2. Put in couscous, ground black pepper, ground coriander, salt, paprika, and turmeric. Put in chickpeas and butter. Mix the mixture well and close the lid.
3. Allow the couscous soak the hot chicken stock for about six minutes.
4. In the meantime, in the mixing container mix together arugula, sun-dried tomatoes, and Feta cheese.
5. Put in cooked couscous mixture and canola oil.
6. Mix up the salad well.

Nutritional Info: Calories 18 || Fat: 9 || Fiber: 3.6 || Carbs: 21.1 || Protein: 6

CREAMY POLENTA

Time To Prepare: 8 minutes

Time to Cook: forty-five minutes

Yield: Servings 4

Ingredients:

- ½ cup cream
- 1 ½ cup water
- 1 cup polenta
- 1/3 cup Parmesan, grated
- 2 cups chicken stock

Directions:

1. Put polenta in the pot.
2. Put in water, chicken stock, cream, and Parmesan. Mix up polenta well.
3. Then preheat oven to 355F.
4. Cook polenta in your oven for about forty-five minutes.
5. Mix up the cooked meal with the help of the spoon cautiously before you serve.

Nutritional Info: Calories 208 || Fat: 5.3 || Fiber: 1 || Carbs: 32.2 || Protein: 8

CRISPY CORN

Time To Prepare: 8 minutes

Time to Cook: five minutes

Yield: Servings 3

Ingredients:

- ½ teaspoon ground paprika
- ½ teaspoon salt
- ¾ teaspoon chili pepper
- 1 cup corn kernels
- 1 tablespoon coconut flour
- 1 tablespoon water
- 3 tablespoons canola oil

Directions:

1. In the mixing container, mix together corn kernels with salt and coconut flour.
2. Put in water and mix up the corn with the help of the spoon.
3. Pour canola oil in the frying pan and heat it.
4. Put in corn kernels mixture and roast it for about four minutes. Stir it occasionally.
5. When the corn kernels are crispy, move them in the plate and dry with the paper towel's help.
6. Put in chili pepper and ground paprika. Mix up well.

Nutritional Info: Calories 179 || Fat: fifteen || Fiber: 2.4 || Carbs: 11.3 || Protein: 2.1

CUCUMBER YOGURT SALAD WITH MINT

Time To Prepare: ten minutes

Time to Cook: 0 minutes

Yield: Servings 2

Ingredients:

- ¼ cup organic coconut milk
- ¼ cup organic mint leaves
- ¼ teaspoon pink Himalayan sea salt
- ½ cup chopped organic red onion
- 1 tablespoon extra virgin olive oil
- 1 tablespoon plain organic goat yogurt
- 1 teaspoon organic dill weed
- 2 chopped organic cucumbers
- 3 tablespoons fresh organic lime juice

Directions:

1. Cut the red onion, dill, cucumbers, and mint and mix them in a big container.
2. Blend them until they're smooth.
3. Top the dressing onto the cucumber salad and mix meticulously. Chill for minimum 1 hour and serve.
4. Enjoy!

Nutritional Info: || Calories: 207 kcal || Protein: 6.9 g || Fat: 13.87 g || Carbohydrates: 18.04 g

CURRY WHEATBERRY RICE

Time To Prepare: ten minutes

Time to Cook: 1 hour fifteen minutes

Yield: Servings 5

Ingredients:

- ¼ cup milk
- ½ cup of rice
- 1 cup wheat berries
- 1 tablespoon curry paste
- 1 teaspoon salt
- 4 tablespoons olive oil
- 6 cups chicken stock

Directions:

1. Put wheatberries and chicken stock in the pan.
2. Close the lid and cook the mixture for an hour over the moderate heat.
3. Then put in rice, olive oil, and salt.
4. Stir thoroughly.
5. Mix up together milk and curry paste.
6. Put in the curry liquid in the rice-wheatberry mixture and stir thoroughly.
7. Boil the meal for fifteen minutes with the closed lid.
8. When the rice is cooked, all the meal is cooked.

Nutritional Info: Calories 232 ‖ Fat: fifteen ‖ Fiber: 1.4 ‖ Carbs: 23.5 ‖ Protein: 3.9

FARRO SALAD WITH ARUGULA

Time To Prepare: ten minutes

Time to Cook: thirty-five minutes

Yield: Servings 2

Ingredients:

- ½ cup farro
- ½ teaspoon ground black pepper

- ½ teaspoon Italian seasoning
- ½ teaspoon olive oil
- 1 ½ cup chicken stock
- 1 cucumber, chopped
- 1 tablespoon lemon juice
- 1 teaspoon salt
- 2 cups arugula, chopped

Directions:

1. Mix up together farro, salt, and chicken stock and move mixture in the pan.
2. Close the lid and boil it for a little more than half an hour.
3. In the meantime, place all rest of the ingredients in the salad container.
4. Chill the farro to the room temperature and put in it in the salad container too.
5. Mix up the salad well.

Nutritional Info: Calories 92 || Fat: 2.3 || Fiber: 2 || Carbs: 15.6 || Protein: 3.9

FETA CHEESE SALAD

Time To Prepare: ten minutes

Time to Cook: 0 minutes

Yield: Servings 2

Ingredients:

- 1 tbsp. olive oil (extra virgin)
- 1 tsp balsamic vinegar
- 2 cucumbers
- 30 g feta cheese
- 4 spring onions
- 4 tomatoes
- Salt

Directions:

1. Cube the tomatoes and cucumbers.
2. Thinly slice the onions.
3. Crush the feta cheese.

4. Mix tomatoes, onions, and cucumbers.
5. Put olive oil, vinegar, and a small amount of salt.
6. Put in feta cheese.
7. Enjoy your meal!

Nutritional Info: || Calories: 221 kcal || Protein: 9.24 g || Fat: 13.84 g || Carbohydrates: 17.18 g

FRESH STRAWBERRY SALSA

Time To Prepare: ten minutes

Time to Cook: 0 minutes

Yield: Servings 6-8

Ingredients:

- ¼ cup fresh lime juice
- ½ cup fresh cilantro
- ½ cup red onion, finely chopped
- ½ teaspoon lime zest, grated
- 1-2 jalapeños, deseeded, finely chopped
- 2 kiwi fruit, peeled, chopped
- 2 pounds fresh ripe strawberries, hulled, chopped
- 2 teaspoons pure raw honey

Directions:

1. Put in lime juice, lime zest and honey into a big container and whisk well.
2. Put in remaining ingredients then mix thoroughly. Cover and set aside for a while for the flavors to set in and serve.

Nutritional Info: || Calories: 119 kcal || Protein: 9.26 g || Fat: 4.38 g || Carbohydrates: 11.73 g

GOAT CHEESE SALAD

Time To Prepare: fifteen minutes

Time to Cook: thirty minutes

Yield: Servings 4

Ingredients:

- ½ cup of walnuts
- ½ head of escarole (medium), torn
- 1 bunch of trimmed and torn arugula
- 1/3 cup extra virgin olive oil
- 2 bunches of medium beets (~1 ½ lbs.) with trimmed tops
- 2 tbsp. of red wine vinegar
- 4 oz. crumbled of goat cheese (aged cheese is preferred)
- Kosher salt + freshly ground black pepper

Directions:

1. Place the beets in water in a deep cooking pan and apply salt as seasoning. Now, boil them using high heat for approximately twenty minutes or until they're soft. Peel them off when they're cool using your fingers or use a knife.
2. To taste, whisk the vinegar with salt and pepper in a big container. Then mix in the olive oil for the dressing. Toss the beets with the dressing, so they're uniformly coated and marinate them for approximately fifteen minutes – 2 hours.
3. Set the oven to 350F. Bring the nuts on a baking sheet and toast them for approximately 8 minutes (stirring them once) until they turn golden brown. Let them cool.
4. Mix and toss the escarole and arugula with the beets and put them in four plates. Put in the walnuts and goat cheese as toppings before you serve.
5. Enjoy!

Nutritional Info: ‖ Calories: 285 kcal ‖ Protein: 11.85 g ‖ Fat: 25.79 g ‖ Carbohydrates: 2.01 g

---

GREEN BEANS

Time To Prepare: five minutes

Time to Cook: ten minutes

Yield: Servings 5

Ingredients:

- ½ teaspoon kosher salt
- ½ teaspoon of red pepper flakes

- 1½ lbs. green beans, trimmed
- 2 garlic cloves, minced
- 2 tablespoons of extra-virgin olive oil
- 2 tablespoons of water

Directions:

1. Heat oil in a frying pan on medium temperature.
2. Include the pepper flake. Stir to coat in the olive oil.
3. Include the green beans. Cook for seven minutes.
4. Stir frequently. The beans must be brown in some areas.
5. Put in the salt and garlic. Cook for a minute, while stirring.
6. Pour water and cover instantly.
7. Cook covered for 1 more minute.

Nutritional Info: Calories 82 || Carbohydrates: 6g || Total Fat: 6g || Protein: 1g || Fiber: 2g || Sugar: 0g || Sodium: 230mg

GREEN, RED AND YELLOW RICE

Time To Prepare: five minutes

Time to Cook: fifteen minutes

Yield: Servings 10

Ingredients:

- ¼ cup garlic, finely chopped
- 1 cup fresh cilantro, chopped
- 2 cups brown rice, washed
- 2 cups frozen corn, thawed
- 2 cups green onions, chopped
- 2 cups red bell pepper, chopped
- 2 tablespoons olive oil
- Cayenne pepper to taste
- Pepper to taste
- Salt to taste

Directions:

1. Put a big deep cooking pan on moderate heat. Put in 4 cups water and brown rice and cook in accordance with the instructions on the package. Once cooked, cover and save for later.
2. Put a big frying pan on moderate heat. Put in oil. When the oil is heated, put in garlic and sauté for approximately one minute until aromatic.
3. Put in corn, red bell pepper, green onion, salt, pepper and cayenne pepper and sauté for at least two minutes.
4. Put in rice and cilantro. Mix thoroughly and heat meticulously.
5. Serve.

Nutritional Info: || Calories: 89 kcal || Protein: 2.41 g || Fat: 4.01 g || Carbohydrates: 11.26 g

HOT PINK COCONUT SLAW

Time To Prepare: five minutes

Time to Cook: 0 minutes

Yield: Servings 3

Ingredients:

- ¼ cup fresh cilantro, chopped
- ¼ teaspoon salt
- ½ cup big coconut flakes, unsweetened or shredded coconut, unsweetened
- ½ cup radish, thinly cut or shredded carrots
- ½ small jalapeño, deseeded, discard membranes, chopped
- ½ tablespoon honey or maple syrup
- 1 cup red onion, thinly cut
- 1 tablespoon olive oil
- 2 cups purple cabbage, thinly cut
- 2 tablespoons apple cider vinegar
- 2 tablespoons lime juice

Directions:

1. Combine all ingredients into a container and toss thoroughly. Cover and set aside for about forty minutes.
2. Toss thoroughly before you serve.

Nutritional Info: || Calories: 179 kcal || Protein: 3.92 g || Fat: 10.64 g || Carbohydrates: 18.53 g

---

LENTIL SALAD

Time To Prepare: ten minutes

Time to Cook: 0 minutes

Yield: Servings 2

Ingredients:

- ½ cup parsley
- 1 red bell pepper
- 1 tbsp. lime juice
- 1 tbsp. olive oil
- 2 cups lentil
- 3 spring onions
- A pinch of salt
- fifteen basil leaves
- Turmeric – to your taste

Directions:

1. Cook the lentils based on the package instructions. Put in a garlic clove while cooking.
2. When cooled, remove the garlic clove and put the lentils into a big container.
3. Chop all the vegetables then put in them to the lentils.
4. Put in lime juice, a small amount of salt, and olive oil.
5. Mix thoroughly.

Nutritional Info: || Calories: 207 kcal || Protein: 11.53 g || Fat: 10.49 g || Carbohydrates: 22.37 g

---

MASCARPONE COUSCOUS

Time To Prepare: fifteen minutes

Time to Cook: 7.5 hours

Yield: Servings 4

Ingredients:

- ½ cup mascarpone
- 1 cup couscous
- 1 teaspoon ground paprika
- 1 teaspoon salt
- 3 ½ cup chicken stock

Directions:

1. Put chicken stock and mascarpone in the pan and bring the liquid to boil.
2. Put in salt and ground paprika. Stir gently and simmer for a minute.
3. Take off the liquid from the heat and put in couscous. Stir thoroughly and close the lid.
4. Leave couscous for about ten minutes.
5. Mix the cooked side dish well before you serve.

Nutritional Info: Calories 227 || Fat: 4.9 || Fiber: 2.4 || Carbs: 35.4 || Protein: 9.7

MOROCCAN STYLE COUSCOUS

Time To Prepare: ten minutes

Time to Cook: ten minutes

Yield: Servings 4

Ingredients:

- ½ teaspoon ground cardamom
- ½ teaspoon red pepper
- 1 cup chicken stock
- 1 cup yellow couscous
- 1 tablespoon butter
- 1 teaspoon salt

Directions:

1. Toss butter in the pan and melt it.
2. Put in couscous and roast it for a minute over the high heat.
3. Then put in ground cardamom, salt, and red pepper. Stir it well.
4. Pour the chicken stock and bring the mixture to boil.
5. Simmer couscous for five minutes with the closed lid.

Nutritional Info: Calories 196 || Fat: 3.4 || Fiber: 2.4 || Carbs: 35 || Protein: 5.9

MUSHROOM MILLET

Time To Prepare: ten minutes

Time to Cook: fifteen minutes

Yield: Servings 3

Ingredients:

- ¼ cup mushrooms, cut
- ½ cup millet
- ¾ cup onion, diced
- 1 cup of water
- 1 tablespoon olive oil
- 1 teaspoon butter
- 1 teaspoon salt
- 3 tablespoons milk

Directions:

1. Pour olive oil in the frying pan then put the onion.
2. Put in mushrooms and roast the vegetables for about ten minutes over the moderate heat. Stir them occasionally.
3. In the meantime, pour water in the pan.
4. Put in millet and salt.
5. Cook the millet with the closed lid for fifteen minutes over the moderate heat.
6. Then put in the cooked mushroom mixture in the millet.
7. Put in milk and butter. Mix up the millet well.

Nutritional Info: Calories 198 || Fat: 7.7 || Fiber: 3.5 || Carbs: 27.9 || Protein: 4.7

ONION AND ORANGE HEALTHY SALAD

Time To Prepare: ten minutes

Time to Cook: 0 minutes

Yield: Servings 3

Ingredients:

- ¼ cup of fresh chives, chopped
- 1 cup olive oil
- 1 red onion, thinly cut
- 1 teaspoon of dried oregano
- 3 tablespoon of red wine vinegar
- 6 big orange
- 6 tablespoon of olive oil
- Ground black pepper

Directions:

1. Peel the orange and cut each of them in 4-5 crosswise slices
2. Move the oranges to a shallow dish
3. Sprinkle vinegar, olive oil and drizzle oregano
4. Toss
5. Chill for thirty minutes
6. Position cut onion and black olives on top
7. Garnish with an additional drizzle of chives and a fresh grind of pepper
8. Serve and enjoy!

Nutritional Info: || Calories: 120 || Fat: 6g || Carbohydrates: 20g || Protein: 2g

PARMESAN ROASTED BROCCOLI

Time To Prepare: ten minutes

Time to Cook: twenty minutes

Yield: Servings 6

Ingredients:

- ½ teaspoon of Italian seasoning
- 1 tablespoon of lemon juice
- 1 tablespoon parsley, chopped
- 3 tablespoons of olive oil
- 3 tablespoons of vegan parmesan, grated
- 4 cups of broccoli florets

- Pepper and salt to taste

Directions:

1. Preheat the oven to 450 degrees F. Apply cooking spray on your pan.
2. Keep the broccoli florets in a freezer bag.
3. Now put in the Italian seasoning, olive oil, pepper, and salt.
4. Seal your bag. Shake it. Coat well.
5. Pour your broccoli on the pan. It must be in a single layer.
6. Bake for about twenty minutes. Stir midway through.
7. Take out from the oven. Drizzle parsley and parmesan.
8. Sprinkle some lemon juice.
9. You can decorate with lemon wedges if you wish.

Nutritional Info: Calories 96 || Carbohydrates: 4g || Cholesterol: 2mg || Total Fat: 8g || Protein: 2g || Sugar: 1g || Fiber: 1g || Sodium: 58mg || Potassium: 191mg

QUINOA SALAD

Time To Prepare: ten minutes

Time to Cook: 0 minutes

Yield: Servings 2

Ingredients:

- ¼ tsp sea salt
- ½ cup quinoa (uncooked)
- 1 carrot
- 1 tbsp. apple cider vinegar
- 1 tbsp. flaxseed oil
- 2 brussels sprouts

Directions:

1. Wash quinoa meticulously.
2. Dice the carrots and brussels sprouts to minuscule pieces.
3. Cook the quinoa based on the instruction on the packaging.
4. Mix flaxseed oil, sea salt, and apple cider vinegar.
5. Sauté brussels sprouts and carrots on a small amount of olive oil for a few minutes.

6. After both brussels sprouts and carrots, and quinoa are ready, combine them all in a container.
7. Put in the dressing and mix meticulously.
8. Serve warm.

Nutritional Info: ‖ Calories: 280 kcal ‖ Protein: 10.15 g ‖ Fat: 12.52 g ‖ Carbohydrates: 31.99 g

---

RED CABBAGE WITH CHEESE

Time To Prepare: five minutes

Time to Cook: twelve minutes

Yield: Servings 4

Ingredients:

- ¼ cup & 1 tbsp. of extra virgin olive oil
- ¼ tsp of freshly ground pepper
- ¼ tsp of salt
- 1 cup of walnuts
- 1 Tbsp. of crumbled blue cheese
- 1 tbsp. of Dijon mustard
- 1 tsp of butter
- 2 thinly cut scallions
- 3 tbsp. of pure maple syrup
- 3 tbsp. of red wine vinegar
- 8 cups of red cabbage, thinly cut

Directions:

For the vinaigrette:

1. Combine the blue cheese, ¼ cup of olive oil, mustard, vinegar, salt, and pepper in a food processor or blender until the mixture has a creamy consistency.

For the salad:

1. Put a parchment paper near the stove.
2. Heat 1 tbsp. Of oil on moderate heat in a moderate-sized frying pan and mix in the walnuts, cooking them for approximately 2 minutes.

3. Now mix salt and pepper, sprinkle maple syrup and cook for approximately three to five minutes while stirring the mixture up to the nuts are uniformly coated.
4. Move to the paper and pour the rest of the syrup over them using a spoon. Separate the nuts and cool down for approximately five minutes.
5. In a big container, put in the cabbage and scallions and toss them with the vinaigrette. Put in the walnuts and blue cheese as toppings.

Nutritional Info: Calories 232 || Fat: 19 gram Saturated || Fat: 4 gram || Sodium: 267 gram || Carbs: 12 gram || Fiber: 2 gram sugar || 8 gram Added sugar 5 gram || Protein: 4 gram

RICE WITH PISTACHIOS

Time To Prepare: ten minutes

Time to Cook: twenty minutes

Yield: Servings 6

Ingredients:

- ¼ cup of raw pistachios (or more for decoration)
- ½ cup of chopped and packed dill leaves
- ½ teaspoon of turmeric
- 1 ½ cups of Basmati rice (rinsed in a colander and soaked in water for approximately 30 minutes, or more)
- 1 teaspoon of vegetable oil
- 1 thinly cut medium onion
- 2 dry baby leaves
- 3 cups of vegetable stock or water
- 5 pods of slightly crushed green cardamom
- Ground black pepper (to taste)
- Salt, to taste

Directions:

1. In a big deep cooking pan, warm the oil and put in the cardamom. Heat it for approximately 1 minute until it turns smildly brown and put in the onion. Sauté for approximately 1-2 minutes.
2. Mix in the dill leaves, turmeric and pistachios. Then put in the rice and stir-fry for approximately one minute.

3. Combine the vegetable stock, black pepper and salt to taste, stir it well and bring it to its boiling point.
4. Cover the pan using lid and cook on moderate to low heat for approximately fifteen minutes.
5. Take it off from the heat then set aside the rice (covered) for approximately ten minutes. Then fluff it using a fork and put in more pistachios as decorate, if you desire.
6. Enjoy!

Nutritional Info: || Calories: 90 kcal || Protein: 3.36 g || Fat: 5.08 g || Carbohydrates: 8.39 g

ROASTED CARROTS

Time To Prepare: ten minutes

Time to Cook: forty minutes

Yield: Servings 4

Ingredients:

- ¼ teaspoon ground pepper
- ½ teaspoon rosemary, chopped
- ½ teaspoon salt
- 1 onion, peeled & cut
- 1 teaspoon thyme, chopped
- 2 tablespoons of extra-virgin olive oil
- 8 carrots, peeled & cut

Directions:

1. Preheat the oven to 425 degrees F.
2. Combine the onions and carrots by tossing in a container with rosemary, thyme, pepper, and salt. Spread on your baking sheet.
3. Roast for forty minutes. The onions and carrots must be browning and soft.

Nutritional Info: Calories 126 || Carbohydrates: 16g || Total Fat: 6g || Protein: 2g || Fiber: 4g || Sugar: 8g || Sodium: 286mg

ROASTED CURRIED CAULIFLOWER

Time To Prepare: five minutes

Time to Cook: thirty minutes

Yield: Servings 4

Ingredients:

- ¾ teaspoon salt
- 1 and ½ tablespoon olive oil
- 1 big head cauliflower, cut into florets
- 1 teaspoon cumin seeds
- 1 teaspoon curry powder
- 1 teaspoon mustard seeds

Directions:

1. Preheat the oven to 375 degrees F
2. Grease a baking sheet with cooking spray
3. Take a container and place all ingredients
4. Toss to coat well
5. Position the vegetable on a baking sheet
6. Roast for thirty minutes
7. Serve and enjoy!

Nutritional Info: || Calories: 67 || Fat: 6g || Carbohydrates: 4g || Protein: 2g

ROASTED PARSNIPS

Time To Prepare: five minutes

Time to Cook: thirty minutes

Yield: Servings 4

Ingredients:

- 1 tablespoon of extra-virgin olive oil
- 1 teaspoon of kosher salt
- 1½ teaspoon of Italian seasoning
- 2 lbs. parsnips
- Chopped parsley for decoration

Directions:

1. Preheat the oven to 400 degrees F.
2. Peel the parsnips. Cut them into one-inch chunks.
3. Now toss with the seasoning, salt, and oil in a container.
4. Spread this on your baking sheet. It must be in a single layer.
5. Roast for half an hour Stir every ten minutes.
6. Move to a plate. Decorate using parsley.

Nutritional Info: Calories 124 || Carbohydrates: 20g || Total Fat: 4g || Protein: 2g || Fiber: 4g || Sugar: 5g || Sodium: 550mg

---

ROASTED PORTOBELLOS WITH ROSEMARY

Time To Prepare: five minutes

Time to Cook: fifteen minutes

Yield: Servings 4

Ingredients:

- ¼ cup extra virgin olive oil
- 1 clove garlic, minced
- 1 sprig rosemary, torn
- 2 tablespoons fresh lemon juice
- 8 portobello mushroom, trimmed
- Salt and pepper, to taste

Directions:

1. Preheat the oven to 450 degrees F
2. Take a container and put in all ingredients
3. Toss to coat
4. Put the mushroom in a baking sheet stem side up
5. Roast in your oven for fifteen minutes
6. Serve and enjoy!

Nutritional Info: || Calories: 63 || Fat: 6g || Carbohydrates: 2g || Protein:1g

SHOEPEG CORN SALAD

Time To Prepare: ten minutes

Time to Cook: 0 minute

Yield: Servings 4

Ingredients:

- ¼ cup Greek yogurt
- ½ cup cherry tomatoes halved
- 1 cup shoepeg corn, drained
- 1 jalapeno pepper, chopped
- 1 tablespoon chives, chopped
- 1 tablespoon lemon juice
- 3 tablespoons fresh cilantro, chopped

Directions:

1. In the salad container, mix up together shoepeg corn, cherry tomatoes, jalapeno pepper, chives, and fresh cilantro.
2. Put in lemon juice and Greek yogurt. Mix yo the salad well.
3. Put in your fridge and store it for maximum 1 day.

Nutritional Info: Calories 49 || Fat: 0.7 || Fiber: 1.2 || Carbs: 9.4 || Protein: 2.7

SPICED SWEET POTATO BREAD

Time To Prepare: fifteen minutes

Time to Cook: 45-55 minutes

Yield: Servings 2

Ingredients:

For dry Ingredients:

- ¼ teaspoon sea salt
- 1 cup coconut flour
- 1 teaspoon ground mace
- 2 tablespoons ground cinnamon

- 2 teaspoons baking powder
- 2 teaspoons baking soda
- 2 teaspoons ground nutmeg

Wet Ingredients:

- 1 cup almond butter
- 2 teaspoons organic almond extract
- 4 big sweet potatoes, peeled, thinly cut
- 4 tablespoons coconut oil
- 8 big eggs
- 8 tablespoons melted grass fed butter, unsalted

Directions:

1. Grease 2 loaf pans of 9 x 5 inches with coconut oil. Coat the bottom of the pan using parchment paper. Set aside.
2. Put a medium deep cooking pan on moderate heat. Put in sweet potatoes. Pour enough water to immerse the sweet potatoes. Cook until the sweet potatoes are soft.
3. Remove the heat and drain the sweet potatoes.
4. Put in the sweet potatoes back into the pan. Mash with a potato masher until the desired smoothness is achieved. Allow it to cool completely.
5. Put all together the dry ingredients into a container and mix thoroughly.
6. Put in eggs into a big container and whisk well. Put in sweet potatoes, butter, almond extract and almond butter and whisk until well blended.
7. Put in the dry ingredients into the container of wet ingredients and whisk until well blended.
8. Split the batter into the prepared loaf pans.
9. Bake in a preheated oven at 350°F for approximately 45 -55 minutes or a toothpick when inserted in the middle of the loaf comes out clean.
10. Remove from oven and cool to room temperature.
11. Slice using a sharp knife into slices of 1-inch thickness.

Nutritional Info: || Calories: 1738 kcal || Protein: 27 g || Fat: 145.92 g || Carbohydrates: 89.58 g

SPICY BARLEY

Time To Prepare: seven minutes

Time to Cook: 42 minutes

Yield: Servings 5

Ingredients:

- ½ teaspoon cayenne pepper
- ½ teaspoon chili pepper
- ½ teaspoon ground black pepper
- 1 cup barley
- 1 teaspoon butter
- 1 teaspoon olive oil
- 1 teaspoon salt
- 3 cups chicken stock

Directions:

1. Put barley and olive oil in the pan.
2. Roast barley on high heat for a minute. Stir it well.
3. Then put in salt, chili pepper, ground black pepper, cayenne pepper, and butter.
4. Put in chicken stock.
5. Close the lid and cook barley for forty minutes over the medium-low heat.

Nutritional Info: Calories 152 || Fat: 2.9 || Fiber: 6.5 || Carbs: 27.8 || Protein: 5.1

SPICY ROASTED BRUSSELS SPROUTS

Time To Prepare: five minutes

Time to Cook: thirty minutes

Yield: Servings 4

Ingredients:

- ½ cup kimchi with juice
- 1 and ¼ pound Brussels sprouts, cut into florets
- 2 tablespoons olive oil
- Salt and pepper, to taste

Directions:

1. Set the oven to 425 F.

2. Toss the Brussels sprouts with pepper, salt, and oil.
3. Bake using your oven for about twenty-five minutes
4. Remove from oven and mix with kimchi
5. Return to the oven
6. Cook for five minutes
7. Serve and enjoy!

Nutritional Info: || Calories: 135 || Fat: 7g || Carbohydrates: 16g || Protein: 5g

SPICY WASABI MAYONNAISE

Time To Prepare: fifteen minutes

Time to Cook: 0 minute

Yield: Servings 4

Ingredients:

- ½ tablespoon wasabi paste
- 1 cup mayonnaise

Directions:

1. Take a container and mix wasabi paste and mayonnaise

Mix thoroughly

2. Allow it to chill, use as required
3. Serve and enjoy

Nutritional Info: || Calories: 388 || Fat: 42g || Carbohydrates: 1g || Protein: 1g

STIR-FRIED ALMOND AND SPINACH

Time To Prepare: ten minutes

Time to Cook: fifteen minutes

Yield: Servings 2

Ingredients:

- 1 tablespoon coconut oil

- 3 tablespoons almonds
- 34 pounds spinach
- Salt to taste

Directions:

1. Put oil to a big pot and place it on high heat
2. Put in spinach and allow it to cook, stirring regularly
3. Once the spinach is cooked and soft, sprinkle with salt and stir
4. Put in almonds and enjoy!

Nutritional Info: || Calories: 150 || Fat: 12g || Carbohydrates: 10g || Protein: 8g

STIR-FRIED FARROS

Time To Prepare: five minutes

Time to Cook: thirty-five minutes

Yield: Servings 2

Ingredients:

- ½ cup farro
- ½ teaspoon ground coriander
- ½ teaspoon paprika
- ½ teaspoon turmeric
- 1 ½ cup water
- 1 carrot, grated
- 1 tablespoon butter
- 1 teaspoon chili flakes
- 1 teaspoon salt
- 1 yellow onion, cut

Directions:

1. Put farro in the pan. Put in water and salt.
2. Close the lid and boil it for half an hour
3. In the meantime, toss the butter in the frying pan.
4. Heat it and put in cut onion and grated carrot.

5. Fry the vegetables for about ten minutes over the moderate heat. Stir them with the help of spatula occasionally.
6. When the farro is cooked, put in it in the roasted vegetables and mix up well.
7. Cook stir-fried farro for five minutes over the moderate to high heat.

Nutritional Info: Calories 129 || Fat: 5.9 || Fiber: 3 || Carbs: 17.1 || Protein: 2.8

TENDER FARRO

Time To Prepare: 8 minutes

Time to Cook: forty minutes

Yield: Servings 4

Ingredients:

- 1 cup farro
- 1 tablespoon almond butter
- 1 tablespoon dried dill
- 1 teaspoon salt
- 3 cups beef broth

Directions:

1. Put farro in the pan.
2. Put in beef broth, dried dill, and salt.
3. Close the lid and put the mixture to boil.
4. Then boil it for a little more than half an hour over the medium-low heat.
5. When the time is done, open the lid and put in almond butter.
6. Mix up the cooked farro well.

Nutritional Info: Calories 95 || Fat: 3.3 || Fiber: 1.3 || Carbs: 10.1 || Protein: 6.4

THYME WITH HONEY-ROASTED CARROTS

Time To Prepare: five minutes

Time to Cook: thirty minutes

Yield: Servings 4

Ingredients:

- ½ teaspoon of sea salt
- ½ teaspoon thyme, dried
- 1 tablespoon of honey
- 1/5 lb. carrots, with the tops
- 2 tablespoons of olive oil

Directions:

1. Preheat the oven to 425 degrees F.
2. Place parchment paper on your baking sheet.
3. Toss your carrots with honey, oil, thyme, and salt. Coat well.
4. Keep in a single layer. Bake in the oven for half an hour
5. Allow to cool before you serve.

Nutritional Info: Calories 85 || Carbohydrates: 6g || Cholesterol: 0mg || Total Fat: 8g || Protein: 1g || Sugar: 6g || Fiber: 1g || Sodium: 244mg

TOMATO BULGUR

Time To Prepare: seven minutes

Time to Cook: twenty minutes

Yield: Servings 2

Ingredients:

- ½ cup bulgur
- ½ white onion, diced
- 1 ½ cup chicken stock
- 1 teaspoon tomato paste
- 2 tablespoons coconut oil

Directions:

1. Toss coconut oil in the pan and melt it.
2. Put in diced onion and roast it until light brown.
3. Then put in bulgur and stir thoroughly.
4. Cook bulgur in coconut oil for about three minutes.

5. Then put in tomato paste and mix up bulgur until homogenous.
6. Put in chicken stock.
7. Close the lid and cook bulgur for fifteen minutes over the moderate heat.
8. The cooked bulgur should soak all liquid.

Nutritional Info: Calories 257 || Fat: 14.5 || Fiber: 7.1 || Carbs: 30.2 || Protein: 5.2

WHEATBERRY SALAD

Time To Prepare: ten minutes

Time to Cook: 50 minutes

Yield: Servings 2

Ingredients:

- ¼ cup fresh parsley, chopped
- ¼ cup of wheat berries
- 1 cup of water
- 1 tablespoon canola oil
- 1 tablespoon chives, chopped
- 1 teaspoon chili flakes
- 1 teaspoon salt
- 2 oz. pomegranate seeds
- 2 tablespoons walnuts, chopped

Directions:

1. Put wheat berries and water in the pan.
2. Put in salt and simmer the ingredients for about fifty minutes over the moderate heat.
3. In the meantime, mix up together walnuts, chives, parsley, pomegranate seeds, and chili flakes.
4. When the wheatberry is cooked, move it in the walnut mixture.
5. Put in canola oil and mix up the salad well.

Nutritional Info: Calories 160 || Fat: 11.8 || Fiber: 1.2 || Carbs: 12 || Protein: 3.4

SAUCES AND DRESSINGS

APPLE AND TOMATO DIPPING SAUCE

Time To Prepare: ten minutes

Time to Cook: 0 minutes

Yield: Servings 2-4

Ingredients:

- ¼ cup of cider vinegar
- ¼ tsp of freshly ground black pepper
- ½ tsp of sea salt
- 1 garlic clove, finely chopped
- 1 large-sized shallot, diced
- 1 tbsp. natural tomato paste
- 1 tbsp. of extra-virgin olive oil
- 1 tbsp. of maple syrup
- 1/8 tsp of ground cloves
- 3 moderate-sized apples, roughly chopped
- 3 moderate-sized tomatoes, roughly chopped

Directions:

1. Put oil into a huge deep cooking pan and heat it up on moderate heat.
2. Put in shallot and cook until light brown for approximately 2 minutes.
3. Stir in the tomato paste, garlic, salt, pepper, and cloves for approximately half a minute. Then put in in the apples, tomatoes, vinegar, and maple syrup.
4. Bring to its boiling point then decrease the heat to allow it to simmer for approximately 30 minutes. Allow to cool for twenty additional minutes before placing the mixture into your blender. Combine the mixture until the desired smoothness is achieved.
5. Keep in a mason jar or an airtight container; place in your fridge for maximum 5 days.
6. Serve it on a burger or with fries.

Nutritional Info: ‖ Calories: 142 kcal ‖ Protein: 3 g ‖ Fat: 3.46 g ‖ Carbohydrates: 26.93 g

BALSAMIC VINAIGRETTE

Time To Prepare: ten minutes

Time to Cook: 0 minutes

Yield: Servings 2-4

Ingredients:

- ¼ tsp of freshly ground black pepper
- ½ cup of extra-virgin olive oil
- ½ cup of rice vinegar
- 1 clove of freshly minced garlic
- 1 tbsp. of honey or maple syrup
- 1 tsp of sea or kosher salt
- 2 tsp of Dijon mustard

Directions:

1. Put all ingredients in a mason jar and cover firmly. Shake thoroughly until all ingredients are blended.
2. Keep in your fridge for minimum 30 minutes before you serve to keep its freshness.
3. Serve with a salad or as your meat marinate.

Nutritional Info: || Calories: 147 kcal || Protein: 1.85 g || Fat: 13.21 g || Carbohydrates: 4.02 g

BEAN POTATO SPREAD

Time To Prepare: twenty-five minutes

Time to Cook: 0 minutes

Yield: Servings 7-8

Ingredients:

- ¼ cup sesame paste
- ½ teaspoon cumin, ground
- 1 cup garbanzo beans, drained and washed
- 1 tablespoon olive oil
- 2 tablespoons lime juice

- 2 tablespoons water
- 4 cups cooked sweet potatoes, peeled and chopped
- 5 garlic cloves, minced
- A pinch of salt

Directions:

1. Throw all the ingredients into a blender and blend to make a smooth mix.
2. Move to a container.
3. Serve with carrot, celery, or veggie sticks.

Nutritional Info: Calories 156 || Fat: 3g || Carbohydrates: 10g || Fiber: 6g || Protein: 8g

CASHEW GINGER DIP

Time To Prepare: five minutes

Time to Cook: 0 minutes

Yield: Servings 1

Ingredients:

- ¼ cup filtered water
- ¼ teaspoon salt
- ½ teaspoon ground ginger
- 1 cup cashews, soaked in water for about twenty minutes and drained
- 1 tablespoon extra-virgin olive oil
- 1 teaspoon lemon juice
- 2 garlic cloves
- 2 teaspoons coconut aminos
- Pinch cayenne pepper

Directions:

1. In a blender or food processor, put together the cashews, garlic, water, olive oil, aminos, lemon juice, ginger, salt, and cayenne pepper.
2. Put in the mix in a container.
3. Cover and place in your fridge until chilled. You can use store it for 4-5 days in your fridge.

Nutritional Info: Calories 124 || Fat: 9g || Carbohydrates: 5g || Fiber: 1g || Protein: 3g

CREAMY AVOCADO DRESSING

Time To Prepare: ten minutes

Time to Cook: 0 minutes

Yield: Servings 2-4

Ingredients:

- ½ cup of extra-virgin olive oil
- 1 clove of garlic, chopped
- 1 tsp of honey or maple syrup
- 2 small or 1 large-sized avocado, pitted and chopped
- 2 tsp of lemon or lime juice
- 3 tbsp. of chopped parsley
- 3 tbsp. of red wine vinegar
- Onion powder
- Some Kosher salt and ground black pepper

Directions:

1. Combine all ingredients into a blender, apart from the oil. As the ingredients are mixed, progressively put in the oil into the mixture. Blend until the desired smoothness is achieved or becomes liquidy.
2. Use as a vegetable or fruit salad dressing. Put in your fridge for maximum 5 days.

Nutritional Info: || Calories: 300 kcal || Protein: 4.09 g || Fat: 27.9 g || Carbohydrates: 11.41 g

CREAMY HOMEMADE GREEK DRESSING

Time To Prepare: ten minutes

Time to Cook: 0 minutes

Yield: Servings 2-4

Ingredients:

- ¼ cup non-dairy milk (e.g., almond, rice milk)

- ½ cup of high-quality mayonnaise, without preservatives
- ½ tsp dried basil
- ½ tsp dried oregano
- ½ tsp parsley
- ½ tsp thyme
- 1/3 cup of extra-virgin olive oil
- 1/4 cup of white wine vinegar
- 2 cloves of garlic, minced
- 2 tbsp. of lemon or lime juice
- 2 tsp of honey
- A few tablespoons of water
- Some Kosher salt and pepper

Directions:

1. Put all together ingredients in a mason jar and shake, cover firmly, and shake thoroughly. Place in your fridge for a few hours before you serve or serve instantly on your favorite vegetable or fruit salad.
2. Shake well before use. Put in your fridge for maximum 5 days.
3. You may put in a few tablespoons of water to tune the consistency as per your preference.

Nutritional Info: ‖ Calories: 474 kcal ‖ Protein: 2.08 g ‖ Fat: 50.1 g ‖ Carbohydrates: 5.31 g

CREAMY RASPBERRY VINAIGRETTE

Time To Prepare: ten minutes

Time to Cook: 0 minutes

Yield: Servings 2-4

Ingredients:

- ½ cup of raspberries
- 1 tbsp. of Dijon mustard
- 1 tbsp. of Greek yogurt
- 1/3 cup of extra-virgin olive oil
- 2 tbsp. of honey or maple syrup

- 2 tbsp. of raspberry vinegar

Directions:

1. Put all together the ingredients apart from the oil into a blender, in accordance with the ordered list. Cover and blend for ten seconds, by slowly increasing the speed.
2. After 10 seconds, reduce the speed and progressively put in the oil into the mixture. Keep the speed at a stable pace until all of the oil has been poured in. Blend until blended.
3. Store in a mason jar then place in your fridge for maximum 5 days. Serve with a vegetable or fruit salad.

Nutritional Info: || Calories: 151 kcal || Protein: 2.22 g || Fat: 9.47 g || Carbohydrates: 14.65 g

CREAMY SIAMESE DRESSING

Time To Prepare: ten minutes

Time to Cook: 0 minutes

Yield: Servings 2-4

Ingredients:

- ¼ cup of non-dairy milk (e.g., almond, rice, soymilk)
- ¼ cup of unsweetened peanut sauce
- 1 cup of mayonnaise
- 1 tbsp. of honey or maple syrup
- 1 tbsps. freshly chopped cilantro
- 2 tbsp. of unsalted peanuts
- 2 tbsp. rice vinegar

Directions:

1. Put all ingredients apart from the cilantro and peanuts into a blender and blend until the desired smoothness is achieved and creamy. Next, put in in the cilantro and peanuts and pulse the blender a few times until completely crushed and well blended. Put in a mason jar and bring it in your fridge.
2. Serve with a garden salad, pasta or as a dipping sauce.

Nutritional Info: || Calories: 525 kcal || Protein: 18.14 g || Fat: 45.55 g || Carbohydrates: 11.01 g

CUCUMBER AND DILL SAUCE

Time To Prepare: ten minutes

Time to Cook: 0 minutes

Yield: Servings 2-4

Ingredients:

- ¼ cup of lemon juice
- 1 cucumber, peeled and squeezed to remove surplus liquid
- 1 cup of freshly chopped dill
- 1 tsp of sea salt
- 450g of Greek yogurt

Directions:

1. In a moderate-sized container, put together the yogurt, cucumber, and dill then stir until well blended. Put in in the lemon juice and salt to taste.
2. Cover and place in your fridge for approximately 1-2 hours before you serve to keep its freshness. Best serve with Mediterranean food, chips, fish, or even bread.

Nutritional Info: || Calories: 97 kcal || Protein: 13.49 g || Fat: 2.1 g || Carbohydrates: 6.34 g

DAIRY-FREE CREAMY TURMERIC DRESSING

Time To Prepare: ten minutes

Time to Cook: 0 minutes

Yield: Servings 2-4

Ingredients:

- ½ cup of extra-virgin olive oil
- ½ cup of tahini
- 1 tbsp. of turmeric powder
- 2 tbsp. of lemon juice
- 2 tsp of honey
- Some sea salt and pepper

Directions:

1. In a container, whisk all ingredients until well blended.
2. Store in a mason jar and place in your fridge for maximum 5 days.

Nutritional Info: || Calories: 328 kcal || Protein: 7.3 g || Fat: 29.36 g || Carbohydrates: 12.43 g

HERBY RAITA

Time To Prepare: ten minutes

Time to Cook: 0 minutes

Yield: Servings 2-4

Ingredients:

- ¼ cup of freshly chopped mint
- ¼ tsp of freshly ground black pepper
- ½ tsp of sea salt
- 1 cup of Greek yogurt
- 1 large-sized cucumber, shredded
- 1 tsp of lemon juice

Directions:

1. Combine the cucumber with ¼ tsp of salt in a sieve and leave to drain for fifteen minutes. Shake to release any surplus liquid and move to a kitchen towel. Squeeze out as much liquid as you can using the paper towel.
2. Put the cucumber into a medium container then mix in the rest of the ingredients until well blended.
3. Put in your fridge for minimum 2 hours to keep its freshness. Best consume with spicy foods as it could relief the spiciness.

Nutritional Info: || Calories: 69 kcal || Protein: 4.33 g || Fat: 3.66 g || Carbohydrates: 4.93 g

HOMEMADE GINGER DRESSING

Time To Prepare: ten minutes

Time to Cook: 0 minutes

Yield: Servings 2-4

Ingredients:

- ¼ cup of chopped celery
- ¼ cup of honey or maple syrup
- ¼ cup of water
- ½ cup of chopped carrots
- ½ tsp of white pepper
- 1 cup of chopped onion
- 1 cup of extra-virgin olive oil
- 1 tsp of freshly minced garlic
- 1 tsp of kosher salt
- 2 ½ tbsp. of unsalted, gluten-free soy sauce
- 2 tbsp. of ketchup
- 2/3 cup of rice vinegar
- 6 tbsp. of freshly grated ginger

Directions:

1. Put the onion, ginger, celery, carrots, and garlic into a blender. Blend until the mixture are fine but still lumpy from the small vegetable chunks.
2. Put in in the vinegar, water, ketchup, soy sauce, honey or maple syrup, lemon juice, salt, and pepper. Pulse until the ingredients are well blended.
3. Slowly put in the oil while blending, until everything is thoroughly combined. The mixture must be runny but still grainy.
4. Serve with a winter salad.

Nutritional Info: ‖ Calories: 389 kcal ‖ Protein: 2.71 g ‖ Fat: 32.08 g ‖ Carbohydrates: 22.14 g

---

HOMEMADE LEMON VINAIGRETTE

Time To Prepare: ten minutes

Time to Cook: 0 minutes

Yield: Servings 2-4

Ingredients:

- ¼ tsp of sea salt
- ½ tsp of Dijon mustard, without preservatives

- ½ tsp of lemon zest
- 1 tsp of honey or maple syrup
- 2 tbsp. of freshly squeezed lemon juice
- 3 tbsp. of extra-virgin olive oil
- Freshly ground black pepper

Directions:

1. Whisk all together the ingredients apart from olive oil and black pepper in a small container. Then progressively put in 3 tbsp. of olive oil while continuously whisking until well blended. Put in some ground black pepper to taste.
2. Put mason jar and place in your fridge for maximum 3 days.
3. Serve with a garden salads.

Nutritional Info: || Calories: 68 kcal || Protein: 1.69 g || Fat: 6.06 g || Carbohydrates: 1.71 g

---

HOMEMADE RANCH

Time To Prepare: ten minutes

Time to Cook: 0 minutes

Yield: Servings 2-4

Ingredients:

- ¼ cup of Greek yogurt
- ¼ tsp Kosher salt
- ½ cup of natural mayonnaise, without preservatives
- ½ tsp of dried dill
- ½ tsp of dried parsley
- ½ tsp of garlic powder
- ½ tsp of onion powder
- ¾ cup of non-dairy milk
- 1/8 tsp Freshly ground black pepper
- 2 tsp of dried chives

Directions:

1. Combine all ingredients apart from the milk into a medium container. Mix together until well blended.

2. Put in in the milk and mix thoroughly.
3. Pour in a mason jar or an airtight container. Serve instantly or place in your fridge for maximum 2 hours to keep the freshness. Put in your refrigerator for maximum 5 days.
4. Serve with a garden or fruit salad.

Nutritional Info: || Calories: 482 kcal || Protein: 3.55 g || Fat: 51.98 g || Carbohydrates: 1.63 g

HONEY BEAN DIP

Time To Prepare: five minutes

Time to Cook: 0 minutes

Yield: Servings 3-4

Ingredients:

- ¼ teaspoon ground cumin
- ¼ teaspoon salt
- 1 (14-ounce) can each of kidney beans and black beans
- 1 tablespoon apple cider vinegar
- 1 teaspoon lime juice
- 2 cherry tomatoes
- 2 garlic cloves
- 2 tablespoons filtered water
- 2 teaspoons raw honey
- Freshly ground black pepper to taste
- Pinch cayenne pepper to taste

Directions:

1. In a blender or food processor, put together the beans, garlic, tomatoes, water, vinegar, honey, lime juice, cumin, salt, cayenne pepper, and black pepper.
2. Blend until it becomes smooth. Put in the mix in a container.
3. Cover and place in your fridge to chill. You can place in your fridge for maximum 5 days.

Nutritional Info: Calories 158 || Fat: 1g || Carbohydrates: 33g || Fiber: 8g || Protein: 9g

SOY WITH HONEY AND GINGER GLAZE

Time To Prepare: ten minutes

Time to Cook: 0 minutes

Yield: Servings 2-4

Ingredients:

- ¼ cup of honey
- 1 tbsp. of rice vinegar
- 1 tsp of freshly grated ginger
- 2 tbsp. gluten-free soy sauce

Directions:

1. Put all together the ingredients into a small container and whisk well.
2. Serve with a vegetables, chickens, or seafood.
3. Keep the glaze in a mason jar, firmly covered, and place in your fridge for maximum four days.

Nutritional Info: || Calories: 90 kcal || Protein: 2.32 g || Fat: 1.54 g || Carbohydrates: 17.99 g

STRAWBERRY POPPY SEED DRESSING

Time To Prepare: ten minutes

Time to Cook: 0 minutes

Yield: Servings 2-4

Ingredients:

- ¼ cup of raspberry vinegar
- ¼ tsp of ground ginger
- ¼ tsp of sea salt
- ½ tsp of onion powder
- ½ tsp of poppy seeds
- 1/3 cup of extra-virgin olive oil
- 1/3 cup of honey
- 2 tbsp. of freshly squeezed orange juice

Directions:

1. Put all ingredients, apart from the poppy seeds and oil into a blender. Blend until the desired smoothness is achieved and creamy. Next, progressively put the oil into the mixture until blended. Put in in the poppy seeds and stir thoroughly.
2. Put in a mason jar then place in your fridge before you serve. Keep for maximum 3 days.
3. Serve with your garden salads.

Nutritional Info: || Calories: 167 kcal || Protein: 1.84 g || Fat: 9.35 g || Carbohydrates: 18.89 g

TAHINI DIP

Time To Prepare: ten minutes

Time to Cook: 0 minutes

Yield: Servings 2-4

Ingredients:

- ¼ cup of tahini
- ½ tsp of maple syrup
- 1 small grated or thoroughly minced clove of garlic (this is optional)
- 1 tbsp. of apple cider vinegar
- 1 tbsp. of freshly squeezed lemon juice
- 1 tbsp. of tamari
- 1 tsp of finely grated ginger, or ½ tsp of ground ginger
- 1 tsp of turmeric
- 1/3 cup of water

Directions:

1. Blend or whisk all ingredients together. Place the dressing in an airtight container then place in your fridge for approximately 5 days.
2. Enjoy!

Nutritional Info: || Calories: 120 kcal || Protein: 4.77 g || Fat: 9.63 g || Carbohydrates: 5.12 g

TOMATO AND MUSHROOM SAUCE

Time To Prepare: ten minutes

Time to Cook: 0 minutes

Yield: Servings 2-4

Ingredients:

- ½ cup of water
- 1 moderate-sized leek, chopped
- 2 moderate-sized carrots, chopped
- 2 stalks of celery, chopped
- 2 tsp of dried oregano
- 4 cloves of garlic, crushed
- 450g of button mushrooms, diced
- 5 tbsp. of coconut milk
- 680g of unsalted tomato puree
- Black pepper, seasoning
- Some sea salt, seasoning

Directions:

1. In a big frying pan, place a few tablespoons of water and heat on moderate heat. Once it sizzles, put in in the mushrooms and Sautee for approximately five minutes, stir once in a while.
2. Next, put in in the leek, carrots, and celery. Stir thoroughly and cook for approximately five minutes or until the vegetables are soft. Put in more water if required.
3. Mix in the tomato puree with ½ cup of water and dried oregano. Bring to its boiling point and then decrease the heat to allow it to simmer for approximately fifteen minutes.
4. Remove from heat and mix in the garlic, coconut milk, and salt and pepper to taste.
5. Put in an airtight container, then store for maximum four days in your fridge or freeze for maximum 1 month. Serve with a pasta.

Nutritional Info: || Calories: 467 kcal || Protein: 16.91 g || Fat: 3.81 g || Carbohydrates: 109.68 g

Seafood

AHI TUNA POKE

Time To Prepare: ten minutes

Time to Cook: 0 minutes

Yield: Servings 2

Ingredients:

- ½ lbs. Ahi tuna
- 1 Avocado
- 1 tbsp. Chili garlic sauce
- 1 tbsp. Sesame oil
- 1 tbsp. Sesame seeds
- 2 scallions
- 2 tbsp. Soy sauce

Directions:

1. Wash the ahi tuna and cut it into bite-sized cubes.
2. Wash the green onions and cut it finely.
3. Mix soy, sesame oil, chili garlic sauce, green onion, and half the sesame seeds in a container.
4. Place the ahi to the dressing and mix thoroughly. Let it sit in your refrigerator for 10-twenty minutes for the flavors to combine.
5. Cut the avocado into little cubes and gently mix it into the remaining dish right before you serve.
6. Drizzle the rest of the sesame seeds on top.
7. Serve with chips or bread and enjoy!

Nutritional Info: Calories: 350 || Fat: 20g || Carbohydrates: 9.5g || Protein: 30g

AMBERJACK FILLETS WITH CHEESE SAUCE

Time To Prepare: ten minutes

Time to Cook: ten minutes

Yield: Servings 4

Ingredients:

- 6 amberjack fillets
- 2 tablespoons olive oil, at room temperature
- Sea salt, to taste
- Ground black pepper, to taste
- For the Sauce:
- 3 teaspoons butter, at room temperature
- 2 garlic cloves, thoroughly minced
- 1/3 cup vegetable broth
- 1/3 cup Romano cheese, grated
- 1/4 cup fresh tarragon chopped
- 3/4 cup twofold cream

Directions:

1. In a non-stick frying pan, warm the olive oil until sizzling.
2. Once hot, fry the amberjack for approximately 6 minutes per side or until the edges are turning opaque. Drizzle them with salt, black pepper, and tarragon. Reserve.
3. To make the sauce, melt the butter in a deep cooking pan over moderately high heat. Sauté the garlic until soft and aromatic or about two minutes.
4. Put in in the vegetable broth and cream and carry on cooking for five to six minutes more; heat off.
5. Mix in the Romano cheese and continue mixing in the residual heat for about 2 minutes more.

Nutritional Info: 285 Calories 20.4g || Fat: 1.2g || Carbs: 23.8g || Protein: 0.1g Fiber

---

AVOCADO & SALMON OMELET WRAP

Time To Prepare: ten minutes

Time to Cook: 20 minutes

Yield: Servings 2

Ingredients:

- .5 of 1 average size Avocado

- 1 Spring onion
- 1 tbsp. Butter or ghee
- 2 tbsp. Chives - freshly chopped
- 2 tbsp. Cream cheese - full-fat
- 3 Large eggs
- oz. Smoked salmon
- Pepper and salt (as you wish)

Directions:

1. Put in a drizzle of pepper and salt to the eggs. Use a fork or whisk—mixing them well. Mix in the chives and cream cheese.
2. Prepare the salmon and avocado (peel and slice or chop).
3. Mix the butter/ghee and the egg mixture in a frying pan. Carry on cooking on low heat until done.
4. Put the omelet on a serving dish with a portion of cheese over it. Drizzle the onion, prepared avocado, and salmon into the wrap.
5. Close and serve!

Nutritional Info: Calories: 765 || Net Carbohydrates: 6 g || Total Fat: Content: 67 g || Protein: 37 g

BACON AND JALAPENO WRAPPED SHRIMP

Time To Prepare: ten minutes

Time to Cook: 20 minutes

Yield: Servings 2

Ingredients:

- ¼ cup shredded pepper jack cheese
- 12 big shrimp, deveined, butterflied, tail-on
- 4 jalapeño peppers, seedless and slice into three to 4 lengthy strips each
- 6 thin bacon slices
- Freshly ground black pepper
- Salt

Directions:

1. Preheat your oven to 350°F.
2. On a baking sheet, position the jalapeño strips in a single layer and roast for about ten minutes.
3. In a small container, flavor the shrimp with salt and pepper.
4. Take away the jalapeño strips from the oven. Put a strip inside each open butterflied shrimp. Cover each shrimp with bacon and insert it using a toothpick. Organize in a single layer on a baking sheet.
5. Cook for eight minutes until the bacon is crunchy.
6. Adjust the oven to broil.
7. Drizzle the cheese on top of the shrimp and broil for approximately 1 minute, until the cheese is bubbling.

Nutritional Info: Calories: 240 ‖ Total Fat: 16 g ‖ Protein: 21 g ‖ Total Carbohydrates: 3g ‖ Fiber: 1g ‖ Net Carbohydrates: 2g

---

BAKED TILAPIA WITH CHERRY TOMATOES

Time To Prepare: ten minutes

Time to Cook: 25-30 minutes

Yield: Servings 2

Ingredients:

- 2 tsp. Butter
- 8 Cherry tomatoes
- .25 cup Pitted black olives
- .5 tsp. Salt
- .25 tsp. Paprika
- .25 tsp. Black pepper
- 1 tsp. Garlic powder
- 1 tbsp. Freshly squeezed lemon juice
- 1 tbsp. Optional: Balsamic vinegar
- 1-4 oz. Tilapia fillets

Directions:

1. Warm the oven to reach 375º Fahrenheit.
2. Grease a roasting pan and put in the butter together with the olives and tomatoes.

3. Flavour the tilapia with the spices. Finally, put in the fish fillets into the pan with a spritz of the lemon juice.
4. Put in a piece of foil over the pan. Bake until the fish easily flakes (25 to 30 min.).
5. Decorate using the vinegar if you wish.

Nutritional Info: Calories: 180 || Net Carbohydrates: 4 g || Total Fat: Content: 8 g || Protein: 23 g

---

BAKED TOMATO HAKE

Time To Prepare: ten minutes

Time to Cook: 20-twenty-five minutes

Yield: Servings 4

Ingredients:

- ½ c. grated cheese
- ½ c. tomato sauce
- 1 tbsp. olive oil
- 2 cut tomatoes
- 4 lbs. de-boned and cut hake fish
- Parsley
- Salt.

Directions:

1. Preheat your oven to 400 0F.
2. Flavour the fish with salt.
3. In a frying pan or deep cooking pan, stir-fry the fish in the olive oil until half-done.
4. Take four foil papers to cover the fish.
5. Shape the foil to resemble containers; put in the tomato sauce into each foil container.
6. Put in the fish, tomato slices, and top with grated cheese.
7. Bake until you get a golden crust, for roughly 20-twenty-five minutes.
8. Open the packs and top with parsley.

Nutritional Info: Calories: 265 || Fat: 15 g || Carbohydrates: 18 g|| Protein: 22 g Sugars: 0.5 g || Sodium: 94.6 mg

BALSAMIC SCALLOPS

Time To Prepare: five minutes

Time to Cook: ten minutes

Yield: Servings 4

Ingredients:

- 1 pound sea scallops
- 1 tablespoon balsamic vinegar
- 1 tablespoon cilantro, chopped
- 2 tablespoons olive oil
- 4 scallions, chopped
- A pinch of salt and black pepper

Directions:

1. Warm a pan with the oil on moderate to high heat, put in the scallops, the scallions, and the other ingredients, toss, cook for about ten minutes, split into bowls before you serve.

Nutritional Info: Calories 300 || Fat: 4 || Fiber: 4 || Carbs: 14 || Protein: 17

BASIL HALIBUT RED PEPPER PACKETS

Time To Prepare: ten minutes

Time to Cook: 20 minutes

Yield: Servings 4

Ingredients:

- ¼ cup chopped fresh basil
- ¼ cup good-quality olive oil
- ½ cup cut sun-dried tomatoes
- 1 cup roasted red pepper strips
- 2 cups cauliflower florets
- 4 (4-ounce) halibut fillets
- Freshly ground black pepper, for seasoning

- Juice of 1 lemon
- Sea salt, for seasoning

Directions:

1. Preheat your oven. Set the oven temperature to 400°F. Cut into four (12-inch) square pieces of aluminium foil. Have a baking sheet ready.
    Make the packets.
2. Split the cauliflower, red pepper strips, and sun-dried tomato between the four pieces of foil, placing the vegetables in the center of each piece. Top each pile with 1 halibut fillet, and top each fillet with equal amounts of the basil, lemon juice, and olive oil. Fold and crimp the foil to make sealed packets of fish and vegetables and put them on the baking sheet.
3. Bake the packets for approximately twenty minutes, until the fish flakes using a fork. Be careful of the steam when you open the packet!
    Serve. Move the vegetables and halibut to four plates, sprinkle with salt and pepper, and serve instantly.

Nutritional Info: Calories: 294 Total fat: 18g Total carbs: 8g || Fiber: 3g Net carbs: 5g || Sodium: 114mg || Protein: 25g

BAVETTE WITH SEAFOOD

Time To Prepare: ten minutes

Time to Cook: ten minutes

Yield: Servings 4

Ingredients:

- ½ Lemon Juice
- 1 clove minced garlic
- 2 tablespoons coarse salt
- 200g clean medium shrimp
- 200g mussel without shell
- 200g of clean octopus
- 200g of clean squid cut into rings
- 350g of Bavette Barilla
- 400g peeled tomatoes

- Black pepper to taste
- Braised olive oil
- Chopped cilantro to taste
- Salt to taste

Directions:

1. In olive oil sauté the shrimp, the octopus, the mussel and the squid separately. Sprinkle with salt and black pepper.
2. In the same pan, sauté the garlic.
3. Put in the peeled tomatoes, mix thoroughly — Cook for a couple of minutes.
4. In a pan of boiling water, position 2 tablespoons of coarse salt and cook Bavette Barilla.
5. Remove Bavette Barilla two minutes before the time indicated on the package. Reserve the pasta cooking water if required.
6. Return the seafood to the sauce.
7. Position 1 scoop of the cooking water in the seafood sauce and put in the drained pasta. Cook for another two minutes.
8. Finish with cilantro and lemon juice.
9. Serve instantly.

Nutritional Info: Calories: 526 kcal || Protein: 40.59 g || Fat: 24 g || Carbohydrates: 38.02 g

BLACKENED FISH TACOS WITH SLAW:

Time To Prepare: 14 minutes

Time to Cook: six minutes

Yield: Servings 4

Ingredients:

- ½ cup red cabbage, shredded
- 1 tablespoon lemon juice
- 1 tablespoon olive oil
- 1 tablespoon olive oil
- 1 teaspoon apple cider vinegar
- 1 teaspoon chili powder
- 1 teaspoon paprika
- 2 tilapia fillets

- 4 low carb tortillas
- Salt and black pepper to taste
- Slaw:

Directions:

1. Flavour the tilapia with chili powder and paprika. Heat the vegetable oil during a frying pan on moderate heat.
2. Put in tilapia and cook until blackened, approximately 3 minutes per side. Cut into strips. Split the tilapia between the tortillas. Blend all the slaw ingredients in a container and top the fish to serve.

Nutritional Info: Calories: 268 || Fat: 20g || Net Carbohydrates: 3.5g || Protein: 13.8g

CHEESE TILAPIA

Time To Prepare: ten minutes

Time to Cook: ten minutes

Yield: Servings 4

Ingredients:

- ¾ cup parmesan cheese, grated
- 1 lb. tilapia fillets
- 1 tbsp. olive oil
- 1 tbsp. parsley, chopped
- 2 tsp. paprika
- Pepper and salt to taste

Directions:

1. Preheat the Air Fryer to 400°F.
2. In a shallow dish, mix the paprika, grated cheese, pepper, salt, and parsley.
3. Puta light sprinkle of olive oil at the tilapia fillets. Cover the fillets with the paprika and cheese mixture.
4. Place the fillets on a sheet of aluminium foil and move to the Air Fryer basket. Fry for about ten minutes. Serve hot.

Nutritional Info: Calories: 246 kcal || Protein: 30.12 g || Fat: 12.22 g || Carbohydrates: 4.35 g

CHEESY TUNA PASTA

Time To Prepare: ten minutes

Time to Cook: 20 minutes

Yield: Servings 2-4

Ingredients:

- ¼ c. chopped green onions
- ¼ tsp. black pepper
- 1 tbs. red vinegar
- 1 tbsp. grated low-fat parmesan
- 1 tbsp. olive oil
- 2 c. arugula
- 2 oz. cooked whole-wheat pasta
- 5 oz. drained canned tuna

Directions:

1. Cook the pasta in unsalted water until ready. Drain and save for later.
2. In a large-sized container, meticulously mix the tuna, green onions, vinegar, oil, arugula, pasta, and black pepper.
3. Toss thoroughly and top with the cheese.
4. Serve and enjoy.

Nutritional Info: Calories: 566.3 ‖ Fat: 42.4 g ‖ Carbohydrates: 18.6 g ‖ Protein: 29.8 g Sugars: 0.4 g ‖ Sodium: 688.6 mg

CHILI HAKE FILLETS

Time To Prepare: twenty-five minutes

Time to Cook: 20 minutes

Yield: Servings 4

Ingredients:

- ¼ cup apple cider vinegar
- ¼ cup soy sauce
- ½ cup olive oil

- 1 red onion, finely chopped
- 1 tsp sea salt
- 2 lbs. hake fillets, skinless
- 2 tbsp. fresh dill, finely chopped
- 2 tsp chili powder
- 2 tsp fresh rosemary
- 3 cups fish stock
- 3 garlic cloves, minced

Directions:

1. Wash fillets using cool running water and place them in a deep container. Sprinkle with olive oil and apple cider vinegar. Drizzle with rosemary, salt, dill, and chili powder. Cover with the lid and save for later.
2. Set the instant pot and grease the inner pot with some oil. Push the "Sauté" button then put onions and garlic. Stir-fry for about four minutes and flavor with some salt and optionally some pepper.
3. Take off the fillets from the container and place it in the pot. Sprinkle about 2 tbsp. of the marinade and pour in the stock. Secure the lid and set the steam release handle.
4. Push the "Manual" button then set the timer for about twelve minutes on HIGH pressure.
5. When done, perform a quick release and cautiously open the lid. Push the "Sauté" button and pour it in the soy sauce.
6. Lightly stir again and cook for minimum 3-4 minutes.
7. Turn off the pot and serve instantly.

Nutritional Info: Calories 46 || Total Fats 30.6g || Net Carbohydrates: 2.6g || Protein: 43.9g || Fiber: 0.5g

---

CHILI SHRIMP AND PINEAPPLE

Time To Prepare: ten minutes

Time to Cook: ten minutes

Yield: Servings 4

Ingredients:

- ½ teaspoon ginger, grated

- 1 cup pineapple, peeled and cubed
- 1 pound shrimp, peeled and deveined
- 1 tablespoon olive oil
- 2 tablespoons chili paste
- 2 tablespoons cilantro, chopped
- 2 teaspoons almonds, chopped
- Pinch of black pepper
- Pinch of sea salt

Directions:

1. Warm a pan with the oil on moderate to high heat, put in the ginger and the chili paste, stir and cook for a couple of minutes.
2. Put in the shrimp and the other ingredients, toss, cook the mix for eight minutes more, split into bowls, before you serve.

Nutritional Info: calories 261 || Fat: 4 || Fiber: 7 || Carbs: 15 || Protein: 8

CHILI SNAPPER

Time To Prepare: ten minutes

Time to Cook: twenty minutes

Yield: Servings 2

Ingredients:

- ½ teaspoon fresh grated ginger
- 1 garlic clove, minced
- 1 green onion, chopped
- 1 tablespoon coconut aminos
- 2 red snapper fillets, boneless and skinless
- 2 tablespoons chicken stock
- 2 tablespoons olive oil
- 2 teaspoons sesame seeds, toasted
- 3 tablespoons chili paste
- A pinch of sea salt
- Black pepper

Directions:

1. Warm a pan with the oil on moderate to high heat, put in the ginger, onion, and the garlic, stir and cook for a couple of minutes. Put in chili paste, aminos, salt, pepper, and the stock stir and cook for about three minutes more. Put in the fish fillets, toss lightly and cook for about five minutes on each side.
2. Split into plates, drizzle sesame seeds on top, before you serve.
3. Enjoy!

Nutritional Info: Calories 261 || Fat: 10 g || Fiber: 7 g || Carbohydrates: 15 g || Protein: 16 g

CHUNKY FISH

Time To Prepare: ten minutes

Time to Cook: 8 minutes

Yield: Servings 4

Ingredients:

- ¼ tsp. freshly cracked black peppercorns
- ½ tsp. sea salt
- 1 cup keto-friendly bread crumbs
- 1 egg, whisked
- 1 tsp. paprika
- 1 tsp. whole-grain mustard
- 2 cans canned fish
- 2 celery stalks, trimmed and finely chopped

Directions:

1. Mix all of the ingredients in which they appear. Mold the mixture into four equal-sized cakes. Leave to chill in your fridge for about fifty minutes.
2. Put on an Air Fryer grill pan. Spritz all sides of each cake with cooking spray.
3. Grill at 360°F for five minutes. Turn the cakes over and resume cooking for another three minutes.
4. Serve with mashed potatoes if you wish.

Nutritional Info: Calories: 245 kcal || Protein: 40.31 g || Fat: 5.67 g || Carbohydrates: 5.64 g

CITRUS & HERB SARDINES

Time To Prepare: five minutes

Time to Cook: 15 minutes

Yield: Servings 2

Ingredients:

- ½ can Chickpeas or Butterbeans, drained and washed
- ½ cup Black Olives (pitted and halves)
- 1 can Tomato, chopped, (not necessary)
- 10 Sardines, scaled and clean
- 2 Garlic cloves, finely chopped
- 2 Whole Lemon zest
- 3 tbsp. Olive oil
- 8 Cherry Tomatoes, halved (not necessary)
- Handful-Flat leafy parsley, chopped
- Pinch of Black Pepper

Directions:

1. In a container, put in the lemon zest to the chopped parsley (save a pinch for decorationing) and half of the chopped garlic, ready for later.
2. Place a very big frying pan on the hob and heat on high.
3. Now put in the oil and once super hot, lay the sardines flat on the pan.
4. Sauté for about three minutes until golden underneath and turn over to fry for another three minutes. Put onto a plate to rest.
5. Sauté the rest of the garlic (add another splash of oil if you need to) for 1 min until tender. Pour in the tin of chopped tomatoes, mix and allow to simmer for 4-5 minutes.
6. If you're avoiding tomatoes, just avoid this step and go straight to chickpeas.
7. Tip in the chickpeas or butter beans and fresh tomatoes and stir until thoroughly heated.
8. Here's when you put in the sardines into the lemon and parsley dressing readied a while back and put in to the pan, cooking for another 3-4 minutes.
9. Once thoroughly heated, serve with a pinch of parsley and remaining lemon zest to decorate.

Nutritional Info: Calories: 493 kcal || Protein: 24.16 g || Fat: 35.67 g || Carbohydrates: 20.92 g

CITRUS SALMON ON A BED OF GREENS

Time To Prepare: ten minutes

Time to Cook: 20 minutes

Yield: Servings 4

Ingredients:

- ¼ cup Extra Virgin Olive Oil, divided
- ½ tsp. Freshly ground black pepper, divided
- 1 Lemon Zest
- 1 tsp. Sea Salt, divided
- 1½ pound Salmon
- 2 Lemon Juice
- 3 Garlic cloves, chopped
- 6 cups Swiss Chard, stemmed and chopped

Directions:

1. In a huge nonstick frying pan at moderate to high heat, heat 2 tablespoons of the olive oil until it shimmers.
2. Flavour the salmon with ½ teaspoon of the salt, ¼ teaspoon of the pepper, and the lemon zest. Place the salmon to the frying pan, skin-side up, and cook for approximately seven minutes until the flesh appears opaque. Flip the salmon and cook for minimum three to four minutes to crisp the skin. Set aside on a plate, cover using aluminium foil.
3. Put back the frying pan to the heat, put in the remaining 2 tablespoons of olive oil, and heat it until it shimmers.
4. Put in the Swiss chard. Cook for approximately seven minutes, once in a while stirring, until tender.
5. Put in the garlic. Cook for half a minute, stirring continuously.
6. Drizzle in the lemon juice, the rest of the ½ teaspoon of salt, and the rest of the ¼ teaspoon of pepper. Cook for a couple of minutes.
7. Serve the salmon on the Swiss chard.

Nutritional Info: Calories: 363 || Total Fat: 25 || Total Carbohydrates: 3g || Sugar: 1g || Fiber: 1g || Protein: 34g || Sodium: 662mg

CLAMS WITH GARLIC-TOMATO SAUCE

Time To Prepare: five minutes

Time to Cook: 20 minutes

Yield: Servings 4

Ingredients:

- ½ lemon, cut into wedges
- ½ teaspoon paprika
- 1 shallot, chopped
- 1/3 cup port wine
- 2 garlic cloves, pressed
- 2 tablespoons olive oil
- 2 tomatoes, pureed
- 40 littleneck clams
- For the Sauce:
- Freshly ground black pepper, to taste
- Sea salt, to taste

Directions:

1. Grill the clams until they are open, for five to six minutes.
2. In a frying pan, heat the olive oil over moderate heat. Cook the shallot and garlic until soft and aromatic.
3. Mix in the pureed tomatoes, salt, black pepper and paprika and carry on cooking an additional ten to twelve minutes, up to well cooked.
4. Heat off and put in in the port wine; stir until blended. Decorate using fresh lemon wedges.

Nutritional Info: 134 Calories 7.8g ‖ Fat: 5.9g ‖ Carbs: 8.3g ‖ Protein: 1g Fiber

---

CLAMS WITH OLIVES MIX

Time To Prepare: ten minutes

Time to Cook: ten minutes

Yield: Servings 2

Ingredients:

- ½ cup veggie stock
- ½ teaspoon dried thyme
- 1 apple, cored and chopped
- 1 shallot, minced
- 2 garlic cloves, minced
- 2 pound little clams, scrubbed
- 3 tablespoons olive oil
- Juice of ½ lemon

Directions:

1. Warm a pan with the oil on moderate to high heat, put in shallot and garlic, stir and cook for about four minutes. Put in the stock, clams, thyme, apple, and lemon juice. Stir and cook for about six minutes more, split into bowls before you serve.
2. Enjoy!

Nutritional Info: Calories 180 || Fat: 9 || Fiber: 2 || Carbs: 8 || Protein: 10

COCONUT MAHI-MAHI NUGGETS

Time To Prepare: ten minutes

Time to Cook: ten minutes

Yield: Servings 2

Ingredients:

- ¼ cup crushed macadamia nuts
- ¼ cup Dairy-Free Tartar Sauce
- ½ cup shredded coconut
- ½ lime, cut into wedges
- 1 cup almond flour
- 1 cup avocado oil or coconut oil, plus more as required
- 1 pound frozen mahi-mahi, thawed
- 2 big eggs
- 2 tablespoons avocado oil mayonnaise
- Freshly ground black pepper

- Salt

Directions:

1. In a frying pan, warm the avocado oil at high heat. You want the oil to be about ½ inch deep, so adjust the amount of oil-based on the size of your pan.
2. Pat the fish to try using paper towels to take off any surplus water.
3. In a small container, put and mix the eggs and mayonnaise.
4. In a moderate-sized mixing container, put and mix the almond flour, coconut, and macadamia nuts. Sprinkle with salt and pepper. Chop the mahi-mahi into nuggets.
5. Place the fish into the egg mixture then dredge in the dry mix. Push into the dry mixture so that "breading" sticks well on all sides.
6. Put in the fish into the hot oil. It should sizzle when you put in the nuggets. Cook for a couple of minutes per side, until golden and crunchy.
7. Put the cooked nuggets on a paper towel-lined plate and squirt the lime wedges over them.

Nutritional Info: Calories: 733|| Total Fat: 53g || Protein: 54g || Total Carbohydrates: 10g || Fiber: 6g || Net Carbohydrates: 4g

COCONUT RICE WITH SHRIMPS IN COCONUT CURRY

Time To Prepare: ten minutes

Time to Cook: forty minutes

Yield: Servings 2-3

Ingredients:

- ⅛ cup Cilantro (chopped)
- ¼ cup Scallions (chopped)
- ½ Lime juice
- 1 ½ cup Water
- 1 cup Jasmine rice
- 16 oz. Shrimp (deveined)
- 2 tbsp.
- 2 tbsp. Ginger (shredded)
- 2 Tsp. Curry powder
- 3 cloves Garlic (chopped)

- Butter
- fifteen oz. Coconut milk
- Salt and red pepper flakes

Directions:

1. On moderate heat, melt 1 tbsp. of butter, then put in rice and stir to coat.
2. Pour 1 cup coconut milk and the water and cook for thirty minutes until rice is cooked.
3. Melt butter in a big pan on moderate heat, put in scallions, garlic, and ginger and leave to cook for about three minutes.
4. In a different container, mix coconut milk and curry powder
5. After the scallions are cooked, put in the shrimps and cook till they are pink.
6. Put in the coconut and curry mixture and cook then season accordingly.
7. Turn off the heat and serve rice mixed with lime juice and cilantro alongside the shrimps.

Nutritional Info: Calories: 400 kcal ‖ Protein: 40.46 g ‖ Fat: 18.01 g ‖ Carbohydrates: 29.99 g

COD CURRY

Time To Prepare: ten minutes

Time to Cook: twenty-five minutes

Yield: Servings 4

Ingredients:

- ¼ cup chopped parsley
- ¼ teaspoon ground cumin
- ½ teaspoon mustard seeds
- 1 small red onion, chopped
- 1 teaspoon curry powder
- 1 teaspoon fresh grated ginger
- 1 teaspoon ground turmeric
- 1½ cups coconut cream
- 2 green chilies, chopped
- 3 garlic cloves, minced
- 4 cod fillets, boneless

- 4 tablespoons olive oil
- Salt and black pepper to the taste

Directions:

1. Heat a pot with half of the oil on moderate heat. Put in mustard seeds and cook for a couple of minutes. Put in ginger, onion, garlic, turmeric, curry powder, chilies, and cumin, stir and cook for ten minutes more.
2. Put in coconut milk, salt and pepper then stir. Bring to its boiling point, cook for about ten minutes and take off the heat. Warm another pan with the remaining oil on moderate heat, put in fish, and then cook for about four minutes. Move the fish on top of the curry mix, toss lightly then cook for 6 more minutes. Split between plates, drizzle the parsley on top before you serve.
3. Enjoy!

Nutritional Info: Calories 210 || Fat: 14 || Fiber: 7 || Carbs: 6 || Protein: 16

COD WITH GINGER AND BLACK BEANS

Time To Prepare: ten minutes

Time to Cook: 15 minutes

Yield: Servings 4

Ingredients:

- ¼ cup Fresh Cilantro Leaves, chopped
- ¼ tsp. Freshly ground black pepper
- 1 (14 oz.) Can Black Beans, drained
- 1 tbsp. Grated fresh ginger
- 1 tsp. Sea Salt, divided
- 2 tbsp. Extra Virgin Olive Oil
- 4 (6 oz.) Cod Fillets
- 5 Garlic cloves, minced

Directions:

1. In a huge nonstick frying pan at moderate to high heat, heat the olive oil until it shimmers.

2. Flavour the cod with the ginger, ½ teaspoon of the salt, and the pepper. Put it in the hot oil then cook for minimum 4 minutes per side until the fish appears opaque. Take off the cod from the pan and set it aside on a platter, tented with aluminium foil.
3. Put back the frying pan to the heat and put in the garlic. Cook for half a minute, stirring continuously.
4. Mix in the black beans and the rest ½ teaspoon of salt. Cook for five minutes, stirring once in a while.
5. Mix in the cilantro and spoon the black beans over the cod.

Nutritional Info: Calories: 419 || Total Fat: 2g || Total Carbohydrates: 33g || Sugar: 1g || Fiber: 8g || Protein: 50g || Sodium: 605mg

CODFISH STICKS

Time To Prepare: 8 minutes

Time to Cook: 15 minutes

Yield: Servings 2

Ingredients:

- ½ tsp paprika
- 2 eggs
- 2 tbsp. coconut flour
- 2 tbsp. ghee butter
- 9 oz. codfish fillet
- Salt and pepper to taste

Directions:

1. Cut the fish into sticks
2. In a container, put and mix the eggs, flour, paprika, pepper, and salt
3. Warm the butter in a frying pan at moderate heat.
4. Immerse each fish slice into the spice mixture
5. Fry in the frying pan using low heat for 4-5 minutes per side

Nutritional Info: Carbohydrates: 1,5 g || Fat: 31 g || Protein: 22,5 g || Calories: 329

CRAB RISSOLES

Time To Prepare: ten minutes

Time to Cook: forty-five minutes

Yield: Servings 5

Ingredients:

- ¼ cup almond milk
- 1 tbsp. almond flour
- 1 tbsp. coconut oil
- 1 tbsp. flax meal
- 1 tbsps. coconut flour
- 1 tsp chives
- 1 tsp ground black pepper
- 1 tsp nutmeg
- 1 tsp onion powder
- 1 tsp salt
- 12 oz. crab meat
- 2 eggs, beaten
- 2 tbsp. butter

Directions:

1. Cut crab meat into tiny pieces.
2. In a container, mix eggs with crab meat, stir to get homogenous mass.
3. Put in flax meal, onion powder, butter, salt, and black pepper, stir.
4. Put in chives and nutmeg. Mix cautiously.
5. Make medium rissoles and dip in almond milk.
6. In a container, mix coconut flour and almond flour.
7. Season rissoles with flour mixture.
8. Heat frying pan with coconut oil on moderate heat.
9. Fry rissoles for about four minutes on both sides.
10. Let them cool for minimum two minutes and serve.

Nutritional Info: Calories 229 || Carbs: 5.98g || Fat: 18g || Protein: 12.95g

CRAB SALAD CAKES

Time To Prepare: ten minutes

Time to Cook: five minutes

Yield: Servings 4

Ingredients:

- .25 cup Red bell pepper, chopped
- .25 tsp. Old Bay seasoning
- .3 cup Celery, chopped
- .5 cup Swiss cheese, shredded
- .5 tsp. Black pepper
- .5 tsp. Salt
- 1 Scallion, chopped
- 1 tbsp. Extra virgin coconut oil
- 1 tbsp. Mayonnaise
- 2 Hot sauce, dashes
- 4 asparagus spears, cut
- 4 tsp. Lemon juice
- 8 oz. Crabmeat

Directions:

1. Pace the rack high in your oven and heat your broiler.
2. Microwave the asparagus in a covered container with 1 tsp. Water for half a minute.
3. Stir in the seasonings as you wish and the mayonnaise, lemon juice, scallion, bell pepper, celery, and crab.
4. For the results into 4 patties and top with the cheese.
5. Broil the patties for about three minutes.

Nutritional Info: Calories: 310 kcal || Protein: 28.19 g || Fat: 12.45 g || Carbohydrates: 24.34 g

---

CRAB STUFFED SALMON

Time To Prepare: ten minutes

Time to Cook: thirty minutes

Yield: Servings 8

Ingredients:

- 2 lbs. Salmon (wider filet works best)
- 2 tbsp. Butter (melted)
- 2 tsp Lemon zest
- Black pepper
- Sea salt

Crab Filling:

- ½ big onion (chopped)
- 1 tbsp. Lemon juice
- 1 tsp Old Bay seasoning
- 2 cloves Garlic (minced)
- 2 tbsp. Fresh parsley (chopped)
- 2 tbsp. Mayonnaise
- 8 oz. Lump crab meat

Directions:

1. Preheat your oven to 400°F. Coat a baking sheet using foil or parchment paper.
2. In a pan at moderate heat, sauté onion for approximately 7-ten minutes, until translucent and browned (or cook longer to caramelize if you wish).
3. On the other hand, whisk together the mayonnaise, minced garlic, fresh parsley, lemon juice, and Old Bay seasoning.
4. Mix in the sautéed onion. Cautiously fold in the lump crab meat, without breaking up the lumps.
5. Put the salmon fillet on the baking sheet. Organize the crab mixture along the length down the middle of the salmon. Beginning from the thinner sides of the filet, fold over the long way.
6. Mix together the melted butter and lemon zest. Brush the lemon butter at the top of the salmon. Dust lightly with sea salt and black pepper.
7. Bake for minimum 16-twenty minutes, until the fish flakes easily using a fork. Drizzle with additional fresh parsley. Cut crosswise into individual filets to serve.

Nutritional Info: Calories: 243 || Fat: 13g || Carbohydrates: 1g || Protein: 29g

CRISPY FISH STICK

Time To Prepare: ten minutes

Time to Cook: ten minutes

Yield: Servings 4

Ingredients:

- ¼ cup Dairy-Free Tartar Sauce
- ½ cup grated Parmesan cheese
- ½ cup ground pork rinds
- ½ teaspoon chili powder
- ½ teaspoon chopped fresh parsley
- 1 cup almond flour
- 1 cup avocado oil or other cooking oil, plus more as required
- 1 pound frozen cod, thawed
- 2 big eggs
- 2 tablespoons avocado oil mayonnaise
- Freshly ground black pepper
- Salt

Directions:

1. In a frying pan, heat the avocado oil at high heat. You want the oil to be about ½ inch deep, so adjust the amount of oil-based on your pan's size.
2. Pat the dry fish using paper towels to remove any surplus water.
3. In a small container, put the eggs and mayonnaise then whisk.
4. In another container, put the almond flour, Parmesan, pork rinds, chili powder, and parsley and mix thoroughly. Sprinkle with salt and pepper.
5. Chop the cod into strips.
6. Place the fish into the egg mixture then dredge in the dry mixture. Push the strips into the dry mixture so that the "breading" sticks well on all sides.
7. Put in 3 to 4 fish sticks at a time to the hot oil. The oil should sizzle when you put the fish sticks. Cook for minimum 2 minutes each side, or until golden and crunchy.
8. Put the cooked fish sticks on a paper towel-lined plate while you continue to fry the remaining fish sticks.
9. Serve with the tartar sauce.

Nutritional Info: Calories: 402 || Total Fat: 30g || Protein: 30g || Total Carbohydrates: 3g || Fiber: 1g || Net Carbohydrates: 2g

CUCUMBER GINGER SHRIMP

Time To Prepare: five minutes

Time to Cook: ten minutes

Yield: Servings 1

Ingredients:

- 1 big cucumber, cut into ½-inch round
- 1 teaspoon (1 g) fresh ginger, grated
- 10-fifteen big shrimp/prawns
- Coconut oil to cook with
- Salt to taste

Directions:

1. Pour 1 Tablespoon (fifteen ml) of coconut oil into a frying pan on moderate heat.
2. Place the ginger and the cucumber and sauté for at least two minutes.
3. Put in in the shrimp then cook until they turn pink and are no longer translucent.
4. Put in salt to taste before you serve.

Nutritional Info: Calories: 250 || Fat: 16 g || Net Carbohydrates: 4 g || Protein: 20 g

CURRIED FISH

Time To Prepare: ten minutes

Time to Cook: thirty-five minutes

Yield: Servings 4

Ingredients:

- ½ teaspoon cayenne pepper, optional
- ½ teaspoon ground coriander
- ½ teaspoon ground cumin
- 1 ½ cups basmati rice
- 1 bell pepper, cored and thinly chopped
- 1 tablespoon curry powder
- 1 yellow onion, finely chopped

- 1/4 cup hot water
- 1/4 teaspoon turmeric
- 2 big tomatoes, diced
- 2 tablespoons canola oil
- Four 5-ounce fish fillets

Directions:

1. Put the rice in a pan, put in roughly 3 cups water, then leave to come to its boiling point; then decrease the heat and simmer for about twenty minutes until all of the liquid is assimilated.
2. In a different pan, heat canola oil using high heat. Put in the onions and sauté for about 2 minutes. Put in spices and bell pepper, and cook one to two minutes longer, stirring continually. Put fillets in the pan and spoon seasoning mixture over the top, then mix tomatoes and water to the dish. Once the liquid comes a to simmer, turn the heat down and cover. Cook 8 to ten minutes longer.
3. Serve with rice.

Nutritional Info: Calories: 362 kcal || Protein: 14.26 g || Fat: 24.98 g || Carbohydrates: 35.58 g

CURRY TILAPIA AND BEANS

Time To Prepare: five minutes

Time to Cook: 20 minutes

Yield: Servings 4

Ingredients:

- 1 cup canned red kidney beans, drained
- 1 tablespoon olive oil
- 1 tablespoon parsley, chopped
- 2 tablespoons green curry paste
- 4 tilapia fillets, boneless
- Juice of ½ lime

Directions:

1. Warm a pan with the oil on moderate heat, put the fish, and cook for minimum five minutes on each side.

2. Put the remaining ingredients, toss lightly, cook on moderate heat for about ten minutes more, split between plates before you serve.

Nutritional Info: Calories 271 || Fat: 4 || Fiber: 6 || Carbs: 14 || Protein: 7

DARING SHARK STEAKS

Time To Prepare: thirty-five minutes

Time to Cook: forty minutes

Yield: Servings 2

Ingredients:

- ¼ cup Worcestershire sauce
- 1 Garlic clove, minced
- 1 tbsp. Ground black pepper
- 2 Shark steak, skinless
- 2 tbsp. Onion powder
- 2 tbsp. Thyme, chopped
- 2 tsp. Chili powder

Directions:

1. In a container, put then mix all of the seasonings and spices to make a paste before setting aside.
2. Spread a slim layer of paste on all sides of the fish, cover, and chill for thirty minutes (If possible).
3. Preheat your oven to 325°F/150°C/Gas Mark 3.
4. Bake the fish in parchment paper for about forty minutes, until well cooked.
5. Serve on a bed of quinoa or whole-grain couscous and your favorite salad.

Nutritional Info: Calories: 112 kcal || Protein: 4.87 g || Fat: 3.65 g || Carbohydrates: 16.78 g

DELICIOUS OYSTERS AND PICO DE GALLO

Time To Prepare: ten minutes

Time to Cook: ten minutes

Yield: Servings 6

Ingredients:

- ½ cup Monterey Jack cheese; shredded
- 1 jalapeno pepper; chopped.
- 1/4 cup red onion; finely chopped.
- 18 oysters; scrubbed
- 2 limes; cut into wedges
- 2 tomatoes; chopped.
- Handful cilantro; chopped.
- Juice from 1 lime
- Salt and black pepper to the taste.

Directions:

1. In a container, combine the onion with jalapeno, cilantro, tomatoes, salt, pepper, and lime juice and stir thoroughly.
2. Put oysters on preheated grill on moderate to high heat; cover grill and cook for seven minutes until they open.
3. Move opened oysters to a heatproof dish and discard unopened ones
4. Top oysters with cheese then put on the preheated broiler for a minute
5. Position oysters on a platter, top each with tomatoes mix you've made earlier and serve with lime wedges on the side

Nutritional Info: Calories: 70 || Fat: 2 Fiber: 0 || Carbohydrates: 1 || Protein: 1

DILL HADDOCK

Time To Prepare: ten minutes

Time to Cook: thirty minutes

Yield: Servings 4

Ingredients:

- 1-pound haddock fillets
- 2 tablespoons lemon juice
- 2 tablespoons mayonnaise
- 2 teaspoons chopped dill
- 3 teaspoons veggie stock

- A sprinkle of olive oil
- Salt and black pepper to the taste

Directions:

1. Grease a baking dish with the oil, put in the fish, also put in stock mixed with lemon juice, salt, pepper, mayo, and dill.
2. Toss a small amount and place in your oven at 350 degrees F to bake for half an hour Split between plates before you serve.

Nutritional Info: Calories: 214 || Fat: 12 Cal || Fiber: 4 g || Carbohydrates: 7 g || Protein: 17 g

EASY CRUNCHY FISH TRAY BAKE

Time To Prepare: ten minutes

Time to Cook: 20 minutes

Yield: Servings 4

Ingredients:

- ½ small red onion
- 1 lemon, cut into wedges
- 1 tablespoon parmesan
- 180g baby stuffed peppers
- 2 teaspoons oregano leaves
- 2 x 250g punnets tomatoes
- 2 zucchini
- 600g frozen crumbed whiting fish fillets

Directions:

1. Preheat the stove to 400F. Oil an enormous preparing plate. Spot the fish filets on the readied plate. Disperse the oregano & parmesan over the fish.
2. Put in the zucchini, tomatoes & stuffed peppers to the plate. Disperse the onion rings over the top. Season well. Splash with olive oil. Heat until the fish is brilliant & thoroughly cooked.
3. Split the fish & vegetables among plates & present with the rocket & lemon wedges.

Nutritional Info: Calories: 346 kcal || Protein: 3.67 g || Fat: 2.8 g || Carbohydrates: 81.77 g

FISH & CHICKPEA STEW

Time To Prepare: five minutes

Time to Cook: ten minutes

Yield: Servings 4

Ingredients:

- 1 brown onion
- 1 carrot, peeled
- 2 cups fish stock
- 2 garlic clove
- 4 kale leaves
- 400g can chickpeas
- 400g can tomatoes
- 500g firm white fish fillets
- Finely grated parmesan
- Salt & pepper to taste
- Sliced Coles Bakery Stone

Directions:

1. Spray a frying pan with olive oil shower. Spot over moderate-low warmth. Include the carrot & onion & cook, mixing, until delicate & brilliant. Include garlic & cook, blending, until sweet-smelling.
2. Put in the chickpeas stock & tomato, & to the onion mix in the frying pan. Bring to the bubble. Lessen warmth to moderate-low & stew until the blend thickens fairly.
3. Put in the kale & fish to the dish & stew until the fish is simply thoroughly cooked. Season.
4. Split the stew among serving bowls. Drizzle with parmesan & present with the bread.

Nutritional Info: Calories: 1447 kcal || Protein: 42.1 g || Fat: 127.85 g || Carbohydrates: 32.4 g

---

FISH CAKES

Time To Prepare: 2 hours and thirty minutes

Time to Cook: ten minutes

Yield: Servings 4

Ingredients:

- .5 cup Bread crumbs
- .5 Onion
- 1 Egg
- 1 tbsp. Italian seasoning
- 2 Chili pepper, seeded
- 4 cloves Garlic
- 4 tbsp. Coconut oil
- 4 tbsp. Whole wheat flour
- 5 Sun-dried tomatoes, chopped
- 6 Basil leaves
- 6 oz. Scallops
- 9 oz. Tuna
- oz. Shrimp

Directions:

1. Coat a pan in 1 T oil and place it on the stove above a burner that has been turned to a high/moderate heat.
2. Put in in the scallops and allow them to cook until they are completely white.
3. Use a food processor to mix in 1 T coconut oil, the egg, tomatoes, garlic, and onion before you put in in the seasoning, chilies, basil and parsley, and medium setting process.
4. Put in in the shrimp, scallops, and tuna and process on a low setting.
5. Put in in the breadcrumbs and keep processing until everything binds together.
6. Make the results into patties before you put in them to a plate and placing the plate in your fridge for minimum 2 hours.
7. Coat a pan in the rest of the oil and place it on the stove above a burner that has been turned to moderate heat.
8. Cook the patties in the pan until both sides have turned a golden brown.

Nutritional Info: Calories: 396 kcal || Protein: 35.52 g || Fat: 19.68 g || Carbohydrates: 22.73 g

---

FISH CASSEROLE WITH CREAM CHEESE SAUCE

Time To Prepare: ten minutes

Time to Cook: thirty-five minutes

Yield: Servings 4

Ingredients:

- 1 liter of water
- 1 tbsp. butter
- 1 tsp. chopped green onions
- 1/4 tsp. chopped garlic
- 1/8 tsp. Chile
- 119 ml of || Fat: cream
- 2 tbsp. grated Parmesan cheese
- 280 g broccoli
- 280 g cooked fish
- 56.7 g cream cheese
- 85 g grated Gouda cheese
- For the sauce:
- Sea salt and black pepper to taste

Directions:

1. Preheat your oven to 350° F.
2. Set all the sauce ingredients into a deep cooking pan and simmer for about three minutes, stirring once in a while.
3. In another deep cooking pan, bring the water to its boiling point and cook the broccoli for about three minutes or until soft.
4. Mash the fish using a fork.
5. Place the broccoli in a casserole dish, put the chopped fish on top, pour the sauce and drizzle with grated cheese.
6. Bake for minimum twenty minutes or until a golden-brown color is achieved.
7. Allow to stand for five minutes, drizzle with chopped green onions and enjoy!

Nutritional Info: Carbohydrates: 9 g || Fat: 36 g || Protein: 32 g || Calories: 474

FISH FINGERS

Time To Prepare: ten minutes

Time to Cook: forty minutes

Yield: Servings 2

Ingredients:

- ¼ tsp. baking soda
- ½ Lemon, juiced
- ½ tsp. Black pepper
- ½ tsp. Red Chili Flakes
- ½ tsp. sea salt
- ½ tsp. Turmeric Powder
- 1 – 2 tbsp. olive oil
- 1 + 1 tsp. Garlic Powder, separately
- 1 + 1 tsp. mixed dried herbs
- 1 cup keto-friendly bread crumbs
- 1 tsp. Ginger garlic paste
- 10 oz. Fish, such as mackerel, cut into fingers
- 2 eggs
- 2 tbsp. Maida
- 3 tsp. Keto almond flour
- Ketchup or tartar sauce [optional]

Directions:

1. Place the fish fingers in a container. Cover with 1 teaspoon of mixed herbs, 1 teaspoon of garlic powder, salt, red chili flakes, turmeric powder, black pepper, ginger garlic paste, and lemon juice. Leave to absorb for roughly ten minutes.
2. In a different container, combine the keto almond flour and baking soda. Beat the eggs in the mixture and stir once more.
3. Throw in the marinated fish and set aside again for minimum ten minutes.
4. Mix the bread crumbs and the rest of the teaspoon of mixed herbs and teaspoon of garlic powder.
5. Roll the fish sticks with the bread crumb and herb mixture.
6. Preheat the Air Fryer at 360°F.
7. Coat the basket of the fryer using a sheet of aluminium foil. Put the fish fingers inside the fryer and pour over a sprinkle of the olive oil.

8. Cook for about ten minutes, making sure the fish is brown and crunchy before you serve. Enjoy with ketchup or tartar sauce if you wish.

Nutritional Info: Calories: 534 kcal || Protein: 40.85 g || Fat: 34.52 g || Carbohydrates: 13.52 g

FISH MEATBALLS

Time To Prepare: twelve minutes

Time to Cook: 15 minutes

Yield: Servings 6

Ingredients:

- ¼ cup fish stock
- ½ tsp chili flakes
- 1 tbsp. dill, chopped
- 1 tsp garlic, minced
- 1 tsp kosher salt
- 1 tsp parsley, chopped
- 2 eggs, beaten
- 4 tbsp. butter
- 8 oz. almond flour
- fifteen oz. salmon, chopped roughly

Directions:

1. Put salmon in blender or food processor and pulse until the desired smoothness is achieved.
2. In a moderate-sized container, mix chili flakes, parsley, dill, and salt.
3. Put in mixed salmon to spice mixture and stir thoroughly.
4. Put in garlic and eggs, stir cautiously until get a consistent mass.
5. Shape mixture into meatballs 1½ inch in diameter and save for later.
6. Drizzle meatballs with almond flour.
7. Preheat pan on moderate heat and melt butter.
8. Put fish meatballs in the pan and cook on high heat for a minute on both sides.
9. Next, put in fish stock and close lid. Simmer for about ten minutes on moderate heat.
10. Serve hot.

Nutritional Info: Calories 209 || Carbs: 1.75g || Fat: 16.1g || Protein: 16.8g

---

FISH SANDWICH

Time To Prepare: ten minutes

Time to Cook: ten minutes

Yield: Servings 4

Ingredients:

- .5 cup Red onion, cut thin
- 1 cup Arugula
- 1 lb. quartered Salmon fillet
- 1 pitted Avocado, peeled
- 2 Plum tomatoes, cut thin
- 2 tbsp. Coconut oil
- 2 tbsp. Mayonnaise
- 2 tsp. Cajun seasoning
- 4 Wheat rolls

Directions:

1. Coat the grill in coconut oil before making sure it is heated to high heat.
2. Coat the fish using the seasoning before you put in it to the grill and allow it to cook for roughly three minutes on each side.
3. Mash the avocado before blending it with the mayonnaise and spreading on the rolls before you serve.
4. Season as needed, serve hot and enjoy.

Nutritional Info: Calories: 389 kcal || Protein: 26.88 g || Fat: 26.27 g || Carbohydrates: 12.21 g

---

FRIED BALL OF COD

Time To Prepare: ten minutes

Time to Cook: ten minutes

Yield: Servings 4

Ingredients:

- ½ cup cut black olive
- 1 red onion cut into strips
- 2 cloves garlic, minced
- 3 minced boiled eggs
- 700g desalted and shredded cod
- Black pepper
- Braised olive oil
- Parsley to taste
- Salt to taste

Directions:

1. In a hot frying pan, position the olive oil and sauté the onion and then the garlic.
2. Put in cod and sauté well.
3. Remove the heat, then put the olives, the chopped eggs, and the parsley.
4. Correct salt if required, put in pepper, and allow to cool.
5. Fill the pastry dough and close by brushing water and kneading using a fork.
6. Fry in hot oil by dipping until a golden-brown color is achieved.
7. Drain over paper towels before you serve.

Nutritional Info: Calories: 253 kcal || Protein: 35.45 g || Fat: 9.61 g || Carbohydrates: 3.86 g

FRIED CODFISH WITH ALMONDS

Time To Prepare: 8 minutes

Time to Cook: eighteen minutes

Yield: Servings 3

Ingredients:

- ½ tsp chili pepper
- ½ tsp onion powder
- 1 egg
- 1 tbsp. chopped fresh dill
- 1 tbsp. ghee butter
- 1 tsp minced garlic
- 1 tsp psyllium

- 16 oz. codfish fillet
- 3 oz. chopped almonds
- 3 oz. cream
- 3 tbsp. keto mayo
- Salt and pepper to taste

Directions:

1. In a small mixing container, mix the psyllium, onion powder, chili, and almonds
2. Beat the eggs in a different container, mix thoroughly
3. Warm the butter in a frying pan at moderate heat.
4. Chop the fillet into 3 slices
5. Immerse into the egg mixture, then into almonds and spices
6. Fry in the frying pan for approximately seven minutes each side
7. In the meantime, in a different container mix the cream, garlic, dill, and salt, stir thoroughly
8. Serve the fish with this sauce

Nutritional Info: Carbohydrates: 4,9 g || Fat: 63 g || Protein: 33,6 g || Calories: 709

GARLIC & LEMON SHRIMP PASTA

Time To Prepare: ten minutes

Time to Cook: thirty minutes

Yield: Servings 4

Ingredients:

- .5 of 1 Lemon
- .5 tsp. Paprika
- 1 lb. Large raw shrimp
- 2 pkg. Miracle Noodle Angel Hair Pasta
- 2 tbsp. Butter
- 2 tbsp. Olive oil
- 4 Garlic cloves
- Fresh basil (as you wish)
- Pepper and salt (to taste)

Directions:

1. Drain the water from the package of noodles and wash them in cold water. Toss into a pot of boiling water for a couple of minutes. Move to a hot frying pan on moderate heat to remove the surplus liquid (dry roast). Set them aside.
2. Use the same pan to warm the butter, oil, and mashed garlic. Sauté for a few minutes but do not brown.
3. Cut the lemon into rounds and put in them to the garlic together with the shrimp. Sauté for roughly three minutes on each side.
4. Fold in the noodles and spices and stir to combine the flavors.

Nutritional Info: Calories: 360 ‖ Net Carbohydrates: 3.5 g ‖ Total Fat: Content: 21 g ‖ Protein: 36 g

---

GARLIC BUTTER SHRIMPS

Time To Prepare: 13 minutes

Time to Cook: 16 minutes

Yield: Servings 3

Ingredients:

- ½ pound shrimp, peeled and deveined
- ½ white onion
- 1 lemon (peeled)
- 1 tsp black pepper
- 2 garlic cloves
- 3 tbsp. ghee butter
- Himalayan rock salt to taste

Directions:

1. Preheat your oven to 425F
2. Mince the garlic and onion, chop the lemon in half
3. Flavour the shrimps with pink salt and pepper
4. Slice one-half of the lemon thinly, chop the other half into 2 pieces
5. Grease a baking dish with the butter; mix the shrimp with the garlic, onion and lemon slices, put in the baking dish

6. Bake the shrimps for fifteen minutes, stirring midway through
7. Take away the shrimps from the oven and squeeze the juice from 2 lemon pieces over the dish

Nutritional Info: Carbohydrates: 3,9 g || Fat: 19,8 g || Protein: 32 g || Calories: 338

GARLIC CRAB LEGS

Time To Prepare: ten minutes

Time to Cook: 20 minutes

Yield: Servings 2

Ingredients:

- ½ lemon, juiced and zested
- 1 tablespoon red pepper flakes
- 2 pounds crab legs
- 2 tablespoons chopped fresh parsley
- 2 tablespoons extra-virgin olive oil
- 2 teaspoons Old Bay Seasoning
- 4 garlic cloves, crushed and minced
- 4 tablespoons butter or ghee

Directions:

1. Preheat your oven to 375°F.
2. Heat a big oven-safe frying pan at medium-low heat. Put in the butter, olive oil, lemon juice, lemon zest, garlic, Old Bay, and red pepper flakes. Sauté for a couple of minutes.
3. Put in the crab legs and parsley to the frying pan. Ladle the butter mixture over the crab and coat for about three minutes.
4. Bring the frying pan in your oven then bake for fifteen minutes, coating every five minutes.
5. Put the crab legs on a platter and pour the butter mixture into a small dish for dipping.

Nutritional Info: Calories: 514 || Total Fat: 38g || Protein: 41g || Total Carbohydrates: 2g || Fiber: 0g || Net Carbohydrates: 2g

GINGER & CHILI SEA BASS FILLETS

Time To Prepare: five minutes

Time to Cook: ten minutes

Yield: Servings 2

Ingredients:

- 1 Garlic cloves, finely slice
- 1 Red chili, deseeded and thinly cut
- 1 tbsp. Extra virgin olive oil
- 1 tsp Ginger, peeled and chopped
- 1 tsp. Black pepper
- 2 Green onion stemmed, chopped
- 2 Sea bass fillet

Directions:

1. Get a frying pan and heat the oil on a moderate-high heat.
2. Drizzle black pepper over the Sea Bass and score the fish's skin a few times using a sharp knife.
3. Put in the sea bass fillet to the super hot pan with the skin side down.
4. Cook for five minutes and turn over.
5. Cook for another two minutes.
6. Remove seabass from the pan and rest.
7. Place the chili, garlic, and ginger and cook for roughly two minutes or until golden.
8. Turn off the heat and put in the green onions.
9. Spread the vegetables over your sea bass to serve.
10. Try with a steamed sweet potato or side salad.

Nutritional Info: Calories: 306 kcal || Protein: 29.92 g || Fat: 8.94 g || Carbohydrates: 26.59 g

GINGER SALMON AND BLACK BEANS

Time To Prepare: ten minutes

Time to Cook: thirty minutes

Yield: Servings 4

Ingredients:

- ¼ cup chopped scallions
- ¼ cup grated carrots
- ¼ cup grated radishes
- ½ cup olive oil
- 1 ½ cup chicken stock
- 1 cup canned black beans, drained
- 1 tablespoon fresh grated ginger
- 2 garlic cloves, minced
- 2 tablespoons coconut aminos
- 2 teaspoons white wine vinegar
- 6 ounces salmon fillets, boneless

Directions:

1. In the meantime, in a container, combine the aminos with half of the oil and whisk. Cut midway into each salmon fillet, put them in a baking dish and pour the aminos mixture all over. Toss and keep in your refrigerator for about ten minutes to marinate. Heat a pan with the remaining oil on moderate heat, put in garlic, ginger, and black beans. Stir and cook for about three minutes.
2. Put in vinegar and stock, stir, bring to its boiling point, cook for about ten minutes, and split between plates. Broil fish for about four minutes per side on moderate to high heat then place a fillet next to the black beans and top with grated scallions, radishes, and carrots.
3. Enjoy!

Nutritional Info: Calories 200 || Fat: 7 || Fiber: 2 || Carbs: 9 || Protein: 9

GINGERED TILAPIA

Time To Prepare: 15 minutes

Time to Cook: six minutes

Yield: Servings 5

Ingredients:

- 2 tablespoons coconut aminos
- 2 tablespoons coconut oil

- 2 tablespoons unsweetened coconut, shredded
- 3 garlic cloves, minced
- 4-ounce freshly ground ginger
- 5 tilapia fillets
- 8 scallions, chopped

Directions:

1. In a huge frying pan, melt coconut oil on moderate heat.
2. Put in tilapia fillets and cook for approximately 2 minutes.
3. Flip the side and put in garlic, coconut, and ginger and cook for approximately one minute.
4. Put in coconut aminos and cook for approximately one minute.
5. Put in scallion and cook for approximately 1-2 minutes more.
6. Serve instantly.

Nutritional Info: Calories: 135 || Fat: 3g || Carbohydrates: 2g || Protein: 26g

GLAZED HALIBUT STEAK

Time To Prepare: ten minutes

Time to Cook: 15 minutes

Yield: Servings 3

Ingredients:

- 1 lb. halibut steak
- ½ cup mirin
- 2 tbsp. lime juice
- ¼ cup stevia
- ¼ tsp. crushed red pepper flakes
- ¼ cup orange juice
- 1 garlic clove, smashed
- ¼ tsp. ginger, ground
- 2/3 cup low-sodium soy sauce

Directions:

1. Make the teriyaki glaze by mixing all of the ingredients apart from for the halibut in a deep cooking pan.
2. Put it to a boil and reduce the heat, continually stirring until the mixture reduces by half. Take off from the heat and leave to cool.
3. Pour half of the cooled glaze into a Ziploc bag. Put in in the halibut, ensuring to coat it thoroughly in the sauce. Put in your fridge for half an hour
4. Preheat the Air Fryer to 390°F.
5. Place the marinated halibut in the fryer and let it cook for ten – twelve minutes.
6. Use any the rest of the glaze to brush the halibut steak with lightly.
7. Serve with white rice or shredded vegetables.

Nutritional Info: Calories: 357 kcal ‖ Protein: 29.34 g ‖ Fat: 23.16 g ‖ Carbohydrates: 7.15 g

GRILLED CALAMARI

Time To Prepare: ten minutes

Time to Cook: five minutes

Yield: Servings 4

Ingredients:

- ⅛ teaspoon freshly ground black pepper
- ¼ teaspoon sea salt
- ½ cup good-quality olive oil
- 1 tablespoon minced garlic
- 2 pounds calamari tubes and tentacles, cleaned
- 2 tablespoons chopped fresh oregano
- Zest and juice of 2 lemons

Directions:

1. Prepare the calamari. Score the top layer of the calamari tubes approximately two inches apart.
2. Marinate the calamari. In a big container, mix together the olive oil, lemon zest, lemon juice, oregano, garlic, salt, and pepper. Put in the calamari and toss to coat it thoroughly, then place it in your fridge to marinate for minimum 30 minutes to an hour. Grill the calamari. Preheat a grill to high heat. Grill the calamari, flipping over once, for approximately 3 minutes total, until it's soft and mildly charred.

3. Serve. Split the calamari between four plates and serve it hot.

Nutritional Info: Calories: 455 Total fat: 30g Total carbs: 8g ‖ Fiber: 1g; Net carbs: 7g ‖ Sodium: 101mg ‖ Protein: 35g

GRILLED FISH TACOS

Time To Prepare: ten minutes

Time to Cook: ten minutes

Yield: Servings 8

Ingredients:

- ½ teaspoon crushed red pepper
- ½ teaspoon garlic powder
- ½ teaspoon ground cumin
- ½ teaspoon oregano
- 1 pound mahimahi fillets
- 1 teaspoon chili powder
- 1 teaspoons salt, divided
- 1/4 cup cilantro, chopped
- 2 mangoes
- 2 tablespoons canola oil
- 2 tablespoons omega-3-rich margarine
- 8 wheat flour tortillas
- Juice of 1 lime

Directions:

1. In a moderate-sized-size container, whisk together the canola oil, margarine, lime juice, one teaspoon of salt, and the residual dried spices. Pour mix over the fish. Cover and marinate for about forty-five minutes in your refrigerator.
2. Meanwhile, peel mangoes and slice into cubes. Combine with cilantro and remaining salt.
3. Preheat grill to moderate-high. Remove fish from the marinade, put on the grill, and cook two to three minutes on both sides. Put tortillas on the grill and heat ten to fifteen seconds on each side. Fill with fish fillets and mango topping.

Nutritional Info: Calories: 231 kcal ‖ Protein: 13.99 g ‖ Fat: 17.04 g ‖ Carbohydrates: 6.02 g

GRILLED SALMON WITH CAPONATA

Time To Prepare: 15 minutes

Time to Cook: twenty minutes

Yield: Servings 4

Ingredients:

- ¼ cup cider vinegar
- ¼ cup good-quality olive oil, divided
- ¼ cup pitted green olives, chopped
- ½ cup chopped marinated artichoke hearts
- 1 onion, chopped
- 1 tablespoon minced garlic
- 2 celery stalks, chopped
- 2 tablespoons chopped fresh basil
- 2 tablespoons chopped pecans
- 2 tablespoons white wine
- 2 tomatoes, chopped
- 4 (4-ounce) salmon fillets
- Freshly ground black pepper, for seasoning

Directions:

1. Make the caponata. In a big frying pan at moderate heat, warm 3 tablespoons of the olive oil. Put in the onion, celery, garlic, and sauté until they have become tender, approximately 4 minutes. Mix in the tomatoes, artichoke hearts, olives, vinegar, white wine, and pecans. Put the mixture to its boiling point, then decrease the heat to low and simmer until the liquid has reduced, six to seven minutes. Take off the frying pan from the heat and set it aside.
2. Grill the fish. Preheat a grill to moderate-high heat. Pat the fish dry using paper towels then rub it with the rest of the 1 tablespoon of olive oil and season lightly with black pepper. Grill the salmon, flipping over once, until it is just thoroughly cooked, approximately eight minutes total.

3. Serve. Split the salmon between four plates, top with a generous scoop of the caponata, and serve instantly with fresh basil.

Nutritional Info: Calories: 348 Total fat: 25g Total carbs: 7g || Fiber: 3g Net carbs: 4g || Sodium: 128mg || Protein: 24g

GRILLED SQUID WITH GUACAMOLE

Time To Prepare: **15** minutes

Time to Cook: **15** minutes

Yield: Servings 3

Ingredients:

- ½ tsp olive oil
- 1 onion, peeled and chopped
- 1 tomato, cored and chopped
- 2 avocados, pitted
- 2 medium squids
- 2 red chilies, chopped
- For the guacamole:
- Fresh coriander, chopped
- Juice from 1 lime
- Juice from 2 limes
- Salt and ground black pepper to taste

Directions:

1. Separate tentacles from squid and score tubes along the length.
2. Rub squid and tentacles with black pepper, salt, and olive oil.
3. Heat grill on moderate to high heat and put squid and tentacles score side down.
4. Cook for a couple of minutes, flip, and cook for a couple of minutes more.
5. Move to container and drizzle all parts with lime juice.
6. Peel and cut avocado.
7. In a moderate-sized container, purée avocado using a fork.
8. Put in tomato, the juice from 2 limes, coriander, onion, and chilies. Mix thoroughly.
9. Serve squid with guacamole.

Nutritional Info: Calories 498 || Carbs: 6.95g || Fat: 44.5g || Protein: 19.9g

GRILLED SWORDFISH

Time To Prepare: ten minutes

Time to Cook: ten minutes

Yield: Servings 3

Ingredients:

Ingredients:

- ½ teaspoon marjoram; dried
- ½ teaspoon rosemary; dried
- ½ teaspoon sage; dried
- 1 lemon; cut into wedges
- 1 tablespoon parsley; chopped.
- 1/3 cup chicken stock
- 1/4 cup lemon juice
- 3 garlic cloves; minced
- 3 tablespoons olive oil
- 4 swordfish steaks
- Salt and black pepper to the taste.

Directions:

1. In a container, mix chicken stock with garlic, lemon juice, olive oil, salt, pepper, sage, marjoram, and rosemary and whisk well.
2. Put swordfish steaks, toss to coat and keep in your refrigerator for around three hours
3. Put marinated fish steaks on preheated grill on moderate to high heat and cook for five minutes on each side
4. Position on plates, top with parsley, then serve with lemon wedges on the side.

Nutritional Info: Calories: 136 || Fat: 5 Fiber: 0 || Carbohydrates: 1 || Protein: 20

HADDOCK WITH SWISS CHARD

Time To Prepare: 15 minutes

Time to Cook: ten minutes

Yield: Servings 1

Ingredients:

- 1 haddock fillet
- 1 teaspoon coconut aminos
- 2 cups Swiss chard, chopped roughly
- 2 minced garlic cloves
- 2 tablespoons coconut oil, divided
- 2 teaspoons fresh ginger, grated finely
- Freshly ground black pepper, to taste
- Salt, to taste

Directions:

1. In a frying pan, put 1 tablespoon of coconut oil then melt it on moderate heat.
2. Put in garlic and ginger and sauté for approximately one minute.
3. Put in haddock fillet and drizzle with salt and black pepper.
4. Cook for minimum about three to five minutes per side or till the desired doneness.
5. In the meantime, in a different frying pan, melt remaining coconut oil on moderate heat.
6. Put in Swiss chard and coconut aminos and cook for approximately 5-10 minutes.
7. Serve the salmon fillet over Swiss chard.

Nutritional Info: Calories: 486 kcal ‖ Protein: 39.68 g ‖ Fat: 34.34 g ‖ Carbohydrates: 5.57 g

HALIBUT CURRY

Time To Prepare: ten minutes

Time to Cook: ten minutes

Yield: Servings 4

Ingredients:

- ¼ tsp. Freshly ground black pepper
- ½ tsp. Sea Salt
- 1 (14 oz.) can Lite coconut milk

- 1½ pound Halibut, skin, and bones removed, cut into an inch pieces
- 2 tbsp. Extra Virgin Olive Oil
- 2 tsp. Curry Powder
- 2 tsp. Ground Turmeric
- 4 cups No-salt added chicken broth

Directions:

1. In a huge nonstick frying pan at moderate to high, heat the olive oil until it shimmers.
2. Put in the turmeric and curry powder. Cook for a couple of minutes, continuously stirring, to bloom the spices.
3. Put in the halibut, chicken broth, coconut milk, salt, and pepper. Put to a simmer then reduce the heat to moderate. Simmer for six to seven minutes, stirring once in a while, until the fish appears opaque.

Nutritional Info: Calories: 429 || Total Fat: 47g || Total Carbohydrates: 5g || Sugar: 1g || Fiber: 1g || Protein: 27g || Sodium: 507mg

HALIBUT STIR FRY

Time To Prepare: five minutes

Time to Cook: 20 minutes

Yield: Servings 6

Ingredients:

- 1 onion, cut 2 stalks celery, chopped
- 2 pounds halibut fillets
- 2 tablespoons capers
- 2 tbsp. olive oil ½ cup fresh parsley
- 4 cloves of garlic minced
- Salt and pepper to taste

Directions:

1. Put a heavy-bottomed pot on high fire and heat for a couple of minutes. Put in oil and heat for two more minutes.
2. Mix in garlic and onions. Sauté for five minutes. Put in rest of the ingredients except for the parsley and stir fry for about ten minutes or until fish is cooked.

3. Tweak seasoning to taste and serve with a drizzle of parsley.

Nutritional Info: Calories 331 Cal || Fat: 26 g || Carbs: 2 g || Protein: 22 g || Fiber: 0.5 g

HEALTHY FISH NACHO BOWL

Time To Prepare: 13 minutes

Time to Cook: 20 minutes

Yield: Servings 4

Ingredients:

- 1 big lime, rind finely grated, juiced
- 1 small avocado
- 1 tablespoon olive oil
- 1 tablespoon yogurt
- 1/3 cup fresh coriander leaves
- 200g cherry tomatoes
- 2-3 teaspoons gluten-free chipotle seasoning
- 3 green shallots
- 400g red cabbage
- 425g can black beans
- 500g white fish fillets
- 50g gluten-free corn chips

Directions:

1. Mix the fish, stew powder/chipotle flavoring & 2 tsp oil in a container
2. Shred the cabbage in a nourishment processor fitted with the cutting connection. Move to a huge container with the tomato, lime skin, dark beans, yogurt, 2 tbs lime juice, 2 shallots, & the remaining oil. Hurl well to consolidate.
3. Heat a huge non-stick frying pan over high warmth. Cook the fish, turning until simply thoroughly cooked. Move to a plate.
4. In the meantime, consolidate the avocado, coriander, remaining shallot & 1 tbs remaining lime squeeze in a little container.
5. Split the cabbage blend, fish, guacamole & corn chips among serving bowls. Drizzle with additional coriander & present with additional lime wedges.

Nutritional Info: **Calories:** 388 kcal || Protein: 28.17 g || Fat: 16.64 g || Carbohydrates: 35.72 g

HERBED COCONUT MILK STEAMED MUSSELS

Time To Prepare: ten minutes

Time to Cook: 15 minutes

Yield: Servings 4

Ingredients:

- ½ sweet onion, chopped
- ½ teaspoon turmeric
- 1 cup coconut milk
- 1 scallion, finely chopped
- 1 tablespoon chopped fresh thyme
- 1 teaspoon grated fresh ginger
- 1½ pounds fresh mussels, scrubbed and debearded
- 2 tablespoons chopped fresh cilantro
- 2 tablespoons coconut oil
- 2 teaspoons minced garlic
- Juice of 1 lime

Directions:

1. Sauté the aromatics. In a huge frying pan, warm the coconut oil.
2. Put in the onion, garlic, ginger, and turmeric and sauté until they have become tender, approximately 3 minutes. Put in the liquid. Stir in the coconut milk, lime juice then bring the mixture to its boiling point. Steam the mussels. Place the mussels to the frying pan, cover, and steam until the shells are open, approximately ten minutes.
3. Take the frying pan off the heat and throw out any unopened mussels. Put in the herbs. Mix in the scallion, cilantro, and thyme and serve. Split the mussels and the sauce into 4 bowls and serve them instantly.

Nutritional Info: Calories: 319 Total fat: 23g Total carbs: 8g || Fiber: 2g; Net carbs: 6g || Sodium: 395mg || Protein: 23g

HERBED ROCKFISH

Time To Prepare: ten minutes

Time to Cook: 20 minutes

Yield: Servings 8

Ingredients:

- ½ tablespoons canola oil
- 1 ½ pounds rockfish fillets
- 1 ½ tablespoons nonfat milk
- 1 cup nonfat plain yogurt
- 1 pint cherry tomatoes, chopped
- 1 tablespoon fresh parsley, chopped
- 1 tablespoon lemon juice
- 1 tablespoon oregano
- 1 tablespoon pimento, minced
- 1 teaspoon garlic, minced
- 1 teaspoon ground black pepper
- 1/4 cup extra virgin olive oil
- 1/4 cup flaxseed, ground fresh
- 2 egg whites
- 2 fresh lemons, wedges
- 6 slices wheat bread, toasted

Directions:

1. Clean rockfish fillets in cold water, take off the skin and remove any bones — Pat dry using paper towels. In a moderate-sized-size container, mix egg whites, nonfat milk, yogurt, canola oil, and lemon juice — put in a pie pan.
2. Place the next 8 ingredients (oregano-flaxseed) in a food processor until thoroughly ground — put in a separate dish.
3. Heat the olive oil in a pan. First, soak the fillets in the spice mixture, succeeded by the yogurt blend, and then once again in the spice mixture, compressing the crumbs slowly into the fish for the final layer.
4. Put the fillets in hot olive oil. When the underneath starts to brown, flip the fillets over, and decrease the heat — Cook for another fifteen to twenty minutes.
5. Complete with tomatoes and lemon wedges.

Nutritional Info: Calories: 178 kcal || Protein: 19.62 g || Fat: 8.96 g || Carbohydrates: 4.73 g

HONEY CRUSTED SALMON WITH PECANS

Time To Prepare: 20 minutes

Time to Cook: 20 minutes

Yield: Servings 6

Ingredients:

- ½ cup chopped pecans
- 3 tablespoons mustard
- 3 tablespoons olive oil
- 3 teaspoons chopped parsley
- 5 teaspoons raw honey
- 6 salmon fillets, boneless
- Salt and black pepper to the taste

Directions:

1. In a container, whisk the mustard with honey and oil. In another container, combine the pecans with parsley and stir.
2. Season salmon fillets with salt and pepper, arrange them on a baking sheet, brush with mustard mixture, top with the pecans mix, and put them in your oven at 400 degrees F to bake for about twenty minutes. Split into plates and serve with a side salad.
3. Enjoy!

Nutritional Info: Calories 200 || Fat: 10 || Fiber: 5 || Carbs: 12 || Protein: 16

HOT TUNA STEAK

Time To Prepare: ten minutes

Time to Cook: twenty-five minutes

Yield: Servings 6

Ingredients:

- ¼ c. whole black peppercorns

- 2 tbsps. Extra-virgin olive oil
- 2 tbsps. Fresh lemon juice
- 6 cut tuna steaks
- Pepper.
- Roasted orange garlic mayonnaise
- Salt

Directions:

1. Bring the tuna in a container to fit. Place the oil, lemon juice, salt, and pepper. Turn the tuna to coat well in the marinade.
2. Rest for minimum fifteen to twenty minutes, flipping over once.
3. Place the peppercorns in a twofold thickness of plastic bags. Tap the peppercorns with a heavy deep cooking pan or small mallet to crush them crudely. Put on a big plate.
4. Once ready to cook the tuna, immerse the edges into the crushed peppercorns. Heat a nonstick frying pan on moderate heat. Sear the tuna steaks, in batches if required, for about four minutes per side for medium-rare fish, putting in two to three tablespoons of the marinade to the frying pan if required, to stop sticking.
5. Serve dolloped with roasted orange garlic mayonnaise

Nutritional Info: Calories: 124 || Fat: 0.4 g || Carbohydrates: 0.6 g || Protein: 28 g Sugars: 0 g || Sodium: 77 mg

IRISH STYLE CLAMS

Time To Prepare: five minutes

Time to Cook: 15 minutes

Yield: Servings 4

Ingredients:

- 1 bottle infused cider
- 1 small green apple; chopped.
- 1 tablespoon olive oil
- 2 garlic cloves; minced
- 2 pounds clams; scrubbed
- 2 thyme springs; chopped.
- 3 ounces pancetta

- 3 tablespoons ghee
- Juice of ½ lemon
- Salt and black pepper to the taste.

Directions:

1. Heat a pan with the oil on moderate to high heat; put in pancetta, brown for about three minutes and decrease temperature to moderate.
2. Put in ghee, garlic, salt, pepper, and shallot; stir and cook for about three minutes
3. Raise the heat again, put in cider; stir thoroughly and cook for a minute
4. Put in clams and thyme, cover the pan and simmer for five minutes
5. Discard unopened clams, put in lemon juice and apple pieces; stir and split into bowls. Serve hot.

Nutritional Info: Calories: 100 || Fat: 2 || Fiber: 1 || Carbohydrates: 1 || Protein: 20

ITALIAN HALIBUT CHOWDER

Time To Prepare: five minutes

Time to Cook: 20 minutes

Yield: Servings 8

Ingredients:

- ½ cup apple juice, organic and unsweetened
- ½ teaspoon dried basil
- 1 cup tomato juice
- 1 onion, chopped
- 1 red bell pepper, seeded and chopped
- 1/8 teaspoon dried thyme
- 2 ½ pounds halibut steaks, cubed
- 2 tablespoons olive oil
- 3 cloves of garlic, minced
- 3 stalks of celery, chopped
- Salt and pepper to taste

Directions:

1. Put a heavy-bottomed pot on moderate to high fire and heat pot for a couple of minutes. Put in oil and heat for one minute.
2. Sauté the onion, celery, and garlic until aromatic.
3. Mix in the halibut steaks and bell pepper. Sauté for about three minutes.
4. Pour in the remaining ingredients and mix thoroughly.
5. Cover and bring to its boiling point. Once boiling, lower fire to a simmer and simmer for about ten minutes.
6. Tweak seasoning to taste.
7. Serve and enjoy.

Nutritional Info: Calories: 318 Cal || Fat: 23g || Carbohydrates: 6g || Protein: 21g || Fiber: 1g

KETO SALMON TANDOORI WITH CUCUMBER SAUCE

Time To Prepare: 15 minutes

Time to Cook: 20 minutes

Yield: Servings 4

Ingredients:

- ½ shredded cucumber (squeeze out the water completely)
- ½ teaspoon salt (not necessary)
- 1 1/4 cup sour cream or mayonnaise
- 1 tablespoon tandoori seasoning
- 1 yellow bell pepper (diced)
- 2 avocados (cubed)
- 2 minced garlic cloves
- 2 tablespoons coconut oil
- 25 ounces salmon (bite-sized pieces)
- 3 ½ ounces lettuce (torn)
- 3 scallions (finely chopped)
- For the crunchy salad
- For the cucumber sauce
- Juice of ½ lime
- Juice of 1 lime

Directions:

1. Preheat your oven to 350 degrees Fahrenheit
2. Combine the tandoori seasoning with oil in a small container and coat the salmon pieces with this mixture.
3. Coat the baking tray using parchment paper and spread the coated salmon pieces in it.
4. Bake for about twenty minutes until tender and the salmon flakes using a fork
5. Take another container and put the shredded cucumber in it. Put in the mayonnaise, minced garlic, and salt (if the mayonnaise doesn't have salt) to the shredded cucumber. Mix thoroughly. Squeeze the lime juice at the top and set the cucumber sauce aside.
6. Combine the lettuce, scallions, avocados, and bell pepper in a different container. Sprinkle the contents with the lime juice.
7. Move the veggie salad to a plate and put the baked salmon over it. Top the veggies and salmon with cucumber sauce.
8. Serve instantly and enjoy!

Nutritional Info: Calories 847 Kcal || Fat: 73 g || Protein: 35 g Net carb: 6 g

KETO ZOODLES WITH WHITE CLAM SAUCE

Time To Prepare: ten minutes

Time to Cook: ten minutes

Yield: Servings 4

Ingredients:

- ½ cup dry white wine
- 1 tablespoon garlic (minced)
- 1 teaspoon kosher salt
- 1 teaspoon lemon zest (grated)
- 1/4 cup butter
- 1/4 cup fresh parsley (chopped)
- 1/4 teaspoon black pepper (ground)
- 2 pounds small clams
- 2 tablespoons lemon juice
- 2 tablespoons olive oil
- 8 cups zucchini noodles

Directions:

1. In a pan at moderate heat, put the olive oil, butter, pepper, and salt. Stir to melt the butter.
2. Put in the garlic. Sautee the garlic until aromatic for minimum 2 minutes
3. Set in the lemon juice and wine. Cook for minimum 2 minutes, until the liquid is slightly reduced
4. Put in the clams. Cook the clams until they are all opened (about three minutes). Discard any clam that does not open after three minutes.
5. Take away the pan from the heat. Put in the zucchini noodles. Toss the mixture to blend well. Allow the zoodles rest for about 2 minutes to tenderize them.
6. Put in the lemon zest and parsley. Stir and serve.

Nutritional Info: Calories: 311 || Carbohydrates: 9 g || Fat: 19 g || Protein: 13 g || Fiber: 2 g

LEMON BUTTER TILAPIA

Time To Prepare: ten minutes

Time to Cook: 10-twelve minutes

Yield: Servings 4

Ingredients:

- 1/4 cup unsalted butter, melted
- 2 tablespoons chopped fresh parsley leaves
- 2 tablespoons freshly squeezed lemon juice
- 3 cloves garlic, minced
- 4 (6-ounce) tilapia fillets
- Freshly ground black pepper, to taste
- Kosher salt, to taste
- Zest of 1 lemon

Directions:

1. Set oven to 425°F. Lightly grease using oil a 9×13 baking dish or coat with nonstick spray.
2. In a small container, put butter, garlic, lemon juice, and lemon zest, whisk together and save for later.
3. Spice the tilapia with salt and pepper to taste and place onto the readied baking dish. Sprinkle with butter mixture.

4. Bring into the oven and bake until fish flakes easily using a fork, approximately 10-twelve minutes.
5. Serve instantly, decorated with parsley, if you wish.

Nutritional Info: Calories: 276 || Fat: 14.5g || Carbohydrates: 1.8g || Protein: 35.5g

LEMON-CAPER TROUT WITH CARAMELIZED SHALLOTS

Time To Prepare: ten minutes

Time to Cook: 20 minutes

Yield: Servings 2

Ingredients:

For the Shallots

- 1 teaspoon ghee
- 2 shallots, thinly cut
- Dash salt

For the Trout

- ¼ cup freshly squeezed lemon juice
- ¼ teaspoon salt
- 1 lemon, thinly cut
- 1 tablespoon plus 1 teaspoon ghee, divided
- 2 (4-ounce) trout fillets
- 3 tablespoons capers
- Dash freshly ground black pepper

Directions:

To make the Shallot:

1. In a huge frying pan on moderate heat, cook the shallots, ghee, and salt for about twenty minutes, stirring every five minutes, until the shallots have fully wilted and caramelized.

To make the Trout:

1. While the shallots cook, in another big frying pan on moderate heat, heat 1 teaspoon of ghee.
2. Put in the trout fillets. Cook for minimum 3 minutes each side, or until the center is flaky. Move to a plate and save for later.
3. In the frying pan used for the trout, put in the lemon juice, capers, salt, and pepper. Heat it until it simmers. Whisk in the rest of the 1 tablespoon of ghee. Ladle the sauce over the fish.
4. Decorate the fish with the lemon slices and caramelized shallots before you serve.

Nutritional Info: Calories: 399 || Total Fat: 22g || Saturated Fat: 10g || Cholesterol: 46mg || Carbohydrates: 17g || Fiber: 2g || Protein: 21g

LEMONY MACKEREL

Time To Prepare: ten minutes

Time to Cook: 15 minutes

Yield: Servings 4

Ingredients:

- 1 tablespoon minced chives
- 2 tablespoons olive oil
- 4 mackerels
- Juice of 1 lemon
- Pinch black pepper
- Pinch of sea salt
- Zest of 1 lemon

Directions:

1. Warm a pan with the oil on moderate to high heat, put in the mackerel and cook for about six minutes on each side. Put in the lemon zest, lemon juice, chives, salt, and pepper then cook for two more minutes on each side. Split everything between plates before you serve.
2. Enjoy!

Nutritional Info: Calories: 289 Cal || Fat::20 g || Fiber: 0 g || Carbohydrates: 1 g || Protein: 21 g

LEMONY MUSSELS

Time To Prepare: five minutes

Time to Cook: five minutes

Yield: Servings 4

Ingredients:

- 1 tbsp. extra virgin extra virgin olive oil
- 2 lbs. scrubbed mussels
- 2 minced garlic cloves
- Juice of one lemon

Directions:

1. Put some water in a pot, put in mussels, bring with a boil on moderate heat, cook for five minutes, discard unopened mussels and move them with a container.
2. In another container, combine the oil with garlic and freshly squeezed lemon juice, whisk well, and put in over the mussels, toss before you serve.
3. Enjoy!

Nutritional Info: Calories: 140 || Fat: 4 g || Carbohydrates: 8 g || Protein: 8 g Sugars: 4g || Sodium: 600 mg

---

LEMONY TROUT

Time To Prepare: ten minutes

Time to Cook: 20 minutes

Yield: Servings 2

Ingredients:

- 1 lemon
- 1 tsp rosemary
- 2 garlic cloves
- 2 tbsp. capers
- 5 oz. trout fillets
- 5 tbsp. ghee butter
- Salt and pepper to taste

Directions:

1. Preheat your oven to 400F
2. Peel the lemon, mince the garlic cloves and cut the capers
3. Flavour the trout fillets with salt, rosemary, and pepper
4. Grease a baking dish with the oil and put the fish onto it
5. Warm the butter in a frying pan on moderate heat
6. Put in the garlic and cook for 4-5 minutes until golden
7. Turn off the heat, put in the lemon zest and 2 tablespoons of lemon juice, stir thoroughly
8. Pour the lemon-butter sauce over the fish and top with the capers
9. Bake for 14-fifteen minutes. Serve hot

Nutritional Info: Carbohydrates: 3,1 g || Fat: 25 g || Protein: 15,8 g || Calories: 302

LIME COD MIX

Time To Prepare: ten minutes

Time to Cook: 15 minutes

Yield: Servings 4

Ingredients:

- ½ cup chicken stock
- ½ teaspoon cumin, ground
- 1 tablespoon olive oil
- 2 tablespoons lime juice
- 2 teaspoons lime zest, grated
- 3 tablespoons cilantro, chopped
- 4 cod fillets, boneless
- A pinch of salt and black pepper

Directions:

1. Set the instant pot on Sauté mode, put oil, heat it, put in the cod and cook for a minute on each side.
2. Put in the rest of the ingredients, put the lid on, and cook on High for 13 minutes.

3. Release the pressure naturally for around ten minutes, split the mix between plates before you serve.

Nutritional Info: Calories 187 || Fat: 13.1 || Fiber: 0.2 || Carbohydrates: 1.6 || Protein: 16.1

MACKEREL BOMBS

Time To Prepare: 15 minutes

Time to Cook: ten minutes

Yield: Servings 4

Ingredients:

- ¼ cup spinach, chopped
- ½ tsp thyme
- 1 egg, beaten
- 1 tsp chili flakes
- 1 tsp garlic, minced
- 1 tsp mustard
- 1 tsp salt
- 1 white onion, peeled and diced
- 1/3 cup almond flour
- 10 oz. mackerel, chopped
- 4 tbsp. coconut oil

Directions:

1. Put mackerel in blender or food processor and pulse until texture is smooth.
2. In a container, mix onion with mackerel.
3. Put in garlic, flour, egg, thyme, salt, and mustard, stir thoroughly.
4. Put in chili flakes and mix up the mixture until get homogenous mass.
5. Put in spinach and stir.
6. Heat a pan at moderate heat then put in oil.
7. Shape fish mixture into bombs 1½ inch in diameter.
8. Put bombs on a pan and cook for five minutes on all sides.
9. Move to paper towels and drain grease and serve.

Nutritional Info: Calories 318 || Carbs: 3.45g || Fat: 26.5g || Protein: 20.1g

MANHATTAN-STYLE SALMON CHOWDER

Time To Prepare: ten minutes

Time to Cook: 15 minutes

Yield: Servings 4

Ingredients:

- ¼ cup Extra Virgin Olive Oil
- ¼ tsp. Freshly Ground Black Pepper
- ½ tsp. Sea Salt
- 1 Pound Skinless Salmon. Pin Bones removed, chopped into ½ inch
- 1 Red Bell Pepper, Chopped
- 1 tsp. Onion Powder
- 2 (28 oz.) Cans Crushed Tomatoes, 1 Drained, 1 undrained
- 2 cups diced (½ inch) Sweet Potato
- 6 cups No salt added chicken broth

Directions:

1. Put in the red bell pepper and salmon. Cook for minimum five minutes, once in a while stirring, until the fish appears opaque and the bell pepper is tender.
2. Mix in the tomatoes, chicken broth, sweet potatoes, onion powder, salt, and pepper. Put to a simmer then reduce the heat to moderate. Cook for minimum ten minutes, once in a while stirring, until the sweet potatoes are tender.

Nutritional Info: Calories: 570 ‖ Total Fat: 42 ‖ Total Carbohydrates: 55g ‖ Sugar: 24g ‖ Fiber: 16g ‖ Protein: 41g ‖ Sodium: 1,249mg

---

MARINATED FISH STEAKS

Time To Prepare: ten minutes

Time to Cook: 15 minutes

Yield: Servings 4

Ingredients:

- 1 lb. fresh swordfish
- 1 tbsp. snipped fresh oregano

- 1 tsp. lemon-pepper seasoning
- 2 minced garlic cloves
- 2 tbsps. Lime juice
- 2 tsp. Olive oil
- 4 lime wedges

Directions:

1. Wash fish steaks; pat dry using paper towels. Cut into four serving-size pieces, if required.
2. In a shallow dish, put and mix lime juice, oregano, oil, lemon-pepper seasoning, and garlic. Put in fish; turn to coat with marinade.
3. Cover and marinate in your fridge for thirty minutes to 1½ hours, turning steaks once in a while. Drain fish, saving for later marinade.
4. Place the fish on the greased unheated rack of a broiler pan.
5. Broil 4 inches from the heat for minimum 8 to twelve minutes or until fish begins to flake when tested using a fork, flipping over once and brushing with reserved marinade midway through cooking.
6. Take off any remaining marinade.
7. Before you serve, squeeze the lime juice on each steak.

Nutritional Info: Calories: 240 || Fat: 6 g || Carbohydrates: 19 g || Protein: 12 g Sugars: 3.27 g || Sodium: 325 mg

MEXICAN SALAD WITH MAHI-MAHI

Time To Prepare: 20 minutes

Time to Cook: 75 minutes

Yield: Servings 4

Ingredients:

- .25 cup Cilantro, chopped
- .5 cup Coconut oil
- .5 cup Red wine vinegar
- .5 tbsp. Cumin, ground
- .5 tsp. Chili powder

- 1 clove Garlic, crushed
- 1 Green bell pepper, chopped
- 1 lb. Ground beef
- 1 Red bell pepper, frozen
- 1 Red onion, chopped
- 1 tbsp. Lemon juice
- 10 oz. Corn kernels, frozen
- 2 tbsp. Agave sweetener
- 2 tbsp. Lime juice
- 32 oz. Mahi-mahi
- fifteen oz. Black beans, washed and drained
- fifteen oz. Cannellini beans, washed and drained
- fifteen oz. Kidney beans, washed and drained
- Hot pepper sauce (as you wish)
- Pepper (as you wish)
- Salt (as you wish)

Directions:

1. In a serving container, mix the red onion, frozen corn, bell peppers, and beans and mix thoroughly.
2. In a smaller separate container, mix the pepper, cumin, cilantro, hot pepper sauce, garlic, salt, sugar, lemon juice, lime juice, red wine vinegar, and coconut oil and whisk well.
3. Pour the dressing over the salad and toss thoroughly to coat, cover the salad using plastic wrap, and chill in your fridge and serve chilled.
4. Prior to serving Flavour the fish as you wish.
5. Put in the coconut oil to a pan before placing the pan on the stove over a moderate heat burner.
6. Put in in the fish and allow it to cook for roughly five minutes on each side.

Nutritional Info: Calories: 709 kcal || Protein: 39.23 g || Fat: 47.12 g || Carbohydrates: 36.61 g

MOZZARELLA FISH

Time To Prepare: five minutes

Time to Cook: 10-fifteen minutes

Yield: Servings 6-8

Ingredients:

- ½ teaspoon dried oregano
- 1 big fresh tomato, cut thinly
- 1 cup grated mozzarella cheese
- 2 lbs. of bone gold sole
- Salt and pepper to taste

Directions:

1. Excellent source of cooking the butter. Organize a single layer of trout. Put in salt, pepper, and oregano.
2. Top with cut cheese slices and tomatoes.
3. Cook, covered, for ten to fifteen minutes at 425°F.

Nutritional Info: Calories: 156 || Fat: 6g || Net Carbohydrates: 5g || Protein: 8g

MUSSEL CHOWDER

Time To Prepare: ten minutes

Time to Cook: 20 minutes

Yield: Servings 4

Ingredients:

- ¼ cup olive oil
- ¼ cup Parmesan cheese, grated
- 1 cup celery stalk, chopped
- 1 cup heavy cream
- 1 lb. fresh mussels, cleaned
- 2 big onions, finely chopped
- 2 cups cauliflower, cut into florets
- 2 tbsp. fresh parsley, finely chopped
- 5 cups fish stock

Spices:

- ¼ tsp of chili flakes

- ½ tsp white pepper, freshly ground
- 1 tsp sea salt

Directions:

1. Wash mussels and drain in a big strainer. Put in a deep pot and sprinkle with some olive oil. Sprinkle with chili flakes and white pepper. Mix thoroughly and set aside,
2. Set the instant pot and press the "Sauté" button. Warm the rest of the oil in the instant pot, then put onions and chopped celery stalks. Stir thoroughly, then cook for about five minutes.
3. Put in the cauliflower then cook for two more minutes.
4. Put mussels then place in the fish stock. Push the "Cancel" button.
5. Closed the lid and set the steam release handle to the "Sealing" position. Push the "Manual" button then set the timer for eight minutes on high pressure.
6. When done, perform a quick release and open the lid. Stir in the heavy cream and split the chowder between serving bowls.
7. Drizzle with grated Parmesan and chopped parsley. Serve instantly.

Nutritional Info: Calories 428 || Total Fats 30.3g || Net Carbohydrates: 12.5g || Protein: 25g || Fiber: 3.3g

NUT-CRUST TILAPIA WITH KALE

Time To Prepare: five minutes

Time to Cook: 15 minutes

Yield: Servings 2

Ingredients:

- ½ cup 100% Wholegrain breadcrumbs
- ½ cup Roasted and Ground Brazil Nuts/Hazelnuts/Any other hard nut
- 1 Garlic clove, minced
- 1 Head of kale, chopped
- 1 tbsp. Sesame seeds, mildly toasted
- 2 tbsp. Low-fat hard cheese, grated
- 2 Tilapia Fillet, skinless
- 2 tsp. Extra virgin olive oil
- 2 tsp. Whole grain mustard

Directions:

1. Set the oven to 350°F.
2. Lightly oil a baking sheet with the use of 1 tsp. extra virgin olive oil.
3. Stir in the nuts, breadcrumbs, and cheese in a separate container.
4. Spread a slim layer of the mustard over the fish and then dip into the breadcrumb mixture.
5. Move to baking dish.
6. Bake for minimum twelve minutes, till thoroughly cooked.
7. In the meantime, warm 1 tsp. Oil in a frying pan at moderate heat temperature then sauté the garlic for half a minute, putting in in the kale for another five minutes.
8. Stir in the sesame seeds.

Nutritional Info: Calories: 475 kcal ‖ Protein: 37.14 g ‖ Fat: 33.44 g ‖ Carbohydrates: 11.08 g

---

OCTOPUS SALAD

Time To Prepare: ten minutes

Time to Cook: forty minutes

Yield: Servings 2

Ingredients:

- 21 ounces octopus; washed
- 3 ounces olive oil
- 4 celery stalks; chopped.
- 4 tablespoons parsley; chopped.
- Juice of 1 lemon
- Salt and black pepper to the taste.

Directions:

1. Place the octopus in a pot, put in water to immerse, cover the pot, bring to a boil on moderate heat; cook for forty minutes, drain and leave aside to cool down.
2. Chop octopus and put it in a salad container.
3. Put in celery stalks, parsley, oil, and lemon juice and toss thoroughly.
4. Spice with salt and pepper, toss again and serve

Nutritional Info: Calories: 140‖ Fat: 10 Fiber:3 ‖ Carbohydrates: 6 ‖ Protein: 23

ORANGE AND MAPLE-GLAZED SALMON

Time To Prepare: 15 minutes

Time to Cook: 15 minutes

Yield: Servings 4

Ingredients:

- ¼ cup Pure maple syrup
- 1 Orange Zest
- 1 tsp. Garlic Powder
- 2 Orange Juice
- 2 tbsp. Low Sodium: Soy Sauce
- 4 4-6 oz. Salmon Fillet, Pin bones removed

Directions:

1. Preheat your oven to 400°F.
2. In a small, shallow dish, whisk the orange juice and zest, maple syrup, soy sauce, and garlic powder.
3. Place the salmon pieces, flesh-side down, into the dish. Allow it to marinate for about ten minutes.
4. Move the salmon, skin-side up, to a rimmed baking sheet and bake for approximately fifteen minutes until the flesh appears opaque.

Nutritional Info: Calories: 297 || Total Fat: 11 || Total Carbohydrates: 18g || Sugar: 15g || Fiber: 1g || Protein: 34g || Sodium: 528mg

OVEN-BAKED SOLE FILLETS

Time To Prepare: ten minutes

Time to Cook: 20 minutes

Yield: Servings 4

Ingredients:

- ½ tablespoon Dijon mustard
- ½ tablespoon fresh ginger, minced
- ½ teaspoon paprika

- ½ teaspoon porcini powder
- 1 teaspoon garlic paste
- 1/4 cup fresh parsley, chopped
- 2 tablespoons olive oil
- 4 sole fillets
- Salt and ground black pepper, to taste

Directions:

1. Mix the oil, Dijon mustard, garlic paste, ginger, porcini powder, salt, black pepper, and paprika.
2. Rub this mixture all over sole fillets. Put the sole fillets in a mildly oiled baking pan.
3. Bake in the preheated oven at 400 degrees F for approximately 20 minutes.

Nutritional Info: 195 Calories 8.2g || Fat: 0.5g || Carbs: 28.7g || Protein: 0.6g Fiber

PAN-SEARED SCALLOPS WITH LEMON-GINGER VINAIGRETTE

Time To Prepare: ten minutes

Time to Cook: seven minutes

Yield: Servings 4

Ingredients:

- ⅛ tsp. Freshly Ground Black Pepper
- ¼ cup Lemon Ginger Vinaigrette
- ½ tsp. Sea Salt
- 1½ Pound Sea Scallop
- 2 tbsp. Extra Virgin Olive Oil

Directions:

1. In a huge nonstick frying pan at moderate to high heat, heat the olive oil until it shimmers.
2. Flavour the scallops with pepper and salt and put in them to the frying pan. Cook for minimum 3 minutes per side until just opaque.
3. Serve with the vinaigrette ladled over the top.

Nutritional Info: Calories: 280 || Total Fat: 16 || Total Carbohydrates: 5g || Sugar: 1g || Fiber: 0g || Protein: 29g || Sodium: 508mg

PARMESAN CRUSTED TILAPIA

Time To Prepare: ten minutes

Time to Cook: five minutes

Yield: Servings 4

Ingredients:

- ¾ cup grated parmesan cheese
- 1 tbsp. chopped parsley
- 1 tbsp. olive oil
- 2 tsp. paprika
- 4 tilapia fillets
- Pinch garlic powder

Directions:

1. Preheat your Air Fryer at 350°F.
2. Coat each of the tilapia fillets with a light brushing of olive oil.
3. Mix all of the other ingredients in a container.
4. Cover the fillets with the parmesan mixture.
5. Coat the base of a baking dish using a sheet of parchment paper and put the fillets in the dish.
6. Moved to the Air Fryer and cook for five minutes. Serve hot.

Nutritional Info: Calories: 244 kcal || Protein: 30.41 g || Fat: 12.24 g || Carbohydrates: 3.29 g

POACHED HALIBUT AND MUSHROOMS

Time To Prepare: five minutes

Time to Cook: thirty minutes

Yield: Servings 8

Ingredients:

- ½ teaspoon soy sauce
- 1 teaspoon fresh lemon juice
- 1/8 teaspoon sesame oil
- 2 pounds halibut, cut into bite-sized pieces
- 4 cups mushrooms, cut ¼ cup water
- Salt and pepper to taste ¾ cup green onions

Directions:

1. Put a heavy-bottomed pot on moderate to high fire.
2. Put in all ingredients and mix thoroughly.
3. Cover and bring to its boiling point. Once boiling, lower fire to a simmer. Cook for about twenty-five minutes.
4. Tweak seasoning to taste.
5. Serve and enjoy.

Nutritional Info: Calories: 217 Cal || Fat: 15.8 g || Carbohydrates: 1.1 g || Protein: 16.5 g || Fiber: 0.4 g

POPCORN SHRIMP

Time To Prepare: five minutes

Time to Cook: 20 minutes

Yield: Servings 2

Ingredients:

- ½ lb. (225 g) small shrimp, peeled
- 2 eggs, whisked
- 6 Tablespoons (36 g) cajun seasoning
- 6 Tablespoons (42 g) coconut flour
- Coconut oil for frying

Directions:

1. Warm the coconut oil in a deep cooking pan (use enough coconut oil so that it's ½ inch (1-2 cm) deep) or deep fryer.
2. Put the whisked eggs into a big container, and in another big container, mix the coconut flour and seasoning.

3. Toss a handful of the shrimp into the whisked eggs and stir around so that each shrimp is coated.
4. Then take the shrimp out of the whisked eggs the put into the seasoning container. Coat the shrimp using the coconut flour and seasoning mixture.
5. Bring the coated shrimp into the hot oil and fry until golden. (Do not stir the pot and the shrimp must in deep-fried)
6. Use a slotted spoon to take off the shrimp and place using paper towels to absorb the surplus oil. Repeat for the rest of the shrimp (change the oil if there are too many solids in it).
7. Cool for minimum ten minutes.

Nutritional Info: Calories: 390 || Fat: 23 g || Net Carbohydrates: 3 g || Protein: 30 g

POTATO DUMPLING WITH SHRIMP

Time To Prepare: 15 minutes

Time to Cook: 50 minutes

Yield: Servings 6-8

Ingredients:

- ½ packet of chopped cilantro
- 1 egg
- 1 tbsp. chopped parsley
- 10 units of clean giant tailed shrimp
- 2 tablespoons flour + flour for handling and breading
- 3 tablespoons palm oil
- 4 lemon juice
- 500g of pink potatoes
- black pepper to taste
- frying oil
- salt to taste

Directions:

1. Place the potato to cook for forty minutes.
2. When super soft, turn off the heat, allow to cool and purée potatoes already peeled.

3. Put in the egg and mix thoroughly, sprinkle with salt and parsley and put in the flour. Set aside in your refrigerator for about two hours.
4. Make small transverse cuts on the belly of the shrimp, without cutting to the end. Flavour the shrimp with black pepper, salt chopped coriander, palm oil, and lemon juice. Leave marinating for fifteen minutes.
5. Take a portion of the potato flour dough in your hands and shape around a shrimp leaving the tail out.
6. Wash flour again and fry in hot oil until golden.

Nutritional Info: Calories: 159 kcal || Protein: 6.95 g || Fat: 8.42 g || Carbohydrates: 14.48 g

PROSCIUTTO-WRAPPED COD

Time To Prepare: five minutes

Time to Cook: ten minutes

Yield: Servings 2

Ingredients:

- 2 (6-ounce) cod fillets
- 2 tablespoons butter or ghee
- 4 prosciutto slices
- Freshly ground black pepper

Directions:

1. Pat the dry fish using paper towels to remove any surplus water.
2. Flavour the fillets with pepper and wrap the prosciutto around the fillets.
3. Heat a frying pan at moderate heat then put in the butter.
4. Once the pan is hot, put in the fillets and cook on each side for five minutes, up to the outside is crunchy and the inside is flaky.
5. Put the cooked fish onto a paper towel-lined plate to absorb any surplus oil.

Nutritional Info: Calories: 317 || Total Fat: 18g || Protein: 38g || Total Carbohydrates: 0g || Fiber: 0g || Net Carbohydrates: 0g

PROSCUITTO-WRAPPED HADDOCK

Time To Prepare: ten minutes

Time to Cook: 15 minutes

Yield: Servings 4

Ingredients:

- 3 tablespoons garlic-infused olive oil
- 4 (4-ounce) haddock fillets, approximately 1 inch thick
- 4 slices prosciutto (2 ounces)
- Freshly ground black pepper, for seasoning
- Juice and zest of 1 lemon
- Sea salt, for seasoning

Directions:

1. Preheat your oven. Set the oven temperature to 350°F. Coat a baking sheet using parchment paper.
2. Prepare the fish. Pat the fish dry using paper towels then spice it lightly on both sides with salt and pepper. Cover the prosciutto around the fish firmly but cautiously so it doesn't rip.
3. Bake the fish. Bring the fish on the baking sheet and sprinkle it with the olive oil. Bake for fifteen to 1seven minutes until the fish flakes easily using a fork.
4. Serve. Split the fish between four plates and top with the lemon zest and a sprinkle of lemon juice.

Nutritional Info: Calories: 282 Total fat: 18g Total carbs: 1g ‖ Fiber: 0g; Net carbs: 1g ‖ Sodium: 76mg ‖ Protein: 29g

PUMPKIN SHRIMP

Time To Prepare: 20 minutes

Time to Cook: 1 hour and ten minutes

Yield: Servings 4-6

Ingredients:

- 1 average pumpkin
- 1 box of sour cream
- 1 cup of curd

- 1 cup of white wine
- 1 white onion
- 1kg medium shrimp
- 2 cans of peeled tomatoes
- 3 cloves of garlic
- Aluminum paper
- salt

Directions:

1. Chop the lid off the pumpkin, wrap in foil and bake at 180 degrees for fifteen minutes.
2. Take out of the oven, remove seeds and return to oven for another forty minutes at 180 degrees.
3. In a pan, sauté the chopped onion. When golden, put in the garlic and sauté until the aroma is released.
4. Put in the peeled tomato cans and the white wine. Cook for fifteen minutes on moderate heat. Put in water if it dries too quickly.
5. When the tomato is already well crushed, put in the cream and ½ cup of curd. Let reduce until it becomes thick — sprinkle with salt.
6. In a frying pan with olive oil, cook the prawns using high heat. When they are golden, put in to the sauce. Take away the pumpkin from the oven, pass the rest of the cream cheese on the inner walls, and put the shrimp sauce inside.

Nutritional Info: Calories: 218 kcal ‖ Protein: 29.55 g ‖ Fat: 5.94 g ‖ Carbohydrates: 10.65 g

---

QUICK CHERMOULA FISH PARCELS

Time To Prepare: 15 minutes

Time to Cook: thirty minutes

Yield: Servings 4

Ingredients:

- ½ small red onion
- 1 ½ teaspoons ground cumin
- 1 long red chilli
- 1/4 cup olive oil
- 100g roasted red capsicum

- 2 garlic cloves
- 2 tablespoons lemon juice
- 3/4 cup coriander leaves
- 3/4 cup parsley leaves
- 4 x 150g firm skinless white fish fillets
- 400g can chickpeas
- Baby rocket
- Chermoula
- Lemon wedges

Directions:

1. Preheat a grill barbecue or hotplate on low warmth. Consolidate chickpeas, capsicum, & onion in a container.
2. Make Chermoula. Join all fixings in a container. Sprinkle with salt & pepper.
3. Cut four 30cm bits of foil. Top each with a 15cm bit of heating paper. Separation chickpea blend among bits of paper. Top with fish. Ladle 1⁄3 of chermoula over fish. Overlay up edges of paper & foil to encase fish, scrunching foil at the top to secure. Spot fish divides a foil heating plate. Spot plate on grill barbecue. Cook, with hood shut, until fish is thoroughly cooked.
4. Put fish divides serving plates. Carefully open. Shower fish with remaining chermoula. Serve it.

Nutritional Info: Calories: 316 kcal || Protein: 9.82 g || Fat: 18.27 g || Carbohydrates: 30.9 g

QUICK FISH BOWL

Time To Prepare: 11 minutes

Time to Cook: 15 minutes

Yield: Servings 2

Ingredients:

- 1 avocado
- 1 tbsp. cumin powder
- 1 tbsp. ghee butter
- 1 tbsp. olive oil

- 1 tbsp. paprika
- 1 tbsp. salsa sauce
- 2 cups coleslaw cabbage, chopped
- 2 tilapia fillets
- Black pepper to taste
- Himalayan rock salt, to taste

Directions:

1. Preheat your oven to 425F. Coat a baking sheet with the foil
2. Mash the avocado
3. Brush the tilapia fillets using olive oil, sprinkle with salt and spices
4. Put the fish onto the baking sheet, greased with the ghee butter
5. Bake for fifteen minutes, then remove the fish from the heat and allow it to cool for five minutes
6. In a container, mix the coleslaw cabbage and the salsa sauce, toss lightly
7. Put in the mashed avocado, sprinkle with salt and pepper
8. Cut the fish and put in to the container
9. Bake for 14-fifteen minutes. Serve hot

Nutritional Info: Carbohydrates: 5,2 g || Fat: 24,5 g || Protein: 16,1 g || Calories: 321

QUICK SHRIMP MOQUECA

Time To Prepare: ten minutes

Time to Cook: ten minutes

Yield: Servings 4

Ingredients:

- 1 chopped red pepper
- 1 chopped yellow pepper
- 1 cup tomato passata
- 2 chopped purple onions
- 2 finger peppers
- 2 tablespoons palm oil
- 200ml of coconut milk

- 3 chopped tomatoes
- 4 cloves garlic, minced
- 600g Shrimp Peeled and Clean
- Braised olive oil
- Chopped cilantro to taste
- Juice of 2 lemons
- Salt to taste

Directions:

1. In a container, position shrimp, sprinkle with salt and lemon juice and save for later.
2. In a hot pan, position olive oil and sauté onion and garlic.
3. Put in the chopped tomatoes and sauté well.
4. Put in the peppers and the tomato passata. Allow it to cook for a few minutes.
5. Put in coconut milk, mix thoroughly.
6. Put in the shrimp to the sauce.
7. Finally, put in the finger pepper, palm oil, and chopped coriander.
8. Serve with rice and crumbs.

Nutritional Info: Calories: 426 kcal ‖ Protein: 46.15 g ‖ Fat: 15.46 g ‖ Carbohydrates: 26.26 g

ROASTED SALMON AND ASPARAGUS

Time To Prepare: five minutes

Time to Cook: 15 minutes

Yield: Servings 4

Ingredients:

- ⅛ tsp. freshly ground cracked black pepper
- 1 Lemon, zest, and slice
- 1 pound Asparagus Spears, trimmed
- 1 tsp. Sea Salt, divide
- 1½ pound Salmon, cut into 4 fillets
- 2 tbsp. Extra Virgin Olive Oil

Directions:

1. Preheat your oven to 425°F.

2. Mix the asparagus with the olive oil then put ½ teaspoon of the salt. Put in a single layer on the bottom of a roasting pan.
3. Flavour the salmon with the pepper and the rest of the ½ teaspoon of salt. Put skin-side down on top of the asparagus.
4. Drizzle the salmon and asparagus with the lemon zest and put the lemon slices over the fish.
5. Roast at the oven for minimum twelve to fifteen minutes until the flesh appears opaque.

Nutritional Info: Calories: 308 || Total Fat: 18g || Total Carbohydrates: 5g || Sugar: 2g || Fiber: 2g || Protein: 36g || Sodium: 545mg

ROCKFISH CURRY

Time To Prepare: 15 minutes

Time to Cook: thirty minutes

Yield: Servings 8

Ingredients:

- ¼ cup water
- ¾ teaspoon ground turmeric, divided
- 1 (½-inch) piece fresh ginger, minced
- 1 teaspoon apple cider vinegar
- 1½ (14-ounce) cans coconut milk, divided
- 12 pearl onions, halved
- 2 medium red onions, cut thinly
- 2 pound rockfish
- 2 Serrano peppers halved
- 2 tablespoons coconut oil
- 40 small leaves, divided
- Freshly ground black pepper, to taste
- Salt, to taste

Directions:

1. In a container, flavor the fish with ¼ teaspoon of the turmeric and salt and keep aside.
2. In a huge frying pan, melt coconut oil on moderate heat.

3. Put in pearl onions, red onions, ginger, Serrano peppers, and 20 curry leaves and sauté for approximately fifteen minutes.
4. Put in ginger, remaining turmeric, salt, and black pepper and sauté for approximately 2 minutes.
5. Move half of the mixture into a container and keep aside.
6. Put in remaining curry leaves, fish fillets, water, and 1 can of coconut milk and cook for approximately 2 minutes.
7. Now cook, covered for approximately five minutes.
8. Put in apple cider vinegar and remaining half can of coconut milk and cook for approximately three to five minutes or till done completely.
9. Serve hot with the topping of reserved onion mixture.

Nutritional Info: Calories: 331 kcal ‖ Protein: 24.72 g ‖ Fat: 18.38 g ‖ Carbohydrates: 18.83 g

ROSEMARY-LEMON COD

Time To Prepare: five minutes

Time to Cook: ten minutes

Yield: Servings 4

Ingredients:

- ½ tsp. Ground black pepper, or more to taste
- ½ tsp. Sea Salt
- 1 Lemon Juice
- 1 tbsp. Fresh Rosemary Leaves, chopped
- 1½ pound Cod, Skin and Bone Removed, cut into 4 fillets
- 2 tbsp. Extra Virgin Olive Oil

Directions:

1. In a huge nonstick frying pan at moderate to high heat, heat the olive oil until it shimmers.
2. Flavour the cod with the rosemary, pepper, and salt. Place the fish to the frying pan and cook for three to five minutes per side until opaque.
3. Pour the lemon juice over the cod fillets and cook for a minute.

Nutritional Info: Calories: 246 || Total Fat: 9g || Total Carbohydrates: 1g || Sugar: 1g || Fiber: 1g || Protein: 39g || Sodium: 370mg

SALMON AND CAULIFLOWER

Time To Prepare: ten minutes

Time to Cook: twenty-five minutes

Yield: Servings 4

Ingredients:

- 1 big red onion, cut into wedges
- 1 cauliflower head, florets separated and chopped
- 1 tablespoon olive oil
- 2 tablespoons coconut aminos
- 4 pieces salmon fillets, skinless
- Pinch black pepper
- Pinch of sea salt

Directions:

1. Place the salmon in a baking dish, put the oil all over, and season with salt and pepper. Put in preheated broiler on moderate heat and cook for approximately five minutes. Put in coconut aminos, cauliflower, and onion, then place in your oven and bake at 400 degrees F for fifteen minutes more. Split between plates before you serve.
2. Enjoy!

Nutritional Info: Calories 112 || Fat: 5 || Fiber: 3 || Carbs: 8 || Protein: 7

SALMON AND COCONUT MIX

Time To Prepare: ten minutes

Time to Cook: 20 minutes

Yield: Servings 4

Ingredients:

- ¼ cup coconut cream

- ¼ cup lime juice
- ½ cup coconut, unsweetened and shredded
- 1 tsp. lime zest, grated
- 2 tsp. Cajun seasoning
- 3 tbsp. avocado mayonnaise
- 4 salmon fillets, boneless
- A pinch of salt
- Pinch of black pepper

Directions:

1. Set the instant pot on Sauté mode, put the coconut cream and the remaining ingredients apart from the fish, mix and cook for minimum five minutes.
2. Put in the fish, set the lid on, and cook on High for minimum ten minutes.
3. Release the pressure for about ten minutes, split the salmon and sauce between plates before you serve.

Nutritional Info: Calories 306 ‖ Fat: 17.5 ‖ Fiber: 1.4 ‖ Carbohydrates: 2.5 ‖ Protein: 25.3

SALMON AND ROASTED PEPPERS

Time To Prepare: five minutes

Time to Cook: twenty-five minutes

Yield: Servings 4

Ingredients:

- ¼ cup chicken stock
- 1 cup red peppers, cut into strips
- 1 tablespoon cilantro, chopped
- 1 yellow onion, chopped
- 2 tablespoons olive oil
- 4 salmon fillets, boneless
- Pinch black pepper
- Pinch of sea salt

Directions:

1. Warm a pan with the oil on moderate to high heat; put in the onion and sauté for five minutes.
2. Place the fish and cook for minimum five minutes on each side.
3. Put in the remaining ingredients, introduce the pan in your oven, and cook at 390 degrees F for about ten minutes.
4. Split the mix between plates before you serve.

Nutritional Info: Calories 265 || Fat: 7 || Fiber: 5 || Carbs: 15 || Protein: 16

SALMON AND SHRIMP MIX

Time To Prepare: five minutes

Time to Cook: 20 minutes

Yield: Servings 4

Ingredients:

- ½ cup chicken stock
- 1 pound shrimp, peeled and deveined
- 1 teaspoon Cajun seasoning
- 2 tablespoons olive oil
- 2 tablespoons tomato passata
- 4 salmon fillets, boneless
- A pinch of salt and black pepper
- Juice of 1 lemon

Directions:

1. Set the instant pot on Sauté mode, put the oil, heat it, put in the remaining ingredients apart from the salmon and shrimp and cook for about three minutes.
2. Put in the salmon and cook for a couple of minutes on each side.
3. Place the shrimp, set the lid on, and cook on High for about ten minutes.
4. Release the pressure fast for five minutes, split the mix between plates before you serve.

Nutritional Info: Calories 393 || Fat: 20 || Fiber: 0.1 || Carbohydrates: 2.2 || Protein: 25

SALMON BALLS

Time To Prepare: five minutes

Time to Cook: 13 minutes

Yield: Servings 2

Ingredients:

- ½ cup heavy cream
- ½ tsp dried cilantro
- ½ tsp ginger powder
- ½ tsp paprika
- 1 avocado
- 1 can of tuna
- 1 egg
- 1 garlic clove
- 2 tbsp. keto mayo
- 2 tbsp. lemon juice
- 2 tbsp. water
- 3 tbsp. coconut oil
- Salt and ground black pepper to taste

Directions:

1. Drain the salmon, cut it
2. Mince the garlic clove, peel the avocado
3. In a container, mix the fish, mayo, egg, and garlic, sprinkle with salt, paprika, and ginger, mix thoroughly
4. Make 4 balls of it
5. Warm the oil in a frying pan at moderate heat
6. Place the balls and fry for 4-6 minutes each side
7. In the meantime, put the heavy cream, avocado, cilantro, lemon juice, and 1 tablespoon of oil in a blender. Pulse thoroughly
8. Serve the balls with the sauce

Nutritional Info: Carbohydrates: 3,9 g || Fat: 50 g || Protein: 20,1 g || Calories: 555

SALMON CAKES

Time To Prepare: ten minutes

Time to Cook: ten minutes

Yield: Servings 2

Ingredients:

- 1 big egg
- 1 tbsp. Dijon mustard
- 1 tbsp. ghee butter
- 2 tbsp. pork rinds
- 3 tbsp. keto mayo
- 6 oz. canned salmon
- Salt and ground black pepper to taste

Directions:

1. In a container, mix the salmon (drained), pork rinds, egg, and half of the mayo, sprinkle with salt and pepper. Mix thoroughly
2. With the salmon mixture, form the cakes
3. Heat the ghee butter in a frying pan on moderate to high heat
4. Put the salmon cakes in the frying pan and cook for approximately 3 minutes per side. Moved to a paper towel to get rid of surplus fat
5. In a small container, mix the rest of the half of mayo and the Dijon mustard, mix thoroughly
6. Serve the salmon cakes with the mayo-mustard sauce

Nutritional Info: Carbohydrates: 1,2 g || Fat: 31 g || Protein: 24,2 g || Calories: 370

SALMON CEVICHE

Time To Prepare: ten minutes +20 resting time

Time to Cook: 0 minutes

Yield: Servings 4

Ingredients:

- ¼ cup Fresh Cilantro Leaves, chopped
- ½ cup Fresh squeezed lime juice
- ½ tsp. Sea Salt

- 1 Jalapeno Pepper, seeded and diced
- 1 pound Salmon, skinless & boneless, cut into bite-size pieces
- 2 tbsp. Extra Virgin Olive Oil
- 2 Tomatoes, diced

Directions:

1. In a moderate-sized container, put and mix together the salmon and lime juice. Allow it to marinate for about twenty minutes.
2. Mix in the tomatoes, cilantro, jalapeño, olive oil, and salt.

Nutritional Info: Calories: 222 || Total Fat: 14g || Total Carbohydrates: 3g || Sugar: 2g || Fiber: 1g || Protein: 23g || Sodium: 288mg

SALMON CROQUETTES

Time To Prepare: 8 minutes

Time to Cook: seven minutes

Yield: Servings 4

Ingredients:

- ⅓ cup olive oil
- ½ bunch parsley, chopped
- 1 cup keto-friendly bread crumbs
- 1 lb. can red salmon, drained and mashed
- 2 eggs, beaten

Directions:

1. Preheat the Air Fryer to 400°F.
2. In a mixing container, mix the drained salmon, eggs, and parsley.
3. In a shallow dish, mix together the bread crumbs and oil to blend well.
4. Mold equal-sized amounts of the mixture into little balls and coat each one with bread crumbs.
5. Place the croquettes in the fryer's basket and air fry for seven minutes.

Nutritional Info: Calories: 442 kcal || Protein: 30.48 g || Fat: 32.64 g || Carbohydrates: 5.31 g

SALMON PATTIES

Time To Prepare: five minutes

Time to Cook: 15 minutes

Yield: Servings 4

Ingredients:

- ½ tsp. garlic powder
- 1 egg
- 14 oz. canned salmon, drained
- 2 tbsp. mayonnaise
- 4 tbsp. cup cornmeal
- 4 tbsp. keto almond flour
- 4 tbsp. Onion, minced
- Salt and pepper to taste

Directions:

1. Flake apart the salmon using a fork.
2. Place the flakes in a container and mix with the garlic powder, mayonnaise, keto almond flour, cornmeal, egg, onion, pepper, and salt.
3. Use your hands to shape equivalent portions of the mixture into little patties and put each one in the Air Fryer basket.
4. Air fry the salmon patties at 350°F for fifteen minutes. Serve hot.

Nutritional Info: Calories:

SALMON ROLLS

Time To Prepare: 15 minutes

Time to Cook: ten minutes

Yield: Servings 3

Ingredients:

- ½ cup cream cheese
- ½ tsp garlic, minced
- 1 oz. walnuts, crushed

- 1 tbsp. butter
- 1 tbsp. dill
- 1 tbsp. oregano
- 1 tsp cilantro
- 1 tsp nutmeg
- 1 tsp salt
- 10 oz. smoked salmon, cut

Directions:

1. In a moderate-sized container, using a mixer, put butter and cream cheese, then stir until smooth and fluffy.
2. Put in oregano, cilantro, salt, dill, garlic, and walnuts, stir cautiously.
3. Put in nutmeg and stir until you get homogenous mass.
4. Put this cream mixture on each salmon slice and roll them.
5. Put salmon rolls in your refrigerator and wait for about ten minutes.
6. Take out rolls from the refrigerator before you serve.

Nutritional Info: Calories 349 || Carbs: 3.98g || Fat: 26.9g || Protein: 23.1g

SALMON SKEWERS IN CURED HAM

Time To Prepare: ten minutes

Time to Cook: 15 minutes

Yield: Servings 4

Ingredients:

- 1 tbsp. l Olive oil
- 100 g dried ham cut
- 225 ml mayonnaise
- 450 g salmon
- 60 ml finely chopped fresh basil
- 8 pcs wooden skewers
- Innings
- Salmon Skewers
- salt black pepper

Directions:

1. Soak the skewers in water.
2. Finely cut fresh basil.
3. Cut salmon fillet into rectangular pieces and fasten on skewers.
4. Roll each kebab in the basil and pepper.
5. Chop the cured ham into thin slices and wrap her every kebab.
6. Lubricate with olive oil and fry on in a pan, grill, or in your oven.
7. Serve with mayonnaise or salad

Nutritional Info: Carbohydrates: 1 g || Fat: 62 g || Protein: 28 g || Calories: 680

SALMON SUSHI

Time To Prepare: thirty minutes

Time to Cook: 20 minutes

Yield: Servings 26

Ingredients:

- ½ tablespoons rice vinegar
- ½ teaspoons sugar
- 1 ½ cups water
- 1 cup of sushi rice
- 1 teaspoon salt
- 4 nori seaweed sheets
- 4 ounces smoked salmon
- Optional: low-sodium soy sauce or wasabi paste.

Directions:

1. Using a pot with a lid, bring water to its boiling point. Mix rice, cover, and lessen the temperature.
2. Simmer eighteen to twenty minutes, remove the heat, and leave the rice to cool for about ten minutes. Put the rice in a container and dampen with vinegar, salt, and sugar. Blend using a wooden spoon, and let the rice stand. Chop smoked salmon into strips.
3. Make each sushi roll as follows:
4. Put 1 seaweed layer on a clean, dry surface.

5. Put ½ cup cooked rice over the seaweed, and delicately spread uniformly over the sheet. Place the strips of salmon in a perpendicular line in the middle of the rice.
6. Delicately roll so as not to rip the seaweed, beginning at the left edge, and ending just before the right edge — Tuck rice in at the sides of the roll.
7. Run a damp finger along the exhibited edge of the seaweed, and conclude rolling, pushing down to secure the border to the roll.
8. Cut into pieces using a cutting knife.

Nutritional Info: Calories: 25 kcal || Protein: 1.78 g || Fat: 1.49 g || Carbohydrates: 2.33 g

SALMON WITH MUSTARD CREAM

Time To Prepare: ten minutes

Time to Cook: twelve minutes

Yield: Servings 2

Ingredients:

- ¼ cup keto mayo
- ½ tsp garlic powder
- 1 tbsp. Dijon mustard
- 2 salmon fillets
- 2 tbsp. fresh cilantro, minced
- 2 tbsp. ghee butter
- Salt and pepper to taste

Directions:

1. Preheat your oven to 450F. Grease a baking dish with the ghee butter
2. Flavour the salmon with salt and pepper and put in the baking dish
3. In a mixing container, put and mix the Dijon mustard, mayo, parsley, and garlic powder. Stir thoroughly
4. Top the salmon fillets with the mustard sauce
5. Bake for about ten minutes

Nutritional Info: Carbohydrates: 2 g || Fat: 41,5 g || Protein: 32,9 g || Calories: 505

SARDINE CASSEROLE

Time To Prepare: 15 minutes

Time to Cook: forty minutes

Yield: Servings 4

Ingredients:

- .5 lbs. Cherry tomatoes, diced
- 1 cloves Garlic, chopped
- 1 lb. Russet potatoes
- 1 tbsp. Basil
- 17.5 oz. Sardines
- 2 tbsp. Bread crumbs
- 3 tbsp. Coconut oil

Directions:

1. Put in the potatoes to a pot before covering them with salted water and letting the pot boil.
2. Once it boils, turn the heat to low/medium before placing a lid on it and letting the potatoes cook for about twenty minutes.
3. Drain the potatoes and cover them in cold water to allow them to cool.
4. Slice and peel the potatoes.
5. Ensure the oven is heated to 350F.
6. Put in the coconut oil to a casserole and coat well.
7. Alternate layers of potato and layers of sardine, putting in the tomatoes to the sardine layers. Top with bread crumbs, basil, and garlic.
8. Allow the casserole cook for about twenty minutes, serve hot, and enjoy.

Nutritional Info: Calories: 553 kcal || Protein: 37.22 g || Fat: 26.88 g || Carbohydrates: 40.95 g

---

SARDINE FRITTERS

Time To Prepare: twenty-five minutes

Time to Cook: thirty-five minutes

Yield: Servings 6

Ingredients:

- ¼ cup spinach, chopped roughly
- ½ tbsp. ground ginger
- 1 tsp cilantro
- 1 tsp salt
- 2 lbs. sardines, minced
- 2 tbsp. butter
- 3 tbsp. fish stock
- 4 tbsp. coconut milk

Directions:

1. In a container, mix sardines, salt, cilantro, and ginger. Stir gently.
2. Put spinach in a blender and blend for a minute.
3. Put in spinach in sardine mixture and mix thoroughly.
4. Shape fish mixture into balls and flatten them.
5. Heat pan on moderate heat and melt butter.
6. Put fish fritters on a pan and fry for a couple of minutes on one side.
7. Flip on the other side; pour in fish stock and coconut milk.
8. Then secure the lid and simmer fritters for about ten minutes.
9. Serve hot.

Nutritional Info: Calories 369 || Carbs: 1g || Fat: 24g || Protein: 38g

SEAFOOD NOODLES

Time To Prepare: ten minutes

Time to Cook: 20 minutes

Yield: Servings 2

Ingredients:

- ½ Lemon Juice
- ½ pack of watercress
- 10 clean prawns
- 150g of dried tomatoes
- 200g mussel without shell
- 200g shell-less volley

- 300g of clean squid cut into rings
- 4 cloves garlic, minced
- 500g of pre-cooked noodles
- black pepper to taste
- Braised olive oil
- parsley to taste
- salt to taste

Directions:

1. In olive oil, sauté the garlic and put in the squid, the mussel, the shrimp, and the shrimp.
2. Place the dried tomatoes and sprinkle with salt and pepper.
3. Put in the noodles, watercress, flavor with lemon juice, and parsley.

Nutritional Info: Calories: 2049 kcal || Protein: 56.21 g || Fat: 143.36 g || Carbohydrates: 139.98 g

SEAFOOD PAELLA

Time To Prepare: ten minutes

Time to Cook: 15 minutes

Yield: Servings 2

Ingredients:

- ½ chopped green peppers
- ½ chopped red peppers
- ½ chopped yellow pepper
- ½ packet of chopped parsley
- 1 chopped onion
- 2 cloves minced garlic + 4 whole cloves garlic in shell
- 2 packets of turmeric dissolved in 1.2 liters of fish stock
- 200g of frozen pea
- 4 units pre-cooked whole prawn
- 400g of cut cooked octopus
- 400g of pre-cooked shrimp
- 400g of the pump or parboiled rice

- 400g squid in rings
- 500g mussel
- Black pepper to taste
- Chilies to garnish
- Extra virgin olive oil
- Lemon juice
- Salt to taste

Directions:

1. In olive oil, sauté onion, garlic, peppers, and rice.
2. Put in the octopus, the squid, and half the broth. Adjust salt and pepper.
3. As the liquid dries, put in more broth taking care of the rice point.
4. When the stock is nearly fully dry, put in the shrimp and the pea.
5. Put in the mussels and parsley.
6. Position peppers on top for decoration and prawns
7. Allow it to cook for fifteen minutes with the pan covered.
8. Finish with lemon juice and olive oil.

Nutritional Info: Calories: 1468 kcal ‖ Protein: 177.19 g ‖ Fat: 28.65 g ‖ Carbohydrates: 115.89 g

SEARED AHI TUNA

Time To Prepare: ten minutes

Time to Cook: 15 minutes

Yield: Servings 2

Ingredients:

- 1 clove garlic, minced
- 1 green onion (scallion) thinly cut, reserve a few slices for decoration
- 1 tbsp. of grated fresh ginger
- 1 tsp. lime juice
- 2 (4-ounces each) ahi tuna steaks (3/4-inch thick)
- 2 tbsp. dark sesame oil
- 2 tbsp. soy sauce

Directions:

1. Start by preparing the marinade. In a small container, put together the sesame oil, soy sauce, fresh ginger, minced garlic, green onion, and lime juice. Mix thoroughly.
2. Put tuna steaks into a sealable Ziploc freezer bag and pour marinade over the top of the tuna. Seal bag and shake or massage with hands to coat tuna steaks well with marinade. Bring the bag in a container, in case of breaks, and place tuna in your fridge to marinate for minimum ten minutes.
3. Put a big non-stick frying pan over moderate to high to high heat. Allow the pan heat for a couple of minutes, when hot, remove tuna steaks from the marinade and place them in the pan to sear for 1-1½ minutes on each side.
4. Remove tuna steaks from pan and slice into ¼-inch thick slices. Decorate using a drizzle of cut green onion. Serve instantly.

Nutritional Info: Calories: 213 kcal ‖ Protein: 4.5 g ‖ Fat: 19.55 g ‖ Carbohydrates: 5.2 g

SESAME GINGER SALMON

Time To Prepare: ten minutes

Time to Cook: 20 minutes

Yield: Servings 2

Ingredients:

- 2 tbsp. White wine
- 2 tsp. Sesame oil
- 1 tbsp. Rice vinegar
- 2 tbsp. Keto-friendly soy sauce substitute
- 1 tbsp. Sugar-free ketchup
- 1 tbsp. Fish sauce – Red Boat
- 1-2 tsp. Minced ginger
- 1-10 oz. Salmon fillet

Directions:

1. Mix all fixings in a plastic canister with a tight-fitting lid (omit the ketchup, oil, and wine for now). Marinade them for approximately 1o to fifteen minutes.

2. On the stovetop, prepare a frying pan using the high-heat temperature setting. Pour in the oil. Put in the fish when it's hot, skin side down.
3. Brown each side for three to five minutes.
4. Pour in the marinated juices to the pan to simmer when the fish is flipped. Position the fish on two dinner plates.
5. Pour in the wine and ketchup to the pan and simmer five minutes until it's reduced. Serve with a vegetable.

Nutritional Info: Calories: 370 ‖ Net Carbohydrates: 2.5 g ‖ Total Fat: Content: 24 g ‖ Protein: 33 g

SESAME-TUNA SKEWERS

Time To Prepare: ten minutes

Time to Cook: 15 minutes

Yield: Servings 6

Ingredients:

- ¼ tsp. Ground black pepper.
- ½ tsp. Ground ginger.
- ¾ c. sesame seeds
- 1 tsp. Salt
- 2 tbsps. toasted sesame oil
- 6 oz. cubed thick tuna steaks
- Cooking spray

Directions:

1. Preheat your oven to approximately 4000F.
2. Coat a rimmed baking tray with cooking spray.
3. Soak twelve wooden skewers in water
4. In a small mixing container, mix pepper, ground ginger, salt, and sesame seeds.
5. In another container, toss the tuna with sesame oil.
6. Push the oiled cubes into a sesame seed mixture and put the cubes on each skewer.
7. Place the skewers on a readily readied baking tray and put the tray into the preheated oven.
8. Bake for about twelve minutes and turn once.

9. Serve and enjoy.

Nutritional Info: Calories: 196 kcal || Protein: 14.47 g || Fat: 15.01 g || Carbohydrates: 2.48 g

---

SHERRY AND BUTTER PRAWNS

Time To Prepare: five minutes

Time to Cook: five minutes

Yield: Servings 4

Ingredients:

- ½ stick butter, at room temperature
- ½ teaspoon mustard seeds
- 1 ½ pounds king prawns, peeled and deveined
- 1 ½ tablespoons fresh lemon juice
- 1 tablespoon garlic paste
- 1 teaspoon cayenne pepper, crushed
- 1 teaspoon dried basil
- 2 tablespoons dry sherry

Directions:

1. Whisk the dry sherry with cayenne pepper, garlic paste, basil, mustard seeds, lemon juice and prawns. Allow it to marinate for an hour in your fridge.
2. In a frying pan, melt the butter over moderate to high flame, coating with the reserved marinade.
3. Drizzle with salt and pepper to taste.

Nutritional Info: 294 Calories 14.3g || Fat: 3.6g || Carbs: 34.6g || Protein: 1.4g Fiber

---

SHRIMP AND BEETS

Time To Prepare: ten minutes

Time to Cook: ten minutes

Yield: Servings 4

Ingredients:

- 1 beet, peeled and cubed
- 1 pound shrimp, peeled and deveined
- 1 tablespoon lemon juice
- 1 teaspoon coconut aminos
- 2 garlic cloves, minced
- 2 spring onions, chopped
- 2 tablespoons avocado oil
- Pinch of black pepper
- Pinch of sea salt

Directions:

1. Warm a pan with the oil on moderate to high heat, put in the spring onions and the garlic and sauté for a couple of minutes.
2. Put in the shrimp and the other ingredients, toss, cook the mix for eight minutes, split into bowls before you serve.

Nutritional Info: Calories 281 || Fat: 6 || Fiber: 7 || Carbs: 11 || Protein: 8

SHRIMP AND BLACK BEANS ENCHALADA

Time To Prepare: five minutes

Time to Cook: 15 minutes

Yield: Servings 4

Ingredients:

- 1 lb. shrimp
- 2 cans (10 g) of red or green enchilada sauce
- 2 cans (fifteen oz.) black beans
- 2 cups grated Mexican cheese mixture
- twelve to thirteen small flour tortillas

Directions:

1. Preheat your oven to 400° F. Put ¼ cup sauce (enchiladas) in a deep cooking pan. Raise the heat and put in the shrimp. Cook until the shrimp are clean and no longer transparent for approximately five minutes. Turn off the heated container.

2. Put the enchiladas in a 9 x 13-inch baking dish. Organize a pea breakfast, 3 or 4 shrimp, and a slice of cheese on an omelet. Fold the tortilla edges into the oven dish on the filling and with the seam facing down.
3. Repeat with the rest of the tortillas. Pour out the remaining enchilada sauce after preparing all the enchiladas.
4. Bake until all the cheese has melted for fifteen minutes.

Nutritional Info: Calories: 196 || Fat: 12g || Net Carbohydrates: 4g || Protein: 17g

SHRIMP AND CORN

Time To Prepare: five minutes

Time to Cook: ten minutes

Yield: Servings 4

Ingredients:

- ½ cup veggie stock
- 1 bunch parsley, chopped
- 1 cup corn
- 1 pound shrimp, peeled and deveined
- 2 garlic cloves, minced
- 2 tablespoons olive oil
- Juice of 1 lime
- Pinch of black pepper
- Pinch of sea salt

Directions:

1. Warm a pan with the oil on moderate to high heat, then put the garlic and the corn and sauté for a couple of minutes.
2. Put in the shrimp and the other ingredients, toss, cook everything for eight minutes more, split between plates before you serve.

Nutritional Info: Calories: 343 kcal || Protein: 29.12 g || Fat: 10.97 g || Carbohydrates: 34.25 g

SHRIMP PIE

Time To Prepare: **15** minutes

Time to Cook: thirty-five minutes

Yield: Servings 4-8

Ingredients:

- ¼ cup sour cream
- 1 gem
- 1 minced finger pepper
- 1 teaspoon salt
- 1 tomato without skin and without chopped seed
- 2 cloves garlic, minced
- 2 tbsp. chopped cilantro
- 2 tbsp. coconut milk
- 2 tbsp. olive oil
- 200g of unsalted cold butter
- 250g of flour
- 3 tbsp. water
- 400g peeled clean shrimp
- salt

Directions:

1. Put the flour in a container then put in the diced butter.
2. Knead with fingertips until crumbly.
3. Put in salt and, progressively, water until it turns into dough. Cover with plastic and place in your fridge for an hour.
4. Heat a frying pan, drizzle with olive oil and brown the garlic and prawns.
5. Put in the tomatoes, sauté for about 2 minutes, then put in coconut milk and pepper and cook for an extra two minutes.
6. Sprinkle with salt, put in the cream, remove the heat and put in the cilantro. Set aside to cool.
7. To open the dough in portions and cover the pancakes, stuff with the shrimp, and cover with a circle of dough.
8. Brush with the yolk , preheat your oven and bake at 180 degrees for approximately 30 minutes or until a golden-brown color is achieved.

Nutritional Info: **Calories: 344 kcal || Protein: 15.6 g || Fat: 19.79 g || Carbohydrates: 25.33 g**

SHRIMP RISOTTO

Time To Prepare: ten minutes

Time to Cook: 15 minutes

Yield: Servings 4

Ingredients:

- ½ lemon
- 12 oz. cauli rice
- 14 oz. shrimps, peeled and deveined
- 2 tbsp. coconut oil
- 3 tbsp. ghee butter
- 4 button mushrooms
- 4 stalks green onion
- Salt and black pepper to taste

Directions:

1. Preheat your oven to 400F
2. Place a layer of cauli rice on a sheet pan, sprinkle with salt and spices; drizzle the coconut oil over it
3. Bake using your oven for about ten minutes
4. Chop the green onion, slice up the mushrooms and remove the rind from the lemon
5. Heat the ghee butter in a frying pan on moderate heat. Put in the shrimps; season it and sauté for about five minutes
6. Top the cauli rice with the shrimps, drizzle the green onion over it

Nutritional Info: **Carbohydrates: 9,2 g || Fat: 26,2 g || Protein: 25 g || Calories: 363**

SHRIMP RISSOLES

Time To Prepare: ten minutes

Time to Cook: thirty minutes

Yield: Servings 4

Ingredients:

- ½ diced onion
- ½ packet of chopped parsley
- 1 tbsp. olive oil
- 100 g of curd
- 2 tbsp. tomato extract
- 250ml of milk
- 250ml of water
- 3 beaten eggs
- 3 cups flour
- 400g of shrimp
- 50g of butter
- Breadcrumbs for breading
- Salt to taste

Directions:

1. Sauté with olive oil, onion, and shrimp.
2. Put in tomato extract, parsley, and salt. Reserve.
3. In a pan, bring to moderate heat water, milk and butter.
4. When the butter has melted, put in 2 cups of wheat flour at a time and stir until the dough starts to unglue from the bottom of the pan. Set aside until warm.
5. When the dough is warm, knead, putting in the rest of the flour until it is smooth and elastic.
6. Roll the dough into a floured surface.
7. The format in circular portions.
8. Stuff with the shrimp and position a spoonful of curd. Close by tightening the ends.
9. Immerse into beaten egg, breadcrumbs, and fry in hot oil until a golden-brown color is achieved.

Nutritional Info: Calories: 736 kcal || Protein: 42.45 g || Fat: 26.71 g || Carbohydrates: 78.58 g

---

SHRIMP SCAMPI

Time To Prepare: ten minutes

Time to Cook: 15 minutes

Yield: Servings 4

Ingredients:

- ⅛ tsp. Freshly Ground Black Pepper
- ¼ cup Extra Olive Oil
- ½ tsp. Sea Salt
- 1 Onion, Finely Chopped
- 1 Red Bell Pepper, Chopped
- 1½ Pound Shrimp, Peeled and Tails Removed
- 2 Lemon Juices
- 2 Lemon Zest
- 6 Garlic Cloves, Minced

Directions:

1. In a huge nonstick frying pan on moderate to high heat, warm the olive oil until it shimmers.
2. Put in the onion and red bell pepper. Cook for approximately 6 minutes, once in a while stirring, until tender.
3. Put in the shrimp and cook for approximately five minutes until pink.
4. Put in the garlic. Cook for half a minute, stirring continuously.
5. Put in the lemon juice and zest, salt, and pepper. Simmer for about three minutes.

Nutritional Info: Calories: 345 || Total Fat: 16 || Total Carbohydrates: 10g || Sugar: 3g || Fiber: 1g || Protein: 40g || Sodium: 424mg

SHRIMP WITH CINNAMON SAUCE

Time To Prepare: ten minutes

Time to Cook: ten minutes

Yield: Servings 4

Ingredients:

- ¼ tsp. Freshly Ground Black Pepper
- ½ tsp. Sea Salt
- 1 cup No Salt Added Chicken Broth
- 1 tsp. Ground Cinnamon

- 1 tsp. Onion Powder
- 1½ Pound Peeled Shrimp
- 2 tbsp. Dijon Mustard
- 2 tbsp. Extra Virgin Olive Oil

Directions:

1. In a huge nonstick frying pan at moderate to high heat, heat the olive oil until it shimmers.
2. Put in the shrimp. Cook for minimum 4 minutes, once in a while stirring, until the shrimp appears opaque.
3. In a small container, whisk the mustard, chicken broth, cinnamon, onion powder, salt, and pepper. Pour this into the frying pan and carry on cooking for about three minutes, stirring once in a while.

Nutritional Info: Calories: 270 || Total Fat: 11g || Total Carbohydrates: 4g || Sugar: 1g || Fiber: 1g || Protein: 39g || Sodium: 664mg

SHRIMP WITH SPICY SPINACH

Time To Prepare: ten minutes

Time to Cook: 15 minutes

Yield: Servings 4

Ingredients:

- ⅛ tsp. Freshly ground black pepper
- ¼ cup Extra Olive Oil. divided
- ½ cup Freshly Squeezed Orange Juice
- 1 tbsp. Sriracha Sauce
- 1 tsp. Sea Salt, divided
- 1½ Pound Peeled Shrimp
- 4 cups Baby fresh Spinach
- 6 Garlic cloves, minced

Directions:

1. In a huge nonstick frying pan on moderate to high heat, heat 2 tablespoons of the olive oil until it shimmers.

2. Put in the shrimp and ½ teaspoon salt. Cook for minimum 4 minutes, once in a while stirring, until the shrimp are pink. Move the shrimp to a plate, tent with aluminium foil to keep warm, and save for later.
3. Put back the frying pan to the heat and heat the rest of the 2 tablespoons of olive oil until it shimmers.
4. Put in the spinach. Cook for about three minutes, stirring.
5. Put in the garlic. Cook for half a minute, stirring continuously.
6. In a small container, put and combine the orange juice, Sriracha, remaining ½ teaspoon of salt, and pepper. Put in this to the spinach and cook for about three minutes. Serve the shrimp with the spinach on the side.

Nutritional Info: Calories: 317 || Total Fat: 16 || Total Carbohydrates: 7g || Sugar: 3 || Fiber: 1g || Protein: 38g || Sodium: 911mg

---

SIMPLE FOUNDER IN BROWN BUTTER LEMON SAUCE

Time To Prepare: ten minutes

Time to Cook: ten minutes

Yield: Servings 4

Ingredients:

For the Sauce:

- ½ cup unsalted grass-fed butter, cut into pieces
- Freshly ground black pepper, for seasoning
- Juice of 1 lemon
- Sea salt, for seasoning

For the Fish:

1. 4 (4-ounce) boneless flounder fillets
2. Sea salt, for seasoning
3. Freshly ground black pepper, for seasoning
4. ¼ cup almond flour
5. 2 tablespoons good-quality olive oil
6. 1 tablespoon chopped fresh parsley

Directions:

1. To make the Sauce:
2. Brown the butter. In a moderate-sized deep cooking pan at moderate heat, cook the butter, stirring it once in a while, until it is golden brown, minimum 4 minutes.
3. Finish the sauce. Take away the deep cooking pan from the heat and mix in the lemon juice. Spice the sauce with salt and pepper and set it aside.
4. To make a Fish: Flavour the fish. Pat the fish fillets dry then spice them lightly with salt and pepper. Ladle the almond flour onto a plate, then roll the fish fillets through the flour until they are lightly coated. Cook the fish. In a big frying pan at moderate to high heat, warm the olive oil. Put in the fish fillets and fry them until they are crunchy and golden on both sides, two to three minutes per side and serve. Moved the fish to a serving plate and sprinkle with the sauce. Top with the parsley and serve it hot.

Nutritional Info: Calories: 389 Total fat: 33g Total carbs: 1g || Fiber: 0g Net carbs: 1g || Sodium: 256mg || Protein: 22g

SIMPLE SQUID STEW

Time To Prepare: 15 minutes

Time to Cook: twenty-five minutes

Yield: Servings 4

Ingredients:

- ¼ cup olive oil
- 1 cup cabbage, shredded
- 1 moderate-sized yellow bell pepper, cut
- 1 small onion, finely chopped
- 2 cups cherry tomatoes, diced
- 3 cups fish stock
- 7 oz. shrimps, cleaned
- 7 oz. squid rings, defrosted

Spices:

- ½ tsp dried oregano
- 1 tsp rosemary powder
- 1 tsp stevia powder

- 2 tsp pink Himalayan salt

Directions:

1. Grease the inside of the pot with olive oil and heat up on the "Sauté" mode. Put onions and stir-fry until translucent. Put in bell pepper and sprinkle with salt. Stir and cook for a couple of minutes more.
2. Mix in tomatoes and pour ¼ cup of the stock. Cook until the liquid evaporates and press the "Cancel" button.
3. Put the remaining ingredients and flavor with oregano, rosemary, and stevia powder. Stir thoroughly and secure the lid.
4. Put the steam release handle to the "Sealing" position, then press the "Manual" button then set the timer for around twenty minutes on high pressure.
5. When done, perform a quick release and open the lid. Split between serving plates and optionally drizzle a parmesan.
6. Serve instantly.

Nutritional Info: Calories 279|| Total Fats 15.8g || Net Carbohydrates: 8.4g || Protein: 24.5g || Fiber: 2.3g

SOLE WITH VEGETABLES

Time To Prepare: ten minutes

Time to Cook: 15 minutes

Yield: Servings 4

Ingredients:

- ½ c. divided vegetable broth
- 1 thinly cut and divided carrot
- 1 thinly cut and divided zucchini
- 2 cut and thinly divided shallots
- 2 tbsps. divided snipped fresh chives
- 4 tsp. divided extra-virgin olive oil
- 5 oz. sole fillets
- Ground black pepper
- Lemon wedges
- Salt

Directions:

1. Preheat your oven to approximately 4250F.
2. Separate the aluminium foil into moderate-sized pieces
3. Place a fillet on one half of the aluminium foil piece and put in seasonings
4. Put in shallots, zucchini, and ¼ each of the carrot on top of the fillet. Drizzle with 1 ½ teaspoon of chives
5. Sprinkle 2 tablespoons of broth and a tablespoon of olive oil over the fish and vegetables
6. Seal to make a packet and put the packet on a big baking tray.
7. Repeat for the remaining ingredients and make more packets
8. Place the sheet in a preheated oven and bake the packets for fifteen minutes
9. Peel back the foil and put the contents with the liquid onto a serving plate.
10. Decorate using lemon wedges and serve.

Nutritional Info: Calories: 130 kcal ‖ Protein: 9.94 g ‖ Fat: 7.96 g ‖ Carbohydrates: 4.92 g

SOUVLAKI SPICED SALMON BOWLS

Time To Prepare: ten minutes

Time to Cook: 20 minutes

Yield: Servings 4

Ingredients:

For the Salmon:

- ¼ cup good-quality olive oil
- ¼ teaspoon freshly ground black pepper
- ½ teaspoon sea salt
- 1 tablespoon balsamic vinegar
- 1 tablespoon minced garlic
- 1 tablespoon smoked sweet paprika
- 2 tablespoons chopped fresh oregano
- 4 (4-ounce) salmon fillets
- Juice of 1 lemon

For the Bowls:

- ½ cup cut Kalamata olives
- ½ cup sour cream
- 1 big tomato, chopped
- 1 cucumber, diced
- 1 red bell pepper, cut into strips
- 1 yellow bell pepper, cut into strips
- 1 zucchini, cut into ½-inch strips along the length
- 2 tablespoons good-quality olive oil
- 6 ounces feta cheese, crumbled

Directions:

To make the Salmon:

1. Marinate the fish. In a moderate-sized container, put and mix the olive oil, lemon juice, oregano, garlic, vinegar, paprika, salt, and pepper. Place the salmon and turn to coat it thoroughly with the marinade. Cover the container and let the salmon sit marinating for fifteen to twenty minutes.
2. Grill the fish. Preheat the grill to moderate-high heat and grill the fish until just thoroughly cooked, four to five minutes per side. Set the fish aside on a plate.

To make the Bowls:

1. Grill the vegetables. In a moderate-sized container, put the oil, red and yellow bell peppers, and zucchini. Grill the vegetables, flipping over once, until they are mildly charred and soft, approximately 3 minutes per side.
2. Assemble before you serve. Split the grilled vegetables between four bowls. Top each container with cucumber, tomato, olives, feta cheese, and the sour cream. Put 1 salmon fillet on top of every container and serve instantly.

Nutritional Info: Calories: 553 Total fat: 44g Total carbs: 10g || Fiber: 3g; Net carbs: 7g || Sodium: 531mg || Protein: 30g

---

SPECIAL OYSTERS

Time To Prepare: ten minutes

Time to Cook: 0 minutes

Yield: Servings 4

Ingredients:

- ½ teaspoon ginger; grated
- 1 cup tomato juice
- 1 Serrano chili pepper; chopped.
- 1/4 cup cilantro; chopped.
- 1/4 cup olive oil
- 1/4 cup scallions; chopped.
- 1/4 teaspoon garlic; minced
- 12 oysters; shucked
- 2 tablespoons ketchup
- Juice from 1 lime
- Juice from 1 orange
- Juice of 1 lemon
- Salt to the taste.
- Zest from 1 lime
- Zest from 1 orange

Directions:

1. In a container, mix lemon juice, orange juice, orange zest, lime juice and zest, ketchup, chili pepper, tomato juice, ginger, garlic, oil, scallions, cilantro and salt and stir thoroughly.
2. Ladle this into oysters and serve them.

Nutritional Info: Calories: 100 ‖ Fat: 1 Fiber: 0 ‖ Carbohydrates: 2‖ Protein: 5

SPICY HERB CATFISH

Time To Prepare: ten minutes

Time to Cook: twenty-five minutes

Yield: Servings 4

Ingredients:

For the spice mixture:

- ½ cup flaxseed, freshly ground

- ½ tablespoon ground red pepper
- ½ teaspoon crushed cardamom
- ½ teaspoons cumin seeds
- 1 tablespoon kosher salt
- 1 tablespoon raw sugar
- 1 teaspoon ground black pepper
- 1/4 cup coriander seeds
- Canola oil spray
- Four 6-ounce catfish fillets

For the garnish:

1. Several sprigs of fresh cilantro 1 medium tomato and
2. 1 lemon quartered

Directions:

1. Preheat your oven to 350°F. Put the spice blend ingredients into a mixing container, and mix well. Put the mixture inside a pie pan.
2. Clean the catfish fillets and pat dry. Put ground flaxseed into an alternate pie pan. Immerse fillets in the spice mixture first, followed by flaxseed. Spray the baking sheet with canola oil and place fillets on a baking sheet and cook for eighteen minutes. Boil the stock juices for another six minutes.
3. Pour the juices over the fillets and serve decorated with cilantro, a portion of tomato, and a lemon quarter.

Nutritional Info: Calories: 208 kcal || Protein: 13.5 g || Fat: 12.65 g || Carbohydrates: 13.66 g

---

SPICY KINGFISH

Time To Prepare: 15 minutes

Time to Cook: ten minutes

Yield: Servings 2

Ingredients:

- ½ teaspoon ground turmeric
- 1 garlic clove, minced
- 1 lime wedge

- 1 tablespoon fresh lime juice
- 1 tbsp. olive oil
- 1 teaspoon cumin seeds
- 1 teaspoon dried unsweetened coconut
- 1 teaspoon fennel seeds
- 1 teaspoon peppercorns
- 10 curry leaves
- 1½ teaspoons fresh ginger, grated finely
- 4 (4-ounce) kingfish steaks
- Salt, to taste

Directions:

1. Heat a cast-iron frying pan on low heat.
2. Put in coconut, cumin seeds, fennel seeds, peppercorns, and curry leaves and cook, stirring constantly for approximately one minute.
3. Take off from the heat and cool to room temperature.
4. In a spice grinder, put in the spice mixture and turmeric and grind rill powdered finely.
5. Move the mixture toto a big container with ginger, garlic, salt, and lime juice and mix thoroughly.
6. Put in fish fillets and cat with the mixture uniformly.
7. Place in your fridge to marinate for approximately three hours.
8. In a huge nonstick frying pan, warm oil on moderate heat.
9. Place the fish fillets and cook for minimum three to five minutes per side or till the desired doneness.
10. Move onto a paper towel-lined plate to drain.
11. Serve with lime wedges.

Nutritional Info: Calories: 592 kcal ‖ Protein: 67.03 g ‖ Fat: 34.55 g ‖ Carbohydrates: 4.91 g

SPICY SALMON TEMPURA ROLL

Time To Prepare: ten minutes

Time to Cook: 0 minutes

Yield: Servings 8

Ingredients:

- ½ avocado, cut into strips
- ½ tbsp. Sirach
- 1 tbsp. mayonnaise
- 1/4 English cucumber, julienned
- 1/4 tsp ground ginger
- 20 grams pork rinds or cracklings
- 4 ounces canned wild salmon
- Nori sheet
- Pickled ginger (not necessary)
- Sesame seeds (not necessary)
- Soy sauce (not necessary)
- Wasabi (not necessary)

Directions:

1. Put in salmon, mayonnaise, Siracha, and ginger to a container and stir until well blended.
2. Put pork rinds in a plastic bag and crush until you get big crumbs.
3. Put nori sheet on your work surface with the glossy side down.
4. Mix pork rind crumbs into the salmon mixture.
5. Position salmon/pork rind mixture and veggies on the nori, minimum an inch away from the edge closest to you. Roll the nori around the filling firmly, tucking the edge under as you go. Spread a small amount of water on the rest of the "rough" side of the nori and continue rolling to bind together and create a uniform roll.
6. Cut in half, then continue to slice every portion in half until you get 8 pieces
7. Decorate using sesame seeds, soy sauce, wasabi or pickled ginger.
8. Serve.

Nutritional Info: Calories: 243 || Fat: 14g || Carbohydrates: 6g || Protein: 23g

SQUID RINGS WITH POTATO AND SPINACH

Time To Prepare: ten minutes

Time to Cook: 15 minutes

Yield: Servings 3

Ingredients:

- 1 lb. fresh spinach, torn
- 1 lb. squid rings, frozen
- 1 tsp dried rosemary, crushed
- 1 tsp garlic paste
- 1 tsp sea salt
- 2 cups cauliflower, roughly chopped
- 2 tbsp. lemon juice
- 2 thyme sprigs, fresh
- 4 tbsp. extra virgin olive oil

Directions:

1. Put squid rings in a deep container and pour in enough warm water to immerse. Allow it to sit for a while. Moved to a big colander and drain. Set aside.
2. Set the instant pot and grease the inner pot with 2 tbsp. of olive oil. Push the "Sauté" button then put garlic paste and rosemary. Stir-fry for a minute, then put the spinach. Sprinkle with salt and cook for minimum 3-4 minutes or until wilted. Take off the spinach from the pot and save for later.
3. Put the rest of the oil to the pot and heat up on the "Sauté" mode. Put chopped cauliflower, making a uniform layer. Top with squid rings and squezze of lemon juice and optionally some olive oil to taste. Sprinkle with salt, put in thyme sprigs and pour in one cup of water (or fish stock).
4. Secure the lid then set the steam release handle to the "Sealing" position. Push the "Fish" button then set the timer for 9 minutes.
5. When you hear the cooker's end signal, gently move the pressure valve to the "Venting" position to release the pressure.
6. Open the pot and mix in the spinach. Optionally, put some more garlic powder or dried thyme.
7. Serve instantly.

Nutritional Info: Calories 353|| Total Fats 21.5g || Net Carbohydrates: 8.9g || Protein: 29.3g || Fiber: 5g

STEAMED GARLIC-DILL HALIBUT

Time To Prepare: five minutes

Time to Cook: twenty-five minutes

Yield: Servings 4

Ingredients:

- 1 lemon, freshly squeezed
- 1 tablespoon dill weed, chopped
- 1 teaspoon garlic powder
- 1-pound halibut fillet
- Salt and pepper to taste

Directions:

1. Put a big pot on medium fire and fill up to 1.5-inches of water. Put a trivet inside the pot.
2. In a baking dish that fits inside your big pot, put in all ingredients and mix thoroughly. Cover dish using foil. Put the dish on top of the trivet inside the pot.
3. Cover pot and steam fish for fifteen minutes.
4. Let fish rest for minimum ten minutes before removing from pot.
5. Serve and enjoy.

Nutritional Info: Calories: 270 Cal || Fat: 6.5 g || Carbohydrates: 3.9 g || Protein: 47.8 g || Fiber: 2.1 g

STEAMED MUSSELS WITH THYME

Time To Prepare: ten minutes

Time to Cook: ten minutes

Yield: Servings 2

Ingredients:

- ¼ cup Parmesan cheese, grated
- 1 lb. mussels, cleaned
- 2 cups fish stock
- 2 tbsp. lemon juice, freshly squeezed
- 3 tbsp. butter
- 5 garlic cloves, crushed

Spices:

- ½ tsp chili flakes
- 1 tsp dried thyme
- 2 tbsp. fresh parsley, finely chopped

Directions:

1. Wash well the mussels under running water then take off any dirt. Drain and save for later.
2. Set instant pot and press the "Sauté" button. Grease the inner pot with butter and put in garlic. Sauté for minimum 2-3 minutes, then pour in the stock. Sprinkle with lemon juice and flavor with thyme, chili flakes, and parsley.
3. Bring the mussels in a steam basket and moved to the pot. Secure the lid and set the steam release handle to the "Sealing" position.
4. Push the "Manual" button then set the timer for five minutes on high pressure.
5. When done, perform a quick release and open the lid. Take off any mussels that didn't open and move to serving bowls. Sprinkle with the sauce from the pot and serve instantly.

Nutritional Info: Calories 207 Total Fats17.1g || Net Carbohydrates: 5.6g || Protein: 17.1g || Fiber: 0.1g

STUFFED TROUT

Time To Prepare: 20minutes

Time to Cook: 1 hour and fifteen minutes

Yield: Servings 4

Ingredients:

- ½ cup quinoa
- 1 cup (100 g) mushrooms, cut
- 1 cup cherry tomatoes, chopped
- 1 cup chicken broth
- 1 yellow onion, finely dices
- 2 tablespoons canola oil
- 2 tablespoons flour
- 2 tablespoons lemon juice

- 2 tablespoons omega-3-rich margarine
- 2 teaspoons dehydrated tarragon
- 2 whole lake trout
- Salt and pepper

Directions:

1. In a pan, put the chicken broth on to simmer. Mix the quinoa, cover, and decrease the heat to low — Cook for 45 to 60 minutes.
2. Preheat your oven to 400°F and proceed to line a baking tray using parchment paper.
3. To make the stuffing, melt margarine in a wide pan on moderate heat. Sauté the onions and mushrooms till soft. Season by including tarragon, and salt and pepper. Mix cherry tomatoes and sauté one to two minutes further, mixing continually. Take off the heat and mix with cooked quinoa. Put in in lemon juice and stir.
4. Spray the canola oil covering the trout. In a container, blend together flour, salt, and pepper. Glaze the interior and exterior of the trout with the flour batter. Fill the trout with the stuffing blend.
5. Cook uncovered for about ten minutes per inch of trout.

Nutritional Info: Calories: 342 kcal ‖ Protein: 18.76 g ‖ Fat: 19.1 g ‖ Carbohydrates: 24.38 g

SWEET CRAB CAKES

Time To Prepare: 15 minutes

Time to Cook: ten minutes

Yield: Servings 4

Ingredients:

- ¼ cup Classic Aioli
- ¼ cup minced red bell pepper
- ¼ cup shredded unsweetened coconut
- 1 egg, lightly beaten
- 1 pound cooked lump crabmeat, drained and picked over
- 1 scallion, finely chopped
- 1 tablespoon Dijon mustard
- 1 teaspoon lemon zest
- 3 tablespoons coconut flour

- 3 tablespoons coconut oil
- Pinch cayenne pepper

Directions:

1. Make the crab cakes. In a moderate-sized container, combine the crab, coconut, mustard, scallion, red bell pepper, egg, lemon zest, and cayenne until it holds together. Form the mixture into eight equal patties about ¾ inch thick.
2. Chill. Put the patties on a plate, cover the plate using plastic wrap, and chill them in your fridge for around 1 hour to twelve hours.
3. Coat the patties. Spread the coconut flour on a plate. Immerse each patty in the flour until it is lightly coated.
4. Cook. In a big frying pan at moderate heat, warm the coconut oil. Fry the crab-cake patties, turning them once, until they are golden and thoroughly cooked, approximately five minutes per side.
5. Serve. Put two crab cakes on each of four plates and serve with the aioli.

Nutritional Info: Calories: 370 Total fat: 24g Total carbs: 12g ‖ Fiber: 6g Net carbs: 6g ‖ Sodium: 652mg ‖ Protein: 26g

SWORDFISH WITH PINEAPPLE AND CILANTRO

Time To Prepare: ten minutes

Time to Cook: 20 minutes

Yield: Servings 4

Ingredients:

- ¼ c. chopped fresh cilantro
- ¼ tsp. Ground black pepper.
- 1 c. fresh pineapple chunks
- 1 tbsp. coconut aminos
- 1 tbsp. coconut oil
- 1 tsp. Salt.
- 2 lbs. cut swordfish
- 2 minced garlic cloves
- 2 tbsps. Chopped fresh parsley

Directions:

1. Preheat your oven to 4000F.
2. Grease a baking tray with coconut oil
3. Put in cilantro, swordfish, coconut aminos, pepper, salt, garlic, parsley, and pineapple to the dish then mix thoroughly.
4. Place the dish in an already preheated oven and bake for about twenty minutes.
5. Serve and enjoy.

Nutritional Info: Calories: 444 kcal || Protein: 47.53 g || Fat: 20.32 g || Carbohydrates: 16.44 g

---

TENDER CREAMY SCALLOPS

Time To Prepare: 15 minutes

Time to Cook: 21 minutes

Yield: Servings 2

Ingredients:

- ½ cup grated parmesan cheese
- 1 cup heavy cream
- 2 tbsp. ghee butter
- 4 bacon slices
- 8 fresh sea scallops
- Salt and black pepper to taste

Directions:

1. Heat the butter in a frying pan at moderate to high heat
2. Put in the bacon and cook for 4-5 minutes each side (till crunchy)
3. Moved to a paper towel to remove the surplus fat
4. Reduce the heat to moderate, drizzle with more butter. Place the heavy cream and parmesan cheese, sprinkle with salt and pepper
5. Lower the heat to low and cook for 8-ten minutes, continuously stirring, until the sauce thickens
6. In another frying pan, heat the ghee butter on moderate to high heat
7. Put in the scallops to the frying pan, sprinkle with salt and pepper. Cook for a couple of minutes per side until golden

8. Move the scallops to a paper towel
9. Top with the sauce and crumbled bacon

Nutritional Info: Carbohydrates: 11 g || Fat: 72,5 g || Protein: 24 g || Calories: 765

THAI CHOWDER

Time To Prepare: ten minutes

Time to Cook: 20 minutes

Yield: Servings 6

Ingredients:

- ½ cup cabbage, chopped
- ½ teaspoon fresh ginger, diced
- 1 teaspoon dried lemongrass
- 1 teaspoon green curry paste
- 10 small red potatoes, diced
- 2 tablespoons fish sauce
- 3 cobs fresh sweet corn
- 3 cups 98 % fat-free chicken broth
- 3/4 cup bay scallops
- 3/4 cup cilantro, chopped
- 3/4 cup coconut milk
- 3/4 cup fresh shrimp, cleaned, with tails on
- Four 5-ounce tilapia fillets

Directions:

1. In a deep cooking pan, boil chicken stock at high heat until it reaches a simmer. Decrease temperature and put in the cabbage, ginger, coconut milk, lemongrass, sweet corn, lemongrass, curry paste, and potatoes — cover and cook for fifteen minutes.
2. Firstly, mix fish fillets and fish sauce, and cook for about six minutes. Secondly, put in the shrimp, and cook for another two to three minutes. Finally, put in the scallops and cook until scallops are opaque in color.
3. Serve with cilantro.

Nutritional Info: Calories: 761 kcal || Protein: 33.25 g || Fat: 5.34 g || Carbohydrates: 150.45 g

THAI SALMON FISHCAKES

Time To Prepare: ten minutes

Time to Cook: ten minutes

Yield: Servings 2

Ingredients:

- ½ tsp red Thai curry paste
- 1 egg
- 2 green onions roughly chopped
- 2 salmon fillets, skin removed
- 2 tbsp. fresh cilantro roughly chopped
- salt and black pepper to taste

Directions:

1. Set all the ingredients into a food processor and process until the desired smoothness is achieved.
2. Put some wax paper or baking parchment onto a plate. Split the mixture into 4, then spoon each portion onto the paper. Cover with an additional layer of paper and a layer of plastic wrap, and leave in your refrigerator for minimum an hour.
3. Warm, a big non-stick frying pan and fry the fishcakes for five minutes at moderate heat. Turnover and cook for an extra five minutes or until thoroughly cooked.

Nutritional Info: Calories: 278 || Fat: 12g || Carbohydrates: 1g || Protein: 36g

---

TIGER PRAWN PAELLA

Time To Prepare: ten minutes

Time to Cook: twenty-five minutes

Yield: Servings 4

Ingredients:

- 1 lb. tiger prawns, whole
- 1 small red bell pepper, finely chopped
- 1 tsp apple cider vinegar
- 2 cups cauliflower, chopped into florets

- 2 small onion, finely chopped
- 3 garlic cloves, crushed
- 3 tbsp. butter
- 4 cups fish stock
- 5 bacon slices, chopped

Spices:

- ½ tsp black pepper, freshly ground
- ½ tsp saffron threads
- 1 tsp sea salt
- 2 tsp turmeric powder
- 4 tbsp. fresh parsley, finely chopped

Directions:

1. Set the instant pot then put cauliflower. Put in the fish stock and drizzle with salt. Secure the lid and set the steam release handle to the "Sealing" position. Push the "Manual" button then set the timer for five minutes on high pressure.
2. When done, perform a quick release and open the lid. Take off the cauliflower from the pot and drain. Make sure to reserve the stock. Set aside.
3. Push the "Sauté" button then grease the inner pot with butter. Heat up then put in onions and garlic. Stir-fry for 4-5 minutes.
4. Put bell pepper and bacon. Cook and stir for 3-4 more minutes. Flavor it with some more salt, pepper, and turmeric powder.
5. Stir thoroughly and put in prawns and cauliflower. Put in the rest of the stock and secure the lid.
6. Set the steam release handle again and press the "Manual" button. Set the timer for minimum 8 minutes on high pressure.
7. When done, release the pressure and open the lid. Mix thoroughly and drizzle with saffron and fresh parsley. Let it sit for a while before you serve.
8. Optionally, press the "Sauté" button again and simmer until all the liquid evaporates.

Nutritional Info: Calories 419|| Total Fats 22.6g || Net Carbohydrates: 8.5g || Protein: 41.8g || Fiber: 2.5g

TILAPIA AND RED SAUCE

Time To Prepare: ten minutes

Time to Cook: 20 minutes

Yield: Servings 4

Ingredients:

- ¼ cup tomato passata
- ½ cup chicken stock
- 1 cup roasted red peppers, chopped
- 1 tablespoon lemon juice
- 1 teaspoon garlic powder
- 1 teaspoon oregano, dried
- 10 ounces canned tomatoes and chilies, chopped
- 2 spring onions, minced
- 2 tablespoons avocado oil
- 4 tilapia fillets, boneless
- A pinch of salt and black pepper

Directions:

1. Set the instant pot on Sauté mode, put the oil, heat it up, put in the onions, and cook for a couple of minutes.
2. Put the remaining ingredients exclude the fish, and simmer everything for eight minutes more.
3. Place the fish, set the lid on, and cook on High for about ten minutes.
4. Release the pressure naturally for about ten minutes, split everything between plates before you serve.

Nutritional Info: Calories 184 || Fat: 2.2 || Fiber: 1.6 || Carbohydrates: 1.9 || Protein: 22.2

TILAPIA FILLETS

Time To Prepare: ten minutes

Time to Cook: 15 minutes

Yield: Servings 3

Ingredients:

- 1 lb. tilapia fillets, cut
- 1 tbsp. fish sauce
- 1 tbsp. hot sauce
- 1 tbsp. nectar
- 2 egg yolks
- 2 tbsp. mayonnaise
- 3 sweet pickle relish
- 4 wheat buns

Directions:

1. In a container, put and whisk the egg yolks and fish sauce.
2. Throw in the mayonnaise, sweet pickle relish, hot sauce, and nectar.
3. Move the mixture to a round baking tray.
4. Put it in the Air Fryer and line the sides with the tilapia fillets. Cook for fifteen minutes at 300°F.
5. Remove and serve on hamburger buns if you wish.

Nutritional Info: Calories: 248 kcal || Protein: 35.29 g || Fat: 10.79 g || Carbohydrates: 2.15 g

TILAPIA WITH PARMESAN BARK

Time To Prepare: 4 minutes

Time to Cook: twelve minutes

Yield: Servings 4

Ingredients:

- ¾ cup freshly grated Parmesan cheese
- 1 tablespoon chopped parsley
- 2 teaspoons pepper
- 4 tilapia fillets (4 us)
- Lemon cut into pieces

Directions:

1. Set the oven to 400° F. Mix cheese in a shallow dish with pepper and parsley and sprinkle with salt and pepper.

2. Combine the fish in the cheese with olive oil and flirt. Put on a baking sheet using foil and bake for ten to twelve minutes until the fish in the thickest part appears opaque.
3. Serve the lemon slices with the fish.

Nutritional Info: Calories: 210 || Fat: 9.3g || Net Carbohydrates: 1.3g || Protein: 28.9g

TILAPIA WITH SPICY DIJON SAUCE

Time To Prepare: ten minutes

Time to Cook: five minutes

Yield: Servings 4

Ingredients:

- ½ cup dark rum
- 1 cup heavy cream
- 1 cup white onions, chopped
- 1 pound tilapia fish, cubed
- 1 tablespoon butter, room temperature
- 1 teaspoon Dijon mustard
- 1 teaspoon garlic, pressed
- 2 chili peppers, deveined and minced
- Ground black pepper, to taste
- Sea salt, to taste

Directions:

1. Toss the tilapia with salt, pepper, onions, garlic, chili peppers and rum. Allow it to marinate for about two hours in your fridge.
2. In a grill pan, melt the butter over a moderately high heat. Sear the fish in hot butter, coating with the reserved marinade.
3. Put in in the mustard and cream and carry on cooking until everything is meticulously cooked, for two to three minutes.

Nutritional Info: 228 Calories 13g || Fat: 6.5g || Carbs: 13.7g || Protein: 1.1g Fiber

TROUT WITH CHARD

Time To Prepare: ten minutes

Time to Cook: 15 minutes

Yield: Servings 4

Ingredients:

- ¼ c. golden raisins
- ½ c. vegetable broth
- 1 chopped onion
- 1 tbsp. apple cider vinegar
- 1 tbsp. extra-virgin olive oil
- 2 bunches cut chard
- 2 minced garlic cloves
- 4 boneless trout fillets
- Ground black pepper
- Salt

Directions:

1. Preheat your oven to approximately 3750F.
2. Put in seasonings to the trout
3. Put in olive oil in a pan, then heat.
4. Put in garlic and onion, then sauté for about three minutes.
5. Put in chard to sauté for two more minutes.
6. Put in broth, raisins, and cedar vinegar to the pan.
7. Layer a topping of trout fillets
8. Cover the pan and put it in the preheated oven for about ten minutes.
9. Serve and enjoy.

Nutritional Info: Calories: 284 kcal ‖ Protein: 2.07 g ‖ Fat: 30.32 g ‖ Carbohydrates: 3.49 g

TUNA CAKES

Time To Prepare: five minutes

Time to Cook: ten minutes

Yield: Servings 2

Ingredients:

- ½ teaspoon black pepper
- ½ teaspoon paprika
- 1 egg
- 1 tablespoon fresh dill
- 1 tablespoon raw parsley
- 12 ounces canned in water tuna, drained (2 cans)
- 2 tablespoons coconut oil
- 2 tablespoons mayonnaise
- Salt to taste

Directions:

1. Put tuna, egg, salt, pepper, mayo, and paprika in a moderate-sized container. Before putting in tuna, drain the water from the can. Chop parsley and dill and put in them too. Mix everything.
2. Take a shallow frying pan, and put in coconut oil on moderate to high heat. By using hands, split your mixture and form 4 or 8 cakes. Make them around ¾-inch thick.
3. Cook your patties in the coconut oil for about four minutes each side or until you see they are firm and golden brown.

Nutritional Info: Calories: 473 || Total Carbohydrates: 1,1g || Fiber: 0,45g|| Net Carbohydrates: 0,65g || Fat: 30,5g || Protein: 43,5g

---

TUNA HANDROLLS

Time To Prepare: 15 minutes

Time to Cook: two minutes

Yield: Servings 2

Ingredients:

- 1 avocado, pitted, peeled
- 1 teaspoon lemon juice (not necessary)
- 2 ounces cucumber
- 2 tablespoons green onions
- 2 tablespoons mayonnaise
- 4 nori sheets

- 5 oz. canned tuna, drained
- 6 black olives
- Salt to taste

Directions:

1. Chop black olives, green onions, and half of the cucumber; put in everything to a big container. Cut half of the cucumber into thin slices (half-moon slices if your cucumber is big). Thinly slice the avocado too. Set cucumber and avocado slices aside.
2. Put in tuna to the big container and cut it using a fork.
3. Put in lemon juice and mayo to the container. Season everything with salt as preferred; stir everything well.
4. Take 2 nori sheets and line them one upon the other.
5. Now put in ½ of your mixture to the bottom of nori; top everything with a few slices of cucumber and avocado.
6. Roll the nori sheets up and repeat the same with two other pieces of nori and the remaining tuna mixture. Your tuna handrolls are ready to serve. Cut each roll in two pieces and enjoy (the serving size is 1 long roll or 2 smaller ones).

Nutritional Info: Calories: 367 || Total Carbohydrates: 11g || Fiber: 7g || Net Carbohydrates: 4g || Fat: 28g || Protein: 20g

TUNA STEAKS WITH SHIRATAKI NOODLES

Time To Prepare: ten minutes

Time to Cook: 20 minutes

Yield: Servings 4

Ingredients:

- 1 pack (7 oz.) miracle noodle angel hair
- 1 red bell pepper, seeded and halved
- 2 tablespoons chopped cilantro
- 2 tablespoons pickled ginger
- 3 cups water
- 4 tuna steaks
- Olive oil for brushing
- Salt and black pepper to taste

Directions:

1. Cook the shirataki rice based on the package instructions: In a colander, wash the shirataki noodles with running cold water.
2. Put a pot of salted water to its boiling point; blanch the noodles for a couple of minutes.
3. Drain and moved to a dry frying pan on moderate heat.
4. Dry roast for a few minutes until opaque.
5. Grease a grill's grate using a cooking spray and preheat on moderate heat. Spice the red bell pepper and tuna with salt and black pepper, brush with olive oil, and grill covered.
6. Cook both for minimum 3 minutes on each side. Moved to a plate to cool. Dice bell pepper using a knife.
7. Position the noodles, tuna, and bell pepper into the serving plate.
8. Top with pickled ginger and decorate with cilantro.
9. Serve with roasted sesame sauce.

Nutritional Info: Calories: 310 || Fat: 18.2g || Net Carbohydrates: 2g || Protein: 22g

---

TUNA-STUFFED TOMATOES

Time To Prepare: ten minutes

Time to Cook: ten minutes

Yield: Servings 2

Ingredients:

- ¼ tsp. seasoning salt
- ½ tsp. Dijon mustard
- 1 6oz. can tuna, drained and flaked
- 1 medium tomato
- 1 tbsp. celery, chopped
- 2 tbsp. mayonnaise
- Shredded mild cheddar cheese, to decorate

Directions:

1. Preheat your oven to 375°. Rinse tomato and cut in half from the stem. Using a tsp., scoop out tomato pulp and any seeds until you have two ½" shells remaining.

2. In a small mixing container, mix tuna, mayonnaise, celery, mustard, and seasoning salt. Stir until well mixed.
3. Scoop an equal amount of tuna mixture into each ½ tomato shell. Put on a baking sheet and drizzle shredded cheddar cheese over the top of each tuna-stuffed tomato shell. Bake for seven to eight minutes or until cheese is melted and golden-brown in color.
4. Serve instantly. Any remaining mixture can be safely stored, covered, in your refrigerator for maximum 72 hours.

Nutritional Info: Calories: 175 kcal || Protein: 21.24 g || Fat: 8.79 g || Carbohydrates: 3.04 g

VIETNAMESE ROLL AND TARÊ

Time To Prepare: 20 minutes

Time to Cook: ten minutes

Yield: Servings 4

Ingredients:

- 1 ½ cup rice noodles prepared per package instructions
- 1 cup carrot cut into sticks
- 1 cup chopped Japanese cucumber
- 1 cup of sake baby
- 1 cup of soy sauce
- 1 cup of sugar
- 250g sauteed medium prawns
- 6 sheets of rice paper
- 6 shredded lettuce leaves
- Mint leaves
- Warm water

Directions:

1. Bring the soy sauce, sake, and sugar to moderate heat. Stir occasionally and cook the mixture until it reduces to ⅓ of the initial amount and obtain a tender syrup consistency. Set aside to cool.
2. Immerse the rice leaf in warm water for approximately half a minute or until it softens.
3. Position on a flat surface and stuff the center of the rice paper with mint leaves, prawns, carrot, cucumber, lettuce, and pasta.

4. Roll up, cut in half and half once more. Repeat the process with the other sheets of rice paper.
5. Serve with taré sauce.

Nutritional Info: Calories: 552 kcal || Protein: 10.54 g || Fat: 20.48 g || Carbohydrates: 82.12 g

WASABI SALMON BURGERS

Time To Prepare: five minutes

Time to Cook: ten minutes

Yield: Servings 1

Ingredients:

- ½ tsp. Honey
- 1 Beaten free-range egg
- 1 tbsp. Fresh ginger, minced
- 1 tsp. Wasabi powder
- 2 can Wild Salmon, drained
- 2 Scallion, chopped
- 2 tbsp. Coconut Oil
- 2 tbsp. Reduce-salt soy sauce

Directions:

1. Mix the salmon, egg, ginger, scallions, and 1 tbsp. oil in a container, stirring thoroughly with your hands to make 4 patties.
2. In a different container, put in the wasabi powder and soy sauce with the honey and whisk until mixed.
3. Heat 1 tbsp. oil on moderate heat in a frying pan and cook the patties for about four minutes each side until firm and browned.
4. Glaze the top of each patty with the wasabi mixture and cook for an extra fifteen seconds and serve.
5. Serve with a side salad or vegetables for a healthy treat.

Nutritional Info: Calories: 591 kcal || Protein: 63.52 g || Fat: 34.3 g || Carbohydrates: 3.83 g

WHITEFISH CURRY

Time To Prepare: ten minutes

Time to Cook: 15 minutes

Yield: Servings 6

Ingredients:

- ¼ c. chopped fresh cilantro
- ¼ tsp. ground black pepper
- 1 bruised lemongrass
- 1 c. vegetable broth
- 1 chopped onion
- 1 lb. Firm white fish fillets
- 1 tbsp. Minced fresh ginger
- 1 thinly cut scallion
- 1 tsp. Salt
- 2 c. chopped broccoli
- 2 c. cubed butternut squash
- 2 minced garlic cloves
- 2 tbsps. coconut oil
- 2 tsp. curry powder
- Lemon wedges
- oz. coconut milk

Directions:

1. In a pot, put in coconut oil and melt.
2. Put in onion, curry powder, ginger, garlic, and seasonings then sauté for five minutes
3. Put in broccoli, lemongrass and butternut squash and sauté for two more minutes
4. Mix in broth and coconut milk and bring to its boiling point. Reduce the heat to simmer and put in the fish.
5. Cover the pot, then simmer for five minutes, then discard the lemongrass.
6. Ladle the curry into a medium serving container.
7. Put in scallion and cilantro to decorate before you serve with lemon wedges.
8. Enjoy.

Nutritional Info: Calories: 218 kcal || Protein: 18.1 g || Fat: 8.57 g || Carbohydrates: 18.2 g

ABOUT THE AUTHOR

Stephanie Bennett is an American health coach, foodie, and author based in New York. She enjoys sharing simple, delicious recipes with her readers, and coming up with new ways to help people live a healthier life.

Printed in Great Britain
by Amazon